J. M. Synge

The Complete Plays

**In the Shadow of the Glen, Riders to the Sea,
The Tinker's Wedding, The Well of the Saints,
The Playboy of the Western World,
Deirdre of the Sorrows**

This volume contains everything that J. M. Synge wrote
in dramatic form, including his masterpiece, *The Playboy
of the Western World*, and five shorter plays which offer
further evidence of his genius for combining the lyrical
with the comic and the tragic. The introduction is by the
Irish scholar, T. R. Henn.

John Millington Synge was born in 1871, of Anglo-
Irish Protestant land-owning stock. He graduated at
Trinity College, Dublin, and then spent a few years
wandering on the continent. Synge went to the Aran
Islands in 1898, and subsequently revisited them several
times. *In the Shadow of the Glen* and *Riders to the Sea* were
both completed in the summer of 1902, and both were
taken from material he had collected on the islands. *The
Playboy of the Western World*, published in 1907, aroused
a prolonged and bitter controversy, which lasted until his
death in 1909. His other works include a few poems and
two books of travels, *The Aran Islands*. *Deirdre of the
Sorrows* was published posthumously.

J. M. SYNGE

The Complete Plays

In the Shadow of the Glen
Riders to the Sea
The Tinker's Wedding
The Well of the Saints
The Playboy of the Western World
Deirdre of the Sorrows

with an introduction and notes by T. R. Henn

Methuen Drama

METHUEN WORLD CLASSICS

3 5 7 9 10 8 6 4 2

First published in this edition in 1981 by Eyre Methuen Ltd
Reissued with a new cover design 1993, 2001

Methuen Publishing Ltd
215 Vauxhall Bridge Road, London SW1V 1EJ

Based on *The Plays and Poems of J. M. Synge* edited by
T. R. Henn, published by Methuen and Co. Ltd in 1963

Introduction and notes copyright © 1963 by T. R. Henn

Methuen Publishing Ltd Reg. No. 3543167

ISBN 0 413 48520 X

A CIP catalogue record for this book
is available from the British Library

Typeset in Baskerville by MATS, Southend-on-Sea, Essex
Printed and bound in Great Britain by
Cox & Wyman Ltd, Reading, Berkshire

CONTENTS

ABBREVIATIONS USED
IN THE NOTES, etc.

The Aran Islands (Elkin Matthews, and Maunsel,
    Dublin, 1907. Reprinted 1961)   *A.I.*

In Wicklow, West Kerry and Connemara (Maunsel
    & Co., 1911)   *W.W.K.*

LADY GREGORY, *Our Irish Theatre*   *O.I.T.*

The Vanishing Irish (ed. J. A. O'Brien, London,
    1954 edn)   *V.I.*

ELEANOR HULL, *The Cuchullin Saga in Irish
    Literature* (London, 1898)   *Hull*

W. B. YEATS, *Collected Poems* (Macmillan, 1950)   *C.P.*

W. B. YEATS, *Collected Plays* (Macmillan, 1953)   *C. Plays*

In the Shadow of the Glen   *The Shadow*

Riders to the Sea   *Riders*

The Tinker's Wedding   *T.W.*

The Well of the Saints   *W.S.*

The Playboy of the Western World   *The Playboy*

Deirdre of the Sorrows   *Deirdre*

Poems and Translations   *P & T*

*Unless otherwise stated, poems and
translations referred to are by Synge.*

I

GENERAL INTRODUCTION

I. THE PLAYWRIGHT

John Millington Synge was born in 1871, in a Dublin suburb, of Anglo-Irish Protestant landowning stock. His father was a Dublin barrister, who had inherited some property in Co. Galway; his mother was the daughter of a Rector in Co. Cork, and an uncle had, ironically enough, gone to the Aran Islands as a Protestant missionary in an attempt to convert the people. On both sides, therefore, he was 'Protestant Ascendancy'; the family was an ancient one, the name what is called in *The Playboy* a 'quality name', much associated with the Church. His boyhood was spent among the hills and mountains to the south of Dublin; an almost Wordsworthian passion for the countryside, and a knowledge of natural history more intimate than Wordsworth's, are continuously reflected in the imagery and descriptive passages of the Plays.

He went to Trinity College, Dublin, in 1888, obtained prizes in Irish and in History, and was a member of the Dublin Naturalists' Field Club. Another dominant interest was music. After leaving Trinity he spent some wandering years, in conditions of hardship and poverty, on the Continent: the Black Forest, Italy, France; presumably with the idea of becoming a professional musician. His fiddle made him welcome among the peasantry of Aran and of Kerry; and it was perhaps the thought of the wandering musician that made Yeats align him, in imagination, with Oliver Goldsmith. So the verse in 'The Seven Sages:'[1]

> They walked the roads
> Mimicking what they heard, as children mimic;
> They understood that wisdom comes of beggary.

But his interests shifted from music to literature; and, like so many young men of the time – Dowson, Johnson, Wilde, Moore, the

[1] *C.P.*, p. 271.

members of The Rhymers' Club and of Yeats' 'The Tragic Generation' – he drifted to Paris. There he appears to have read widely in European literature; afterwards he translated, into the rhythmical prose that he had made his own, poems or portions of them from three languages. His chief interests seem to have been Petrarch, Villon, the Pléiade, Cervantes, Molière, Racine, and he was well read in Elizabethan and Jacobean literature: 'Friend of Ronsard, Nashe and Beaumont'.[1] We may reflect that the Anglo-Irish literary revival drew much, directly or indirectly, from France; as if some wider vision, a harder edge of perception, were needed to redeem the ever-latent tendency to sentimentality, over-narrow patriotism, and – let us be frank – a humourless provincialism that is all too apparent among the minor writers of that time.

In Paris he was fortunate in meeting the growing interest in Celtic culture and archaeology; and in particular that of Brittany, whose links with Wales and Ireland, in language, myths and monuments, had long been recognized. Synge attended lectures – he was the only pupil – by the famous de Jubainville on ancient Irish, and became interested in the work of Anatole le Braz, who had written much on the folklore and archaeology of Brittany. He had read Pierre Loti, and, though critics today seem to decry the influence of *Le Pêcheur d'Islande*, the book is valuable in helping to an understanding of the background of the Aran Islanders and of the fishermen of West Kerry.

It was in Paris that Yeats found him, either in 1896 or 1897,[2] and gave him his famous advice:

> I said: 'Give up Paris, you will never create anything by reading Racine, and Arthur Symons will always be a better critic of French Literature. Go to the Aran Islands. Live there as if you were one of the people themselves; express a life that has never found expression.' I had just come from Aran, and my imagination was full of those grey islands where men must reap with knives because of the stones.[3]

A number of circumstances combined to make Synge's journey to Aran, in 1898, bear such strange and rich fruit. He alone of the members of the Irish Literary Revival had a university degree, and

---

[1] *P & T*, 'On a Birthday'.
[2] There is some confusion over the exact date.
[3] *Essays and Introductions* (1961), p. 299.

a knowledge of European literature, combined with sufficient Irish to enable him to master the pure but rapid and colloquial language of the islands. His boyhood in Wicklow had given him the basic understanding of the peasantry that is not to be obtained, as Yeats and Lady Gregory had believed, by merely visiting cottages and collecting legends and fairy-lore. (Yeats urged Synge to try to gather this last on Aran, but he resolutely and wisely refused.) He was Protestant by baptism and race, liberal-agnostic from his temperament and study on the Continent; and these qualities, together with a gift for observing the life about him by a quiet and courteous withdrawal of his personality, combined to foster a gentle ironic compassionate viewpoint without mitigating an Elizabethan delight in all that was vital, vigorous, and at times brutal.

The second fortunate circumstance was the precise moment in the history of the Irish Literary Renaissance which brought him to Aran, constrained him to note the life that he saw as material for a series of articles, and allowed time for the dramatic material to crystallize out into plays just when the Abbey wanted them. In the years between 1892 and 1899 Yeats and others had discussed the possibility of opening a small theatre in Dublin: 'We hope to find, in Ireland, an uncorrupted and imaginative audience, trained to listen by its passion for oratory – we will show that Ireland is not the home of buffoonery and of sentiment, as it has been represented, but the home of an ancient idealism.'[1] In 1899 an English company gave a season of Anglo-Irish plays in Dublin, and in 1902 the Irish National Theatre Society was formed.

It was a curious stroke of fate that threw together the promoters of the theatre. They included Miss Horniman, a wealthy English-woman from Manchester, who provided the financial backing; Edward Martyn, a Mayo landowner, who knew a good deal about the theatre, but who was subject to a religious and sensitive conscience which made him unfitted to deal with the troubles that lay ahead; and George Moore, also of landowning stock, liable to enormous and short-lived enthusiasms and with a great capacity for malicious anecdote. Above all there was Lady Gregory, the widow

[1] From the *Prospectus of the Irish Literary Theatre*. Shaw makes this point most forcibly in *John Bull's Other Island* and in *The Matter with Ireland* (q.v.).

of a Clare landowner, who provided much of the practical business intelligence of the theatre, 'mothered' ceaselessly the frail and over-worked Yeats, and made of her home at Coole Park both a *salon* where the great literary figures of the time could meet (so that Yeats wrote of it in terms of Urbino and Castiglione's *The Courtier*) and a refuge for Yeats himself.

We must see, in the first instance, the new drama as in part a revolt against realism and the Ibsen-type drama; in part a rejection of the English commercial theatre of the last two decades of the century; in part a protest against a general Philistinism. To this Ireland, in her literary Renaissance, was to provide a new regenera-tive force.[1] We must quote both Yeats and Synge on this matter:

> Why should we thrust our works, which we have written with imaginative sincerity and filled with spiritual desire, before those quite excellent people who think that Rossetti's women are 'guys', that Rodin's women are 'ugly' and that Ibsen is 'immoral', and who only want to be left at peace to enjoy the works so many clever young men have made specially to suit them? We must make a theatre for ourselves and our friends, and for a few simple people who understand from sheer simplicity what we understand from scholarship and thought.[2]

Beside this we may set a passage from the Preface to *The Playboy*:

> In the modern literature of towns . . . richness is found only in sonnets, or prose poems, or in one or two elaborate books that are far away from the profound and common interests of life. One has, on one side, Mallarmé and Huysmans producing this literature; and on the other, Ibsen and Zola dealing with the reality of life in joyless and pallid words. On the stage one must have reality, and one must have joy; and that is why the modern intellectual drama has failed, and people have grown sick of the false joy of the musical comedy,[3] that has been given them in place of the rich joy found only in what is superb and wild in reality.

There is, then, the revolt against the contemporary English

[1] The same thought made Yeats choose the opposing symbols of Rome and Byzantium, the Imperial power and the last remaining pocket of a unified culture.
[2] W. B. Yeats, *Essays and Introductions*, p. 166.
[3] We may perhaps think of the same contrast in Sir Philip Sidney's *Apologie*: 'Delight hath a joy in it, either permanent or present. Laughter hath only a scornful tickling.'

theatre, of which Edward Martyn wrote slightingly on his return from France and Germany in 1899:

> The contrast has always struck me . . . between the upholstered, drawing-room-like shapelessness of an English theatre, designed for an addled, over-fed audience, who loathe, above all things, any performance on the stage that would appeal to a lofty and aesthetic sense in humanity, and the grand lines and noble austerity of some foreign theatres like, let us say, the Théâtre Français, where the first consideration is not materialism but art.[1]

The first performances of the Irish Literary Theatre were given at the 'Ancient Concert Rooms' in Dublin in 1899; in 1904 the Abbey was opened in a building of mixed character, partly the Mechanics' Institute and partly the old morgue. Many factors contributed to its success; one was a certain notoriety attending the production of Yeats' *Countess Cathleen*, which in 1899 had been violently attacked in the pamphlet called *Souls for Gold*, and which was produced later in the same year with police protection. Another was Yeats' discovery, in 1901, of two highly gifted amateur actors, William and Frank Fay; and of Florence Farr,[2] who seemed in his view likely to popularize a new method of speaking verse; and the consolidation of the Irish National Theatre Society. Synge's contributions began in 1903, with *In the Shadow of the Glen*, followed in 1904 by *Riders to the Sea*, composed in that order. Then come *The Well of the Saints* (1905), *The Playboy* in 1907, and *Deirdre* (posthumously, with a preface by Yeats) in 1910. *The Tinker's Wedding* was not produced.

Synge's contribution differed both from Yeats' proposed ideals and from the general trend of the new movement. To Yeats one function of the theatre was to make the nation conscious of its heritage in history and myth; to provide a point round which the popular imagination might first awaken, and then concentrate its power; and at the last to unify itself for a nationalist effort by the imagery liberated in the drama. His plays were to be popular, not in the middle-class sense, but as representing *das Volk* and Gaelic culture, together with an epic national past. And thus they might

---

[1] cit. Ellis-Fermor, *The Irish Dramatic Movement* (1939), p. 27.
[2] *v.* 'Speaking to the Psaltery': *Essays and Introductions*, p. 13.

serve, with this spiritual awakening, definite political ends; at the end of his life he was to ask, of the 1916 Easter Rising:

> . . . Did that play of mine send out
> Certain men the English shot?

In contrast, Synge's work is non-political,[1] detached, ironic; concerned with this excited yet dispassionate exploration of the world of the western peasantry, and of an imagination that was still 'fiery, magnificent, and tender'. By 1909 the flame of his own life, and perhaps that of the first phase of the Abbey, had guttered and burnt. An idealistic Nationalist movement had become entangled with politics and religion. Miss Horniman withdrew her support in consequence of the decision to open the theatre on the day of King Edward's funeral. Edward Martyn withdrew his because of his religious conscience. The controversy over *The Playboy*, a sequel to other censorship troubles, exacerbated an already sensitive nationalism, which Shaw's *John Bull's Other Island*, and its *Preface*, had done little to mollify.

It is important to attempt a picture of Synge himself. We may start with some personal descriptions:

> He was a gentle fellow, shy, with that deep sense of humour that is sometimes found in the quietest people. His bulky figure and heavy black moustache gave him a rather austere appearance – an impression quickly dispelled when he spoke. His voice was mellow, low; he seldom raised it. But for his quiet personality he might have passed unnoticed in any gathering.[2]

> There was a third man whom she often noticed: his clothing seemed as if it had been put on him a long time ago and had never been taken off again. He had a long, pale face with a dark moustache drooping over a most beautiful mouth. His eyes were very big and lazy, and did not look quite human; they had a trick of looking sideways – a most intimate, personal look. Sometimes he saw nothing in the world but the pavement, and at other times he saw everything. He looked at Mary Makebelieve once, and she got a fright; she had a queer idea that she had known him well hundreds of years before and that he remembered her also. She was afraid of that man, but she liked him because he looked so gentle and so – there was

---

[1] He does reflect the fear of the peasantry for the English soldiery, the legal system, and the police.

[2] Maire Nic Shiubhlaigh and Edward Kenny: *The Splendid Years*.

something else which as yet she could not put a name to, but which her ancestry remembered dimly.[1]

Here is a French eye-witness:

La figure de Synge est typique: une tête longue, un peu carrée, aux traits tourmentés et, par moments, quasi douloureux, pas belle, mais singulièrement expressive. La moustache châtaine voile à demi les lévres épaisses; une manière de goître enfle le côté droit du cou. Il se montre d'une courtoisie charmante, pleine d'aménité, de douceur, légèrement timide. L'intelligence est ouverte, accueillante.[2]

And against this some sentences from Yeats:

He had under modest and charming manners, in almost all things of life, a complete absorption in his own dream. I have never heard him praise any writer, living or dead, but some old French farce-writer. For him nothing existed but his thought. He claimed nothing for it aloud. He never said any of those self-confident things I am enraged into saying, but one knew that he valued nothing else. He was too confident for self-assertion. . . . One did not think of him as an egotist. He was too sympathetic in the ordinary affairs of life and too simple. In the arts he knew no language but his own.[3]

It was this 'absorption in his own dream' that gives rise to his characteristic ambivalence of attitude. There is a profound love and understanding of nature and the Irish landscape, more apparent, perhaps, in the Essays; yet with it a dispassionate realization of its cruelty, loneliness, and the uncertain menaces of mountain and of sea. He is aware of the peasant with his qualities of stoic endurance, his sense of pagan sorrow; and of his brutality and violence in action or in thought.

He told me once that when he lived in some peasant's house, he tried to make those about him forget that he was there, and it is certain that he was silent in any crowded room. It is possible that low vitality helped him to be observant and contemplative. . . .[4]

It was thus that Yeats knew and celebrated him, using his own favourite theme of the loneliness of the creative artist, the images of the heron and the solitary Fisherman, and the quotation from

---

[1] James Stephens: *The Charwoman's Daughter.*
[2] Anatole le Braz: cit. Bourgeois, and Corkery.
[3] *Autobiographies* (1955), p. 512.
[4] *Essays and Introductions*, pp. 320-1.

Proclus: 'The Lonely returns to the Lonely'. So in the 'Elegy on the Death of Major Robert Gregory' Synge is invoked as a mourner at the *Adonais*-like funeral procession:

> And that enquiring man John Synge comes next,
> That dying chose the living world for text . . .[1]

And again:

> . . . John Synge, I and Augusta Gregory, thought
> All that we did, all that we said or sang
> Must come from contact with the soil, from that
> Contact everything Antaeus-like grew strong . . .[2]

We have, then, a solitary and quiet man, of great sensibility, educated in the European tradition, whom chance sent to observe and to make into plays at the turn of the century the virtually untapped springs of peasant life. Many writers had reflected and refracted portions of that life before; but all of them had written from the outside, or from three or four strata *above*, the peasantry itself. In the Ireland of the eighteenth and nineteenth centuries there is no middle class; the chasm across which the writers must observe is correspondingly deep, and the result is mainly superficial comedy and sentimental tragedy. Synge was the first to live among the people, with a relative lack of self-consciousness for which his boyhood in Wicklow had prepared him, but without ties of kinship or marriage or wealth to distort his reception or his observation. After him the revival of Gaelic studies brought scholars and writers to the West to live his kind of life; two autobiographies, translated from the Irish,[3] have given proof, by their immediate popularity, of the appeal of this rude pastoralism.

But it would be wrong to see Synge as unprejudiced. His social standing, the tradition of race, combine with his agnosticism to perceive subtle and pitiful ironies in the life which he depicts. The Irish peasant of the time used, continually and almost without thought of their significance, pious and 'holy' blessings, expletives, interjections; at their best the signs of an inherent and courteous devotion, which one values and respects to the full. A neighbour or

---

[1] *C.P.*, p. 148.
[2] *C.P.*, p. 369.
[3] Tomás O'Crohan, *The Islandman*: Maurice O'Sullivan, *Twenty Years a Growing*.

stranger entering a cottage will say 'God bless the house' or 'God bless all here': the eldest person present replies 'And you too'. We do not pass men cutting turf or making hay without saying, 'God bless the work'. A dead person will seldom be mentioned without the addition of 'God rest his soul'. But in drama there are apt to be metaphysical and incongruous collocations of such expressions in relation to the events of the play. A classic example is from *The Playboy*:

> 'Is it killed your father?'
> 'With the help of God I did, surely, and that the Holy Immaculate Mother may intercede for his soul.'

and from *The Well of the Saints*

> Let me hit her one good one, for the love of the Almighty God . . .

These verbal ironies, ambivalences, are common in the plays; and give grounds for the attacks (and counter-defences) to the charges of Synge's anti-clericalism and even blasphemy.

There are other temperamental qualities which condition some of his attitudes in the plays. There is abundant evidence, in prose, plays and poems, of his morbid horror of death, and even an obsession with the revealed macabre of the Irish graveyards. These he had seen on Aran. There is some grim humour on the subject of hanging; we may remind ourselves that this concerned many writers at the turn of the century,[1] and think, too, of Villon's 'Ballade des Pendus'.

Synge suffered much from sickness, and died before his marriage to Miss Allgood could take place; the marks of this last period of suffering are set deeply upon the posthumous *Deirdre*. His periods of depression have their intense compensations in a perception of the inscape of nature, and his excited delight in all that is 'superb and wild in reality'. (This compensatory aspect of the work of the invalid or sickly is familiar in literary history.)[2] Yeats, who remains the most sensitive critic of Synge, goes some way to justify this:

> All minds that have a wisdom come of tragic reality seem morbid to those who are accustomed to writers who have not faced reality at all . . .[3]

---

[1] e.g. Hardy, Housman, Wilde.
[2] e.g. 'the ferocious invalids', Stevenson, Henley.
[3] *Essays and Introductions*, p. 322.

and again

> Mr Synge, indeed, sets before us ugly, deformed or sinful people, but his people, moved by no practical ambition, are driven by a dream of that impossible life.[1]

On the negative side he avoided, or escaped from, many of the preoccupations of his contemporaries. The Irish land agitation, the rise of Sinn Féin, the Parnell controversy, left him untouched and untroubled. He is moved by no vision of a resurgence of Irish nationalism as a result of the Abbey Plays. He has no concern for the historical and well-nursed grievances of Irish history. The melancholy or sense of tragedy are imminent in the lives which he saw about him, and in the natural surroundings in which these are set. His world, even in *Deirdre*, is narrow and profound, like the world of the Scottish ballads, concerned with emotions that are few and simple. The extension of that world beyond the local or temporal or ephemeral is achieved by its firm anchorage in a few combinations of Dante's triad, Love, War, and Death; the chain's links tested by recorded experience or, as in *Deirdre*, by a faithful recreation, in a historical setting, of matters which had been his concern elsewhere.

Synge's world is made acceptable by the honesty with which it is presented. That honesty does not exclude his own amused delight at its incongruities, his exultation in its strength, his sympathetic pity for its terror (which may sometimes be that of the penumbral world of the unseen), his assent to the observed resignation and poetry of its people.

2. THE LANGUAGE OF THE PLAYS

Much has been written of Synge's language; and the adverse criticisms range from St John Ervine's indictment of him as a 'faker of peasant speech' to T. S. Eliot's more reasonable and more reasoned view:

> The plays of John Millington Synge form rather a special case, because they are based upon the idiom of a rural people whose speech is naturally poetic, both in imagery and in rhythm. I believe

---

[1] *Essays and Introductions*, p. 304.

that he even incorporated phrases which he had heard from these country people of Ireland. The language of Synge is not available except for the plays set among that same people . . . But in order to be poetic in prose, a dramatist has to be so consistently poetic that his scope is very limited. Synge wrote plays about characters whose originals in life talked poetically, so that he could make them talk poetry and remain real people.[1]

Let us admit at the outset the disadvantages and limitations of this diction. It is fatally easy to write – in one kind. It lends itself readily both to parody and to 'imitation' at the hands of inferior dramatists. It is difficult to 'tone down' for the less vital moments of a play. Because of its inversions, ellipses, and occasional unfamiliar constructions it may present real difficulties of meaning to the English reader. In good stage productions it reveals subtleties of cadence and intonation which float, as it were, upon the rhythms. There are clearly variations in the regional accents of actors, but even the early Abbey Company seem to have had difficulties with the cadences:

> When he brought *The Shadow of the Glen*, his first play, to the Irish National Theatre Society, the players were puzzled by the rhythm, but gradually they became certain that his woman of the glens, as melancholy as a curlew, driven to distraction by her own sensitiveness, her own fineness, could not speak with any other tongue, that all his people would change their life if the rhythm changed.[2]

This 'peasant speech' is a selection, refraction, compression of the language that Synge had known from boyhood, among the people of the Dublin, Wicklow and Galway countrysides. It is reinforced and enriched by his life in the Aran Islands and in West Kerry: we may see from his prose the embodiment of whole passages of dialogue, or of their modification for his purposes. He himself tells us that he had learnt much from listening, with his ear to a crack in the floorboards, to the talk in the kitchen of a country farmhouse, and this I see no reason to disbelieve; without a 'stranger' present the talk in such a company would be far more violent and picturesque. But anyone with a sensitive ear will pick up, in youth, the characteristics of the people among whom he has

---

[1] T. S. Eliot, *Poetry and Drama*, pp. 19-20.
[2] Yeats, *Essays and Introductions*, p. 300.

lived, or even shared the life of the country, especially in fishing or shooting or hill-walking. Once known in this way, one falls readily into the idiom when familiar places are revisited, no matter what time has intervened.

This Anglo-Irish, based upon the Gaelic structure, echoing its syntax and above all its *tourneurs de phrases*, was spoken by the peasants and fishermen with a certain hesitation and precision, a kind of deference[1] to the language, a searching for the exact word, that showed the speaker's unfamiliarity and his habit of transposing, often literally, the equivalent Gaelic. We may quote Lady Gregory on this matter:

> The rich abundant speech of the people was a delight to him. When my *Cuchulain of Muirthemne* came out, he said to Mr Yeats that he had been amazed to find in it the dialect he had been trying to master. He wrote to me 'Your *Cuchulain* is part of my daily bread'.[2]

I have said that the language is refracted and compressed; it is also heightened continually, as all dramatic speech must be, by the poet's personality. It is still possible to hear the occasional sentence or phrase that has Synge's music or imaginative splendour, but the occasions are few. Let us admit, too, that it can become stilted and bloodless, as did the form of dialect known contemptuously as 'Kiltartanese';[3] and that the frequent present participles ('and I walking', 'and you coming'), though normal constructions in the Irish and still in constant use, can become tedious, and lend themselves readily to parody. In this respect the language of *The Shadow* is, I think, more open to criticism[4] than that of *Riders*; in which the strong liturgical emotion, together with a vital integration in the life of the islanders, seems to produce its own proper dignity

---

[1] It is of some interest to reflect that the inscriptions on the tombstones in the graveyards of Aran are in English, not Irish; as if the foreign language were a kind of status-symbol.

[2] *O.I.T.*, p. 124.

[3] So called from the village near Lady Gregory's home, Coole Park. *v.* Yeats' 'An Irish Airman Foresees His Death, *C.P.*, p. 152:

> My country is Kiltartan Cross,
> My countrymen Kiltartan's poor . . .

[4] And to parody; among the satires on the Abbey Plays, the Ulster Players produced *The Mist that does be on the Bog*.

and simplicity. But at its best it is an efficient though limited instrument, capable both of 'household speech' and of poetry, fulfilling at least in part Synge's own wish that 'very speech should be as fully flavoured as a nut or an apple'.

Here Yeats' opinion is relevant:

> . . . He made his own selection of word and phrase, choosing what would express his own personality. Above all, he made word and phrase dance to a very strange rhythm, which will always, till his plays have created their own tradition, be difficult to actors who have not learned it from his lips. It is essential, for it perfectly fits the drifting emotion, the dreaminess, the vague yet measureless desire, for which he would create a dramatic form. It blurs definition, clear edges, everything that comes from the will . . . and it strengthens in every emotion whatever comes to it from far off, from brooding memory and dangerous hope.[1]

This is, perhaps, an over-poetical statement; and, rich in suggestion as Synge's language is, I think that we must be careful in our assessment of it. It would be wrong to think of it wholly in Yeats' terms. Synge can be violent and brutal, using to the full the contrast between his lyric structure and 'the illustrious vulgar'. He loves his Elizabethan or Jacobean strokes of *bravura*, which sometimes seem 'tumid' in Longinus' sense. Indeed, we may perceive some reaction against the faint colours and the 'wavering rhythms' of Pre-Raphaelitism; '. . . it is the timber of poetry that wears most surely, and there is no timber that has not strong roots among the clay and worms'.[2]

The Shadow and *Riders* suggest certain subtle differences in their language. Synge himself noted that in Wicklow, originally part of The Pale,[3] the language has a more definitely Elizabethan 'tone' than in the West, where the Gaelic lay far closer to the surface, and where English might be understood with difficulty and spoken (in Synge's time) hardly at all. As recently as half a century ago one was greeted with the Gaelic phrase 'I have no English' in the Clare hills.

Three aspects of Synge's dramatic language invite our special

---

[1] *Essays and Introductions*, p. 299.
[2] Preface to *P & T*.
[3] A belt of country along the eastern coast from Drogheda to Arklow, held as a military and administrative area by the English.

consideration: idiom, imagery and rhythm. The idiom requires some familiarity. Such phrases as:

> 'You to be going'[1] (When I/We consider that you have been going)
> 'It'd be a grand thing if I'd a sup handy the way I wouldn't be destroying myself groping across the bogs in the rain falling'[2] (the way I wouldn't – in order that I might not)
> 'I've made all sure to have you'[3] (I've taken all steps to possess you)
> 'If you're a dunce itself, you'd have a right to know that larceny's robbing and stealing'[4] (You'd have a right – you ought to know from common experience)

But only in a few instances of extreme ellipsis do these present any difficulty in understanding; an attempt has been made to paraphrase or explain them, with certain unfamiliar words, in the Notes.

Synge's imagery is sparsely used. Nor does he attempt, as Yeats does, to 'charge' his symbols with special or personal significance. His basis is the speech of the countryside, in turn founded on the household and husbandman's perception of the natural world. *The Playboy* is in this respect the richest of the plays. If we attempt some rough grouping as a criterion of the efficiency of the images to communicate, there seem to be two main classes, the 'literary' and the 'folk'. Of these I find the latter by far the more successful. A few examples may serve.

> Amn't I after seeing the love-light of the star of knowledge shining from her brow, and hearing words would put you thinking of the holy Brigid speaking to the infant saints –

(We may defend this as a reminiscence by Christy of an ikon or of the devotional manuals that are common in cottages.)

> – and now she'll be turning again, and speaking hard words to me, like an old woman with a spavindy ass she'd have, urging on a hill.[5]

(Here the image is of the folk, a little *nachgesucht* perhaps, but I think valid.)

Again:

> PEGEEN: Providence and Mercy, spare us all!
> CHRISTY: It's that you'd say surely if you seen him and he after drinking for weeks, rising up in the red dawn, or before it maybe,

---

[1] *T.W.*   [2] *W.S.*   [3] *Deirdre.*   [4] *The Playboy.*   [5] ibid.

14

> and going out into the yard as *naked as an ash-tree in the moon of May*, and shying clods against the visage of the stars . . .

'Naked as an ash-tree in the moon of May' suggests initially the Tennysonian memory, and seems to me false; as does the half-Marlovian 'shying clods against the visage of the stars'.

Against these we may set a host of images from the countryside and its life: the old man's chin,

> the way it would take the bark from the edge of an oak board you'd have building a door.

the old man sleeping,

> . . . there'll be no old fellow wheezing, the like of a sick sheep, close to your ear.

– Conchubor's 'mottled goose neck', and Deirdre's 'I have put away sorrow like a show that is worn out and muddy'.

A serious criticism is that Synge does, at times, strain after his rhetorical effects. In this kind we might instance

> . . . till you'd find a radiant lady with droves of bullocks on the plains of Meath, and herself bedizened in the diamond jewelries of Pharaoh's ma.

or the often-quoted

> . . . do be straining the bars of paradise to lay eyes on the Lady Helen of Troy, and she abroad, pacing back and forward, with a nosegay in her golden shawl.

The first passage suggests that dramatic taste and propriety of character have been submerged in the desire to shock by the juxtapositions of *Pharaoh's ma*, and this, I think, fails; the second might be justified in terms of Marlow's lyricism, though a Mayo peasant would be less likely than Pistol or an Elizabethan schoolboy to fling about such allusions. But the description of

> that young gaffer who'd capsize the stars

might again be justified in terms of Marlowe, or of Roy Campbell,[1] and Michael's complaint

> Oh, aren't you a heathen daughter to go shaking the fat of my heart, and I swamped and drowned with the weight of drink?

---

[1] e.g. 'The Flaming Terrapin'.

has at least a precedent, rather improbably, in the Psalms.[1] But it must be admitted that Synge's fondness for violently colliding images often leads to failure.

3. RHYTHM

Synge's rhythms may be thought of as showing four layers or strata. The first is the speech of the peasantry, remembered or recorded; and refracted through the dramatist's evolved style. This is a disjunctive speech, making free use of connectives, well suited for narrative, but often spoken with a precision and strangeness because the speaker is half translating from the second layer of language. On this we may quote Bourgeois:

> The student who knows Gaelic still thinks in Gaelic as he reads or hears Synge's plays. This applies not only to the phraseology used by his characters, but to the syntax of their sentences. An aorist-like 'He is after doing', or co-ordination used instead of subordination in the Irishism 'And he going to the fair . . .' are pure Gaelic constructions. Ancillary clauses, enallages, inversions and hyperbata of all kinds are unusually plentiful.[2]

A further layer suggests echoes of Tudor and Jacobean prose, both before and after the date of the Authorized Version; we may remember such a construction as

> For I determined not to know anything among you, save Jesus Christ, and him crucified.[3]

It is not easy to conjecture whether these rhythms are a relic of English conquests, or the outcome of Synge's Protestant and ecclesiastical background, reinforced by his own reading of the Tudor dramatists. The last determinant is Synge's own preferences for certain rhythmic combinations, certain tastes and flavours of words.

As to the method, Bickley[4] quotes an excellent example of Synge's re-moulding of the noted phrase, and others are suggested in the Notes. The original is given in *The Aran Islands*:

> Listen to what I'm telling you: a man who is not married is no better than an old jackass. He goes into his sister's house, and into his

---

[1] cxix. 70. [2] op. cit., p. 226.
[3] 1 Cor. ii. 2. [4] F. Bickley, *J.M.S.*, p. 29.

brother's house; he eats a bit in this place, and a bit in another place, but he has no home for himself; like an old jackass straying on the rocks.

Now the centre of the image is the correspondence between the unmarried man and the 'old jackass': the rocks may be those of the sea-shore, or of the stony fields of Aran or the Burren country in Clare; the intention is to express the wandering half-starved aimless life, with perhaps a hint of sexual frustration. Synge compresses it, and holds back the key-image for dramatic effect and for the cadence:

> What's a single man, I ask you, eating a bit in one house and drinking a sup in another, like an old braying jackass strayed upon the rocks?

We may well feel uneasy at the jingle of *braying* and *strayed*. All Synge's technique is apparent here, and the accusation of 'literariness' is not without some justification.[1] But one of the intentions in the re-writing was to give the characteristic cadences, and we may examine some of these.

The cadence is the pattern of weak and strong accents at the end of a phrase, and offers, perhaps, some analogies with the resolution of chords in music. It is denoted by counting the stresses backward from the end of the sentence or clause, and is of two main types; the Latin (familiar through the rhythms of the Mass passing over in translation to the English Liturgy) and the native or English cadence. The former ends with an unstressed syllable ('in te sperant Domine', 'tempore opportuno'), the latter with a strong accent. Both are often tightened and given impetus by alliteration.

As examples:

. . . with a nosegay in her golden shawl   (6:3:1)

. . . I'm master of all fights from now   " "

. . . that young gaffer who'd capsize the stars   " "

The alternative form appears thus:

'The blessing of God on you' says he | and I could say nothing.[2]

---

[1] I have noted some of the imagery in *The Playboy* as over-stressed.
[2] There appear to be several alternative combinations of accent, according to the shade of meaning desired.

... and I have a new cake you can eat | while you'll be working.

... and all the coffins | she's seen made already.

In these three we appear to have variants of the traditional *cursus planus*[1] of the general structure ××/×. Often the cadences are counterpointed in a parallel structure, like that of Hebrew poetry, and strengthened by alliteration:

> ... for the *t*ide's *t*urning at the green head,
>> and the hooker's *t*acking from the east.

– where the insertion of the one word *in* (which would be quite logical) to give

> ... and the hooker's / tacking in / from the east

would have introduced too 'poetic' a rhythm.

It is to Synge's credit that the rhythm is varied continually to avoid any suggestion of these obsessive iambics or tri-syllables; an example from *Deirdre* will serve:

> Birds go mating in the spring of the year,
>> and ewes at the leaves falling,
> but a young girl must have her lover in all the course of the sun
>> and moon.

– where the excision of *all* would have set up an unduly repetitive pattern. As a rule, however, the dramatic emphasis seems to lend itself to the heavy final stress:

> It should have been great and bitter torments did rouse your spirits
>> to a deed of blood.

> ... and be looking out day and night upon the holy men of God.

Yet any attempted analysis of technical devices is no more than a gesture that may draw attention to the subtleties of the language; which only attains its full life when spoken in the theatre by those who can command its strange harmonies and overtones. It is true that the strong rhythms may become monotonous in the reading;

---

[1] See N. R. Tempest, *The Rhythm of English Prose*.

but even in amateur productions it will come to life if the imagination allows the prose to speak for itself. One this we may quote Yeats:

> Synge found the check that suited his temperament in an elaboration of the dialects of Kerry and Aran. The cadence is long and meditative, as befits the thought of men who are much alone, and who when they meet in one another's houses – as their way is at the day's end – listen patiently, each man speaking in turn and for some little time, and taking pleasure in the vaguer meaning of the words and in their sound.[1]

The work of Synge is slight in bulk, but it is a unity. As we read *In Wicklow and West Kerry* and *The Aran Islands* we may re-create for ourselves much of the atmosphere that we need for understanding the plays; and they can show us something of how the uncut stone of narrative and dialogue lay in the quarry of his mind. The poems show his concern with Villon and the Elizabethans, and with that timber that 'has its roots among the clay and worms'. The translations from Petrarch and Villon show his use of the new speech and rhythms that he had forged; and their very strict limitations for that purpose. The less famous works illuminate *Riders to the Sea* and *The Playboy* in many ways. *In the Shadow of the Glen* gives us something of a woman's loneliness and defeat, the mystery of the hills and the lament for the passing of youth. Life oscillates between the mystery of the poetic vision and the brutal realities of living, as does *The Well of the Saints*, and both pose the theme of *The Playboy*; do we live by dream or by reality, and is not man's capacity for self-delusion a protection for his meagre happiness?[2] *The Tinker's Wedding* gives us some insight, delicately shadowed, into the mind of woman and of priest, together with the roaring violence of an Elizabethan or medieval farce. *Riders to the Sea* gives us tragedy in its profound and inexorable simplicity; less violent, more elegiac in its tone, achieving depth by common yet complex symbols, against the overwhelming forces of mutability and the sea. *Deirdre* lives, not as a complete success, in a wholly different kind; heroic tragedy re-created in Synge's idiom, but showing his own preoccupation with death and the passing of beauty. It is doubtful whether this kind of

---

[1] Yeats, *Essays and Introductions*, p. 334.
[2] *v.* Ibsen.

tragedy can ever again be made relevant and vital; if Synge had lived to fulfil his original intention, he might have found an edge of satire to give it more definition, but no more pity.

Synge was a solitary man, and no one could follow him. 'Peasant' plays there were and are in plenty, so that 'P.Q.' (peasant quality) is now a term of dramatic classification, and sometimes of contempt. One reason may be that the vein which he worked was small and soon exhausted. His manner, diction, even the general character-types, are fatally easy to imitate. Perhaps it was the individuality of Synge's style that could combine the outrageous and the lyric, realism and irony and pity, in a manner beyond imitation. Yeats (with Lady Gregory's help) could do no more than copy Synge's language, without his insight into character through language. A passage from *The Pot of Broth*[1] may suggest a useful comparison with speeches from *The Shadow* and *The Playboy*.

> TRAMP: Stop till I'll help you, ma'am, you might scald your hand. I'll show it to you in a minute as white as your own skin, *where the lily and the rose are fighting for mastery*. Did you ever hear what the boys in your own parish were singing after you being married from them – such of them as had any voice at all *and not choked with crying, or senseless with the drop of drink they took to comfort them and to keep their wits from going, with the loss of you* . . .

Lady Gregory herself could achieve a comedy as refined as her gay and gracious nature, and a minor tragedy, pathetic or patriotic, fitted to her vision and gifts. It was left for Sean O'Casey to transplant tragedy to the Dublin slums, and to forge a new Anglo-Irish speech for it, being finely touched with the issues of two wars and, after, with the spur of the Irish censorship. None of these, or the many competent dramatists of the Abbey, could achieve those ambivalent complexities of mood, the fierce ironic joy in the brutal or the 'glorious phrase', with the grim detachment of the 'disinterested' artist, manipulating his characters to advance or recede in the total rhythm of each play. But perhaps Synge is also a preacher, agnostic and a-moral, whose text (as Yeats had said) is the living world. It is a world which concerns the tragedy of the common people, and particularly of women; yet its tragedy may be dissolved or accented, momentarily, by laughter, and imagination

[1] *C. Plays*, p. 99.

nourished by its humour. In that world the extremities meet to illumine, however intermittently, the human situation. For valediction we must read Yeats' 'Celebrations' and 'Detractions',[1] and perhaps remember Villon:

> O grace et pitié tres immense,
> L'entrée de paix et la porte,
> Some de benigne clemence,
> Qui noz faultes toult et supporte,
> Se de me louer me deporte,
> Ingrat suis, et je le maintien,
> Dont en ce refrain me transporte:
> On doit dire du bien le bien.

---

[1] *Autobiographies* (1955), pp. 511-12.

II

INTRODUCTIONS TO THE PLAYS

IN THE SHADOW OF THE GLEN

I

Synge has given us the scene – 'The last cottage at the head of a long glen in County Wicklow.' Glenmalure is nearly ten miles long; the River Avonbeg runs through it. The original of Nora's cottage belonged to two brothers called Harney, who lived there with their unmarried sister.[1] 'Here and there in County Wicklow there are a number of little-known places . . . with curiously melodious names, such as Aughavanna, Glenmalure, Annamoe, or Lough Nahanagan – where the people have retained a peculiar simplicity.'[2] The places named in *The Shadow* are within fifteen miles or so of Wicklow town.

It is difficult to convey the extreme influence of place in the lonelier districts of Ireland.

These people live for the most part beside old roads and pathways where hardly one man passes in the day, and look out on unbroken barriers of heath. At every season heavy rains fall for often a week at a time, till the thatch drips with water stained to a dull chestnut and the floor in the cottages seem to be going back to the condition of the bogs near it. Then the clouds break, and there is a night of terrific storm from the south-west . . . when the winds come down through the narrow glens with the congested whirl and roar of a torrent, breaking at times for sudden moments of silence that keep up the tension of the mind. . . . This peculiar climate, acting on a population that is already lonely and dwindling, has caused or increased a tendency to nervous depression among the people, and every degree of madness, from that of the man who is merely mournful to that of the man who has spent half his life in the madhouse, is common among these hills.[3]

---

[1] Greene and Stephens, *J. M. Synge*, p. 68.
[2] *W.W.K.*, p.27.
[3] ibid., pp. 13, 14.

And among such conditions night and mist can grow unbearably sinister.

Thus nature becomes a sort of grim protagonist, as menacing in its own peculiar manner as the sea in *Riders*. The fishermen of Aran at least live in small communities, clusters of houses, where the men can visit by night and the women may 'gather the talk' in the daytime. Here in the hills prolonged storms isolate the lonely farms; the hills take on their own mystery of loneliness, and drive men 'queer' or mad.

This is Nora's lot, and she has to suffer doubly. At best the fate of an Irish 'small farmer's' wife[1] is a ceaseless drudgery, 'sitting up here boiling food for himself, and food for the brood sow, and baking a cake when the night falls'. There are beasts to be fed, cattle to be milked, turf to be carried, whatever the driving rain and the mud; in spring and summer they must help to dig and plant and reap. So it comes about that the women are old before their time; at thirty-five their beauty has gone. The coming of many children may quicken the process; Nora sees Peggy Cavanagh and Mary Brien as symbols both of the time that awaits her, and of the time that passes her by. But above and beyond all this the country is one of loveless marriages, arranged by the matchmakers, dowry balanced against land and cattle. A man will often defer marriage until he is well on in years; either because his parents refuse to accept a possible bride into the house, or because he wishes to accumulate the safety of a 'stocking', or because he feels more secure as a bachelor; and this prolonged repression may and does affect mental stability, let us quote again:

> In no other country in the world is marriage undertaken so late in life, and perhaps in no other country in the world is there so high a proportion of the unmarried. Worse than the number of bachelors and old maids is the custom of deferring marriage until the man is almost sterile and the woman incapable of producing more than one or two children.[2]

and

> ... the very mentality of the people is opposed to youthful unions.

---

[1] 'It would appear that about 60 per cent of Irish farms are below 30 acres in size, while some 40 per cent are actually between 15 and 5 acres; in other words, they are uneconomic.' *V.I.*, p. 165.

[2] ibid., p. 44. In many parts of the country early marriage is thought to

The present faulty system, which originated in the stress and poverty of a bygone age, is now regarded as the ideal system. What was once imposed as a necessity has become the accepted standard. People, especially in the country districts, consider thirty-five the lowest suitable age for a man to marry, while the woman is scarcely considered mature at thirty.[1]

So woman has her peculiar dilemma: young or old, she must take the husband that offers:

What way would I live, and I an old woman, if I didn't marry a man with a bit of a farm, and cows on it, and sheep on the back hills?

If the breadwinner dies, she (like the women of Aran) is helpless; a strict morality, and the very isolation of her life, forbid the mitigation of a lover. There is only the coming of old age.

I have tried to make clear this background of place and custom, of utter loneliness and remoteness, of the loveless marriage. To it we may add the omnipresent land-hunger and greed of the peasant. Only by realizing these things can we understand Nora's despair, her outcry against the husband that was 'always cold'; and perceive the depth of the scene where Nora soliloquizes on her fate, and her lover counts her husband's money, and thinks that her own poetry may have driven her 'queer'.

2. THE PLAY

One day I was travelling on foot from Galway to Dublin, and the darkness came on me and I ten miles from the town I was wanting to pass the night in. then a hard rain began to fall and I was tired walking, so when I saw a sort of a house with no roof on it up against the road, I got in the way the walls would give me shelter.

As I was looking round I saw a light in some trees two perches off, and thinking any sort of a house would be better than where I was, I got over a wall and went up to the house to look in at the window.

I saw a dead man laid on a table, and candles lighted, and a woman watching him. I was frightened when I saw him, but it was raining hard, and I said to myself, if he was dead he couldn't hurt

---

be risky, even a trifle indecent; the proper age is thought to be 45-50 for the man, and at least 35 for the woman.

[1] *V.I.*, p. 45.

me. Then I knocked on the door and the woman came and opened it.

'Good evening, ma'am,' says I.

'Good evening kindly, stranger,' says she. 'Come in out of the rain.'

Then she took me in and told me her husband was after dying on her, and she was watching him that night.

'But it's thirsty you'll be, stranger,' says she. 'Come into the parlour.'

Then she took me into the parlour – and it was a fine clean house – and she put a cup, with a saucer under it, on the table before me with fine sugar and bread.

When I'd had a cup of tea I went back into the kitchen where the dead man was lying, and she gave me a fine new pipe off the table with a drop of spirits.

'Stranger,' says she, 'would you be afeard to be alone with himself?'

'Not a bit in the world, ma'am,' says I; 'he that's dead can do no hurt.'

Then she said she wanted to go over and tell the neighbours the way her husband was after dying on her, and she went out and locked the door behind her.

I smoked one pipe, and I leaned out and took another off the table. I was smoking it with my hand on the back of my chair – the way you are yourself this minute, God bless you – and I looking on the dead man, when he opened his eyes as wide as myself and looked at me.

'Don't be afeard, stranger,' said the dead man; 'I'm not dead at all in the world. Come here and help me up, and I'll tell you all about it.'

Well, I went up and took the sheet off of him, and I saw that he had a fine clean shirt on his body, and fine flannel drawers.

He sat up then, and says he –

'I've got a bad wife, stranger, and I let on to be dead the way I'd catch her goings on.'

Then he got two fine sticks he had to keep down his wife, and he put them at each side of his body, and he laid himself out again as if he was dead.

In half an hour his wife came back and a young man along with her. Well, she gave him his tea, and she told him he was tired, and he would do right to go and lie down in the bedroom.

The young man went in and the woman sat down to watch by the dead man. A while after she got up, and 'Stranger,' says she, 'I'm going in to get the candle out of the room; I'm thinking the young man will be asleep by this time.' She went into the bedroom, but the divil a bit of her came back.

Then the dead man got up, and he took one stick, and he gave the
other to myself. We went in and we saw them lying together with her
head on his arm.

The dead man hit him a blow with the stick so that the blood out
of him leapt up and hit the gallery.[1]

That is my story.[2]

That is the story as it was told to Synge by an old man in Aran,
though it is the English of Kerry rather than of the Islands. In
essence it is a perennial one, to be found in many literatures. We
must examine the peculiar subtlety with which it becomes drama
beyond its own crude latent possibilities of violence and revenge.

The extension or projection of the play takes place in several
dimensions. The most important is language; that is used power-
fully to suggest the strange and numinous atmosphere of the Glen;
for Synge, though he would have no truck with Yeats' fairy world,
was intensely aware of the genius of lonely places.[3] Character is
revealed bit by bit, more often in speech than in the occasional
significant gesture or smile. The mysterious heroic figure of the
dead Patch Darcy is linked, ironically, to the other characters by the
sheep-imagery; and Darcy, Dan, Nora, are all gathered under the
Glen's shadow by the recurrent *queer*; which has overtones of the
fey, the supra-natural, as well as of derangement of the mind.

The potential solemnity of the wake is retained, and amplified by
eerie suggestion; the corpse has not been 'tidied' because of the
curse upon Nora if she touches him, and that might be transferred
– such is the force of curses – to the Tramp. (There is a similar story
told to Synge of a dying woman who forbade her daughter to touch
her hair; a year later the daughter, acting on a hint, dug up the body
and found that the hair had been used to conceal a hoard of
sovereigns.)[4] Patch Darcy moves uneasily in the background; we
feel that Nora's whistle in the night might call him instead of
Michael. The isolation of the cottage, the unpitying rain, is built up
in Nora's speech, which reveals, in the poetry, her own loneliness
and passion. The departure from the original fable begins with the
Tramp's intervention, with a new dignity and authority:

It's a hard thing you're saying for an old man, master of the house,
and what would the like of her do if you put her out on the roads?

[1] i.e. a sort of open attic: *v.* the scene in *Riders.* [2] *A.I.*, pp. 37-9.
[3] *v.*, pp. 68-9. [4] *W.W.K.*, p. 114.

26

He tries a second time:

> Maybe himself would take her.

But there is no solution, and then, suddenly, we have the Tramp's two lyric outbursts; that seem for an instant – we may think of *Antony and Cleopatra* – to lift the play into a world above all morality. To it the poetry in Nora responds; clear-eyed, bitter, she has no illusions as to her future as a tramp's doxy. She makes her impassioned defence:

> What way would a woman live in a lonesome place the like of this place, and she not making a talk with the men passing?[1]

We are left with the second and final reversal; the about-to-be wronged husband sits down to drink with his would-be betrayer. This is an almost Shavian twist, an expression of Synge's delighted irony. I do not find this scene incredible; given the relief of Dan at the expulsion of the 'blathering' Tramp and the 'bad wife' (they both know too much about Patch Darcy anyway) and his knowledge that conventional ethics, the traditional 'turning out of doors', are all on his side; given, too, the relief of Michael at escaping from threatened violence as well as from the obloquy of the seducer,[2] it falls reasonably into place. Here the keyword of the two speeches is *quiet*, which has peculiar overtones of respectability, peace from marital nagging, even enjoyment; as well as of lack of spirit or 'wildness', the sin imputed to the frustrate ghosts of such men.

The Shadow is neither comedy nor tragedy; it has elements of comedy which are not fully exploited in the present, elements of tragedy which are, perhaps, projected into the future after the curtain has fallen. Yet the irony of the ending is the only possible aesthetic resolution of the dilemma that the play presents. Husband and wife are held in a careful dramatic balance. On his side is convention, the practice of the late marriage, the union of January

---

[1] Cf. Yeats'

> For a man's attention
> Brings such satisfaction
> To the craving in my bones.
> (*C.P.*, p. 309)

[2] Which is very much more serious in Ireland than in most other countries.

and May; his right, in a country where divorce is unknown, to turn her out of doors when her prospective unfaithfulness has been made known before witnesses. According to these lights he has not failed; he could still have given her

> the half of a dry bed, and good food in your mouth

To Nora, the loveless marriage (yet it is surprising how admirably most of them turn out) has deprived her of children, brought her to the horrors of loneliness on the hill-farm, to the unending drudgery of its work, to the man who was 'cold' always. Patch Darcy is dead, no more than a memory; Michael Dara is a poor thing, but he is at least male. She has kept a half-humorous flicker of maternal tenderness for the old man:

> Yet, if it is itself, Daniel Burke, who can help it at all, and let you be getting up into your bed, and not be taking your death with the wind blowing on you, and the rain with it, and you half in your skin.

or again –

> And what way will yourself live from this day, with none to care you?

And yet the complexity, the essential femininity of Nora's character is such that she herself does not understand it; and we may quote Yeats again:

> If he see *The Shadow of the Glen*, he will ask. Why does this woman go out of her house? Is it because she cannot help herself, or is she content to go? Why is not all made clearer? And yet, like everybody when caught up into great events, she does many things without being quite certain why she does them. . . . She feels an emotion that she does not understand. She is driven by desires that need for their expression, not 'I admire this man,' or 'I must go, whether I will or no,' but words full of suggestion, rhythms of voice, movements that escape analysis. . . . She is intoxicated by a dream which is hardly understood by herself, but possesses her like something half remembered on a sudden wakening.[1]

Only the Tramp turned poet has anything to offer; and she knows that it will betray her; but it has been a fine bit of talk, and she will go with him.

---

[1] *Essays and Introductions*, pp. 304-5.

3. THE WAKE

So much of the plot hinges upon the ceremony of the wake (Pedrollo called his opera *La Veglia*) that it is well to describe it briefly. The body, dressed in its shroud and 'tidied' – usually by some woman, not of the family, who has known skill in this – is laid on a table in a corner of the room, candles burning at head and feet. As each visitor enters he lifts the cloth from the face of the dead to make his farewell. The Tramp, no doubt from experience, is suspicious ('It's a queer look is on him for a man that's dead') and it is wholly in Michael Dara's character to refuse to pull down the sheet and look. 'I will not, Nora; I do be afeard of the dead.' The visitor kneels down to say a prayer. At one time it was customary to place a conical mound of snuff on the navel of the corpse, from which each took a pinch as he went by. Then, one by one, the callers pass to the group round the fire. Each is given a *new* clay pipe, ready loaded with tobacco; that is why Nora apologizes to the Tramp for having only her husband's pipes available. There is whisky and stout in whatever quantity the means of the relatives allow, and tea for the women.

The talk round the fire develops, first, as a series of praises of the deceased, reminiscences and anecdotes (always favourable) about his or her life; and finally might develop into something like an orgy.[1] The whole ceremony is pagan, down to the symbolism of the new clay pipes,[2] overlaid with Christian ritual. (I can remember being brought, very briefly, by my nurse to the beginnings of a wake in one of the tenants' cottages, and being terrified of the corpse in the corner.) The best modern description is by T. H. White:[3]

> The point was, of course, that everybody was trying to amuse Charlie Plunkett.
> Otherwise, why 'wake' him? We were there to give him company, support, help, love, during his first lost hours straying beside the

---

[1] There is a story of a casual body of a tramp who died in a certain parish whose people proceeded joyfully to 'wake' it. When the wake was over the next parish begged the loan of the body; and so on, till the parish priest had to intervene.

[2] Is tobacco smoke a kind of incense, the new pipe a resurrection symbol?

[3] *The Godstone and the Blackymor*, p. 166 et seq.

body.[1] That was why we were sitting up with him. Obviously the best possible treatment was to entertain him – to flatter him, to keep his heart up, to take his mind from his troubles – and this we did, for pity and protection, by means of song and vulgarity.

Against this we may set the terrible chant, that follows the soul in its progress to the other world, of 'The Lyke-Wake Dirge':

> This ae nighte, this ae nighte,
> *Every night and alle,*
> Fire and fleet and candle-lighte,
> *And Christe receive they saule.*

– and quote the opening of F. R. Higgins' poem on Padraic O'Conaire, the Gaelic storyteller:

> They've paid the last respects in sad tobacco
> And silent is this wake-house in its haze;
> They've paid the last respects; and now their whisky
> Flings laughing words on mouths of prayer or praise;
> And so young couples huddle by the gables,
> O let them grope home through the hedgy night –
> Alone I'll mourn my old friend, while the cold dawn
> Thins out the holy candlelight.[2]

Here is a modern keen, translated from the Irish, from Achill Island:

O Man of the House, you have left us.
Your place by the fire is empty.
We'll be hearing your voice no longer
Praising, or chiding in anger.
We will not tell you any more at the day's end
Of its labours and its joys
Weeping we mourn your passing
The cold ground will cover you, hold you.
The love that went to you and from you
Makes our hearts warm with remembrance
You have left us, O Man of the House, but we do not forget you.

In a production it is highly important that the audience should be prepared for the atmosphere of the wake, whether by music or by some other method.

[1] This is what Yeats means by:
> Ah! when the ghost begins to quicken,
> Confusion of the death-bed over . . .
> 'The Cold Heaven' (*C.P.*, p. 140).

[2] *Oxford Book of Modern Verse*, p. 370.

4. THE CHARACTERS

The Tramp is the central figure of the play. Tramps and tinkers seem to embody, or symbolize, Synge's desire for 'what is superb and wild in reality' and he stresses their vitality and health;[1] his own verses 'The Passing of the Shee' suggest that these people were in some sort a heroic compensation for the dusty Celtic mythology, as well as anti-types of the orthodox.[2] Perhaps Synge's own wandering years in Europe had suggested a sympathetic bond; in his love letters he signed himself 'Your Old Tramp'.[3] Of all the people in the Glen he alone seems to have achieved some kind of harmony with nature, and we may recall Synge's own pseudo-Wordsworthian verses:

> I knew the stars, the flowers, and the birds,
> The grey and wintry sides of many glens,
> And did but half-remember human words,
> In converse with the mountains, moors, and fens.[4]

That melancholy and reserved nature found in Glenmalure something that is echoed in the play:

> In these hills the summer passes in a few weeks from a late spring, full of odour and colour, to an autumn that is premature and filled with the desolate splendour of decay; and it often happens that in moments when one is most aware of this ceaseless fading of beauty, some incident of tramp life gives a local human intensity to the shadow of one's own mood.[5]

In one dimension the Tramp is a link between the sinister Glen and the world outside; he is the eternal wanderer, who has gathered wisdom in his travels. He has both a poet's sensitivity, a sharp practical mind, and a realistic earthiness; but from the outset there

[1] v. W.W.K., pp. 1, 2.
[2] Yeats used them in much the same way. The polar antimonies of King and Beggar are, of course, archetypal: v. Synge's 'Queens'.
[3] v. Greene and Stephens, p. 92.
[4] v. 'Prelude'. It has been suggested that the 'moors and fens' may be a memory of the hymn, 'Lead, kindly light'.
[5] W.W.K., p. 6.

are hints of his poetry, and the whisky releases and reinforces it,[1] without abating his realism:

'What would he do with me now?'
'Give you the half of a dry bed, and good food in your mouth.'

Dan is slightly sketched; the cantankerous old man of Tudor Comedy, wholly conscious of his own mastery, accepting the phenomenon of 'the bad wife' and the traditional remedy. Beside him Michael Dara is a poor thing; timid, boastful, consumed by greed; foreshadowing in himself, as he counts the money, the repetition of the loveless marriage from which Nora has tried to escape into a temporary shadow of romance, and which is broken when he appeals to her to 'get me out of this'. He is not unlike Christy Mahon of *The Playboy* before his redemption by Pegeen.

Nora we have already considered; but only a mature actress can suggest the bitterness of unsatisfied marriage, the poetry that responds to that of the Tramp, the woman's realism that foresees her lot with him, and the woman's dread of old age and the bitter exaltation of

– but you've a fine bit of talk, stranger, and it's with yourself I'll go.

Outside the four characters on the stage move, ghost-like, two others. There is Patch Darcy, who 'died and was eaten by crows in the butt of a ditch'; Nora's first lover, perhaps; a quasi-heroic figure in the play. There is a whole saga about him, and he is drawn in sharp contrast to the timorous Michael; his praises are given by the Tramp, and we feel, uneasily, that this is in some sense Patch Darcy's wake also:

That was a great man, young fellow – a great man, I'm telling you. There was never a lamb from his own ewes he wouldn't know before it was marked, and he'd run from this to the city of Dublin and never catch for his breath.[2]

He seems to be linked both to the Tramp and to Nora by the

[1] We may quote from *A.I.*, p. 165: 'When he had a couple of glasses taken and was warm by the fire, he began making a song.'
[2] The source is in *W.W.K.*, p. 47. 'You've been after sheep since you were that height . . . and yet you're nowhere in the world beside the herds that do be reared beyond on the mountains. Those men are a wonder, for I'm told they can tell a lamb from their own ewes before it is marked. . . .'

recurrent ditch imagery.[1] Then too, there is Peggy Cavanagh, the spectral woman of old age, the living emblem of Nora's own prospective fate:

> – and it's not from the like of them you'll be hearing a tale of getting old like Peggy Cavanagh, and losing the hair off you, and the light of your eyes . . .

So we remember Synge's favourite Villon, and the 'Ballade des Dames du Temps Jadis', and a hundred such-like laments. Finally there is Mary O'Brien, who has at least the consolation of children – though there is a shade of irony and envy combined in Nora's description of her. Just as the significance of *Riders* is extended by its symbols, so these shadow-figures reach out into universality beyond the remote world of the Glen.

RIDERS TO THE SEA

If we are to understand the inwardness of the play, we must try to reconstruct imaginatively something of the life of the islanders as Synge knew it at the turn of the century. The Aran Islands form a small group of three, Inishmore, Inishmaan, and Inisheer, set far out in the Atlantic between the coasts of Galway and Clare. The land is poor and stony; small fields intersected by stone walls which retain this shallow soil, itself formed in part from rotten seaweed. There is not timber or turf for fuel, or grass for the horses in the winter months. Prolonged storms meant that the islands were inaccessible for long periods at a time, and, for lack of the fishing, might bring families near to starvation. The islands shelve upwards from east to west, rising to high cliffs on the open Atlantic; there are many monuments, among them the massive Bronze Age forts of Dún Aengus, ruins of castles and oratories, relics of early Christian settlements. O'Flaherty's film, *Man of Aran*, gave a good picture of the setting and of the life.

In 1897, when Yeats advised Synge to go there, the communities of the islands were probably among the most primitive in western Europe. Synge's temperament, his 'negative capability', and his

---

[1] I am not aware that this has been mentioned in previous comments on the play: but we may remember three poems of Yeats in support, as well as *Macbeth*. Tinkers, tramps, drunkenness, are linked to the ditch (*v.* p. 281).

study of Gaelic made him the friend of the people. It is not too much to suggest that he found himself and his genius among them. It is thus that Yeats speaks of him in the elegy 'In Memory of Major Robert Gregory':[1]

> . . . And never could have rested in the tomb
> But that, long travelling, he had come
> Towards nightfall upon certain set apart
> In a most desolate stony place,
> Towards nightfall upon a race
> Passionate and simple like his heart.

– which we may set against this passage:

> They live in a world of grey, where there are wild rains and mists every week in the year, and their warm chimney corners, filled with children and young girls, grow into the consciousness of each family in a way it is not easy to understand in more civilized places.[2]

The prose sketches of his life in the islands are set out in *The Aran Islands*, later to be supplemented by *In Wicklow, West Kerry and Connemara*. In them he has given us both the raw material, and something of the tensions and emotions, of the life that he wove into the plays. We can trace in the book these sources, and indeed we know more of the prose stuff for *Riders to the Sea* than for any of the other plays. It is pertinent to quote some of the more illuminating passages:

> As they talked to me and gave me a little poteen and a little bread when they thought I was hungry, I could not help feeling that I was talking with men who were under a judgement of death. I knew that every one of them would be drowned in the sea in a few years and battered naked on the rocks, or would die in his own cottage and be buried with another fearful scene in the graveyard I had come from.[3]

Since the sea takes them, the islanders do not learn to swim, for that would only prolong suffering. And there are strange stories connected with the ritual of drowning; of a man's hands being smashed with a stretcher as he clings to the gunwale, for you must not take back what the sea has claimed; how, if your cap blows off, you must not look at it, but ask another whether it is floating crown

[1] *C.P.*, p. 148.   [2] *A.I.*, p. 58.   [3] ibid., p. 141.

or brim uppermost, and if the brown is on top, you must leave it, for the sea may think that you are beneath it, and take it as a simulacrum of you. All are aware of an immanence of the supernatural, of omens, far older than Christianity:

> Before he went out on the sea that day his dog came up and sat beside him on the rocks, and began crying. When the horses were coming down to the slip an old woman saw her son, that was drowned a while ago, riding on one of them. She didn't say what she was after seeing, and this man caught the horse, he caught his own horse first, and then he caught this one, and after that he went out and was drowned.[1]

The Connemara ponies are strong; they are wild and easily frightened:

> The islanders themselves ride with a simple halter and a stick, yet sometimes travel, at least in the larger island, at a desperate gallop. . . . More than once in Aranmor I met a party going out west with empty panniers from Kilronan. Long before they came in sight I could hear the clatter of hoofs, and then a whirl of horses would come round a corner at full gallop with their heads out, utterly indifferent to the slender halter that is their only check. They generally travel in single file with a few yards between them, and as there is no traffic there is little fear of an accident.[2]

Here is the yarn that Synge wove into the 'recognition' scene in the play:

> Now a man has been washed ashore in Donegal with one pampooty[3] on him, and a striped shirt with a purse in one of the pockets, and a box for tobacco.
> For three days the people here have been trying to fix his identity. Some think it is the man from this island, others think that the man from the south answers the description more exactly. Tonight as we were returning from the slip we met the mother of the man who was drowned from this island, still weeping and looking out over the sea. . . .
> Later in the evening, when I was sitting in one of the cottages, the sister of the dead man came in through the rain with her infant, and there was a long talk about the rumours that had come in. She pieced together all she could remember about his clothes, and what

---

[1] ibid., p. 144.
[2] ibid., p. 47.
[3] *Pampooties*: the shoes made of raw cowhide with the hair outwards; they are the only footgear that is relatively safe on slippery rock.

his purse was like, and where he had got it, and the same for his tobacco box, and his stockings. In the end there seemed little doubt that it was her brother.

'Ah!' she said, 'it's Mike sure enough, and please God they'll give him a decent burial.'[1]

Two passages bear on the coffin and the 'white boards':

... When the wind fell a little I could hear people hammering below me to the east. The body of a young man who was drowned a few weeks ago came ashore this morning, and his friends have been busy all day making a coffin in the yard of the house where he lived.[2]

. . . . .

I asked her if the curragh would soon be coming back with the priest. 'It will not be coming soon or at all to-night,' she said. 'The wind has gone up now, and there will come no curragh to this island for may be two days or three. And wasn't it a cruel thing to see the haste was on them, and they in danger all the time to be drowned themselves?'

Then I asked her how the woman was doing.

'She's nearly lost,' said the old woman; 'she won't be alive at all to-morrow morning. They have no boards to make her a coffin, and they'll want to borrow the boards that a man below has had this two years to bury his mother, and she alive still.'[3]

All the ritual connected with death – the laying out, the wake, the scene in the churchyard – is of supreme importance; so is the depth of the grave (in a stony country), and the quality of the coffin boards. I remember how, when my father's grave was opened to take my mother's body, an old retainer told me with pride that the first coffin was as 'sound as the day it was laid in', and expecting that I should find consolation from this. Synge gives two macabre descriptions of burials in Aran; his account of the keen and its inwardness is best given in his own words:

This grief of the keen is no personal complaint for the death of one woman over eighty years, but seems to contain the whole passionate rage that lurks somewhere in every native of the island. In this cry of pain the inner consciousness of the people seems to lay itself bare for an instant, and to reveal the mood of beings who feel their isolation in the face of a universe that wars on them with winds and seas. They are usually silent, but in the presence of death all outward show of indifference or patience is forgotten, and they shriek with pitiable despair before the horror of the fate to which

---

[1] *A.I.*, p.109.   [2] ibid., p. 136   [3] ibid., p. 137.

they all are doomed.

Before they covered the coffin an old man kneeled down by the grave and repeated a simple prayer for the dead.

There was an irony in these words of atonement and Catholic belief spoken by voices that were still hoarse with the cries of pagan desperation.[1]

With these passages before us we may turn to the play itself.

Riders to the Sea is unique in dramatic history, for it is the only one-act play that can be described as a tragedy in the fullest sense. At first sight the plot would seem to be too simple, the characterization too faintly sketched, to enable the playwright to build up and communicate the typical momentum, the high seriousness, proper to the form. Some critics have found, indeed, that it is too fatalistic to be tragic, that it affords no scope for conflict. From the outset the protagonists seem to be enclosed in an inflexible circle of destiny, in which the prayers and consolations of Christianity are powerless; the resolution of the play rests upon a resignation that is more stoic than Christian, a sense of relief that no further loss is possible, when humanity confronts the ultimates of death:

No man at all can be living for ever, and we must be satisfied.

What, then, can make the play great tragedy?

It has something of the simplicity in depth of much Greek drama, and of the Scottish ballads,[2] where the conditions of the essential conflict are known and accepted as an aspect of the human situation; so that we can dispense with detailed exposition of plot or character. The conflict is between the sea and humanity, singly and collectively. The human opponents are on three levels; Bartley who must sell his horses at the fair; his sisters who seem to have a sacrificial-prophetic function, like Antigone and Ismenê; Maurya who speaks the two great elegies for the dead, who are the dead not only of Aran but of the world. The sea is the tyrant-god full of mystery and power, the giver and the taker of life, the enemy and the challenger of the young; it is pre-existent evil and good:

It's the life of a young man to be going on the sea, and who would listen to an old woman with one thing and she saying it over?

---

[1] ibid., p. 43.
[2] We may think, in particular, of 'The Wife of Usher's Well'.

To the old, it is that which takes, sooner or later, all that woman gives:

> I've had a husband, and a husband's father, and six sons in this house – six fine men, though it was a hard birth I had with every one of them, and they coming into the world – and some of them were found, and some of them were not found, but they're gone now the lot of them. . . .

Man's conflict with the sea, and woman's loss, is archetypal; it is everywhere in myth, legend, history, from the Greek Anthology to 'Lycidas':

> Ay me! Whilst thee the shores, and sounding Seas
> Wash far away, where ere they bones are hurl'd,
> Whether beyond the stormy Hebrides,
> Where thou perhaps under the whelming tide
> Visit'st the bottom of the monstrous world . . .

In the play there are in miniature elements of the Greek tragic pattern: the foreboding of Maurya, the ritual elegies for the single and the many dead; the keening women as a chorus; the release of tension in the resigned acceptance of defeat. In structure, language, imagery, as well as by its supreme economy, it has the 'felt authority'[1] of great drama. But 'tragedy is lyrical in origin, and at its great moments it reverts to type'. It is the lyric language, and the complex and yet never wholly explicable significance of the symbols (themselves of great simplicity and of the 'household kind') that elevate the play to tragedy, that 'set the mind wandering from idea to idea, from emotion to emotion', and extend the play from local to universal significance.

The symbol may be considered as the third and last term of the poetic image; the first two being simile and metaphor. We may think of it, very tentatively, as that product of the creative imagination which apprehends and states resemblances or correspondences between myths, legends, events, or things; these being used to define, enlarge, characterize, or evaluate that which is contemplated. But the symbol differs from simile or metaphor in that the correspondences implied are not simple, of the order of one to one (although metaphor may on occasion be highly complex), but pluri-significant; capable of many meanings, and of extending and

[1] I am indebted for this phrase to J. L. Styan, *The Elements of Drama*.

amplifying the significances that the artist perceives. He chooses it because by this means, and by this means only, is it possible to make a gesture, as it were, towards these meanings; yet the symbol, by its very nature, is never susceptible of full explanation or exegesis, and must be thought of as existing in its own right. Symbols which appear to recur persistently throughout human history (such as the many aspects of the sea, the drowned man, the horse that signifies power, fear and strength) are often called archetypal.[1]

Of this archetypal nature is the conflict of man with the sea, the giver and taker of life.[2] The islandmen must be constantly aware of its menace, its moods, its protection. Again and again through the play the characters speak of the tides and their significance. It is the killer of the young, the breadwinners, whose life it is to be upon it. The fishermen are all its riders, mysteriously linked to the human and superhuman riders, here and in tradition.[3] We may if we wish discern, uneasily, some connection between the red mare ridden by Bartley, and the grey mare by Michael's phantasm, for one colour belongs to strength and virility, the other to the dead.[4] The bread that was baked on the table where Bartley's body is laid, that Maurya tries vainly to give to him when she meets him by the spring well,[5] serves to refresh the old men who must make his coffin. At the opening we see the 'fine white boards' bought at a great price for Michael's coffin, and they are instantly recognizable by their size and proportions if one has made such things; the new rope will serve for a halter for the horses, or to lower a coffin. But the nails (they suggest, perhaps, pain, finality) have been forgotten:

> It's a great wonder she wouldn't think of the nails, and all the coffins she's seen made already.

The living and the dead intermingle even in their possessions. The stick that Maurya takes to support her on her way to the spring well

---

[1] See, for example, Maud Bodkin, *Archetypal Patterns in Poetry*; W. H. Auden, *The Enchaféd Flood*.

[2] *v. Henry V*, II iii. 12; and the Scottish ballads, for the belief that birth comes on the flood tide, death on the ebb.

[3] Consider, e.g., the White Horses of *Rosmersholm*, and Wagner.

[4] The red and grey cocks are a cliché-phrase of the Ballad; but Yeats uses this opposition of colour in *A Full Moon in March*. For Death on the Pale Horse, see Revelations vi. 8.

[5] This is an example of the 'unstressed' symbol. There are many biblical precedents.

(itself a life-image) belonged to the dead Michael. Bartley is wearing Michael's second shirt, so that the girls when they open the parcel cannot compare the drowned man's with it. They must find proof instead in the dropped stitches of the stocking, and we feel uneasily that there is more behind this, remembering the Three Fates and the thread of life, and perhaps Donne's image:

> Because such fingers need to knit
> That subtle knot, which makes us man.

The boards, the rope, are new; so are the clothes and shoes that Michael's phantasm wears; and we may think of the new linen in Revelations, and the new shoes of 'The Lyke-Wake Dirge'.

So the symbols, set in their matrix of rhythmical speech of great subtlety and complexity, permeate the play. They dissolve, coalesce, combine in tension or opposition, to give depth or contrapuntal irony, retaining always their essential nature, which is to set the imagination in motion, to extend it beyond the bounds of the apparent simplicity of the plot. And we may quote from Yeats' essay 'The Emotion of Multitude':

> Indeed all the great Masters have understood, that there cannot be great art without the little limited life of the fable, which is always the better the simpler it is, and the rich, far-wandering, many-imaged life of the half-seen world beyond it. There are some who understand that the simple unmysterious things living as in a clear moonlight are of the nature of the sun, and that vague many-imaged things have in them the strength of the moon.[1]

In a production the set should be basically as Synge has given it; a cottage interior with the large open hearth, a small creel or basket of turf beside, a hook in the chimney from which the cast-iron cooking-pots are hung; three or four of the 'sugawn' chairs, with twisted hay-rope for seats; a single long kitchen table on which they cook and eat, where the girls examine the drowned man's clothing, and on which Bartley's body is laid. (It was a touch of genius in a television production when one of the girls quickly washed down the table on which the bread has been baked, just before the men come in.)

There might be a built-in bed with a door to its recess; a short clumsy ladder that leads to the 'loft' below the thatch; a single door

[1] *Essays and Introductions*, p. 216.

with a half-hatch, a window that looks out on the headland. There must be a dresser with china on it; beside it, perhaps hanging on the wall, a little shrine with a red oil lamp under it, and a bowl for the holy water. In a corner, the new boards and coil of rope.

One temptation (as in the production I have mentioned) is to overplay the 'fisherman' setting, and the noise of the sea and surf and wind. For though there is a heavy sea running on 'the white rocks' it is not a full gale, otherwise the hooker going to Galway would not be out of harbour. The play is built upon 'vigour and beauty of speech', and its subtleties, and anything that detracts from these things, by extraneous sight or sound, must be rigorously rejected by the producer.

If the Irish accent (and, even more, the intonation) cannot be found implicit in the actors, it is best spoken as normal poetic prose, and the cadences and rhythms allowed to guide the voices without any attempt at a brogue; taking the speech a little slowly, as native Irish speakers handle English with a sense almost of deference. So, too, the keening, which is difficult to reproduce unless one has heard it,[1] must be given in a subdued pitch by the 'chorus' of the old women, and must not be allowed to drown the speech.

Of the characters, Nora, although the younger, seems to be the more decisive personality. Both should show the exasperated impatience, verging on petulance, of the young for the very old; Maurya belongs to another world. Bartley is lightly sketched; laconic, matter-of-fact, unconcerned with the women and their griefs.

There is one moment that is difficult to produce, and on which the play, in a sense, seems to hinge. This is the shuddering cry, given in the text as 'Uah!' by the two girls together; it is compounded of horror, and the premonition of the supernatural, and a wail of fear. The speeches of Maurya are out of the reach of any but a really great actress, who has knowledge of suffering and loss; she seems to rise gradually through a hieratical dignity of sorrow in word and gesture, to her acceptance of defeat.

---

[1] Vaughan Williams' music gives it well.

THE TINKER'S WEDDING

Then a woman came up and spoke to the tinker, and they went down the road together into the village. 'That man is a great villain,' said the herd when he was out of hearing. 'One time he and his woman went up to a priest on the hills and asked him would he wed them for half-a-sovereign, I think it was. The priest said it was a poor price, but he'd wed them surely if they'd make him a tin can along with it. "I will, faith," said the tinker, "and I'll come back when it's done." They went off then, and in three weeks' time they came back, and they asked the priest a second time would he wed them. "Have you the tin can?" said the priest. "We have not," said the tinker; "we had it made at the fall of night, but the ass gave it a kick this morning the way it isn't fit for you at all." "Go on now," says the priest. "It's a pair of rogues and schemers you are, and I won't wed you at all." They went off then, and they were never married to this day.'[1]

This is the raw material of the play. Synge himself tells us that the first draft was written about the time he was working on *Riders to the Sea* and *In the Shadow of the Glen*. It was re-written many times.[2] In one of his rare Prefaces he hinted, half-apologetically, at its function: ' . . . where a country loses its humour, as some towns in Ireland are doing, there will be morbidity of mind, as Baudelaire's mind was morbid.' But whatever the virtues of *The Tinker's Wedding* it was too strong meat for the Abbey Theatre. The gift for *selbst-ironie* has never been a strong feature of Irish theatrical taste; and the violence inflicted on a caricatured priest made the play impossible to produce. The classic tolerance that sanctioned The Feast of Fools, *The Four P's*, *Sir Thopas*, and a score of such clerical caricatures was absent. One imagines that those who rioted out of shocked propriety at *The Playboy* were joined by the ancillary forces of the Church: and there had been previous difficulties, though of a more subtly theological character, with Yeats' *Countess Cathleen*. Moral indignation at the content of *The Tinker's Wedding* seems to have vitiated much criticism even today, especially that of the extreme 'nationalist' school; we may give examples:

Only in a few passages do we come on the deeper Synge, and those

---

[1] *W.W.K.*, pp. 47-8.
[2] 'The MS includes in an earlier version of the play, an apology to the Irish Clergy' (D. H. Greene, *P.M.L.A.*, article, cit.).

few passages apart, the play is hardly worth considering either as a piece of stage-craft or as a piece of literature.[1]

and

One is sorry Synge wrote so poor a thing, and one fails to understand why it should ever have been staged anywhere.[2]

Greene[3] considers it as an artistic failure, but of interest as a link between the one-act plays of Synge's apprenticeship and the three-act plays of his maturity.

Almost alone of the purely Irish critics E. A. Donoghue[4] has approved the qualities of the play: among his insights are the ironic contrasts (the traditional material of comedy) between the worlds of the tinkers and that of the priest, and the interchange of 'orthodoxies' that are involved. Dr Donoghue's view is stated with perception and delicacy; but I think the play may be presented from a slightly different angle.

It would be idle to pretend that Synge, an Anglo-Irish Protestant, does not show a distinct anti-clerical outlook; it is never overt, save in *The Tinker's Wedding*; but in the Notes and elsewhere I have indicated some of the ironies and ambivalences that are perceptible, more particularly in *The Playboy*. I find that this is no anti-clericalism of a characteristic Anglo-Irish type, but rather that of the liberal-agnostic Continental tradition; cool, on the whole good-humoured, and not emotionally implicated. I believe rather that Synge's attitude is based, here as elsewhere, in a dispassionate observation of both sides; a keen interest in those ironies and overtones to which his ear is perpetually attuned; and a dramatic instinct that welcomes, on occasion, the violence or coarseness of the Elizabethan farcical situation. The tensions of the play lie between the tinkers and the priest; somewhere between them, faintly shadowed but still present, are the common people, the respectable Middle Term. Let us glance for a moment at the two sides, the tinkers' first.

Irish tinkers differ greatly in habits and customs from the English

---

[1] Corkery, *Synge and Anglo-Irish Literature* (1931) p. 149.
[2] ibid., p. 152
[3] In *P.M.L.A.*, cit.
[4] 'Too Immoral for Dublin', *Irish Writing*, No. 30, March 1955.

gypsies,[1] who hold them in some contempt for their squalor and disorder. They move round the countryside, to traditional roadside encampments; there are ponies, herds of donkeys, ramshackle covered wagons, slatternly women. They are great thieves and beggars, violent both in drink and out of it; they pick up a living mainly at fairs, with some work in tin-ware, knife-grinding and the like. Their lives had interested Synge from his earliest writings, and he noted their habit of exchanging 'wives' at certain annual gatherings. They have managed to free themselves, to a greater or less extent, from government and convention, while allowing the maximum freedom to instincts of sexual promiscuity, fighting, drinking; yet they retain a primitive awe of the religious customs which they have themselves abandoned, and a mixture of envy and contempt of settled communities. A verse from Yeats may throw some light on this:

> The Roaring Tinker if you like,
> But Mannion is my name,
> And I beat up the common sort
> And think it is no shame.
> The common breeds the common,
> A lout begets a lout,
> So when I take on half a score
> I knock their heads about.
> *From mountain to mountain ride the fierce horsemen.*[2]

The world of the tinkers is full-blooded, violent, zestful; but they are neither Natural nor Pagan. Nor is it quite true to say that they represent Paganism,[3] to be set against the Christianity of the priest, though the opposition is a neat and attractive one. Synge is more subtle than that. Their life, beliefs, customs, lie rather at an angle to the dull circular world of the peasantry and the priest; half-contemptuous, half-envious of the values of each; oscillating between fear and boldness, cringing and arrogant at once.

The world of the priest is also tangential to the norm of the peasantry (whom he despises); wavering between loneliness and boredom; eager to have a sympathetic ear (particularly the ear of a

---

[1] For a description of their customs, see J. E. M. White's *No Home But Heaven*.

[2] *C.P.*, p. 371; *v.* also Synge's 'The Passing of the Shee'.

[3] The argument in which the Priest describes Mary as a 'flagrant old heathen' seems to me tenuous. It is a normal term of abuse.

woman) for his troubles, and yet half-ashamed of his confidantes; responding readily to Mary's maternal solicitude for his welfare, to the invitation to drink; and then suddenly recalling his ecclesiastical duties. Between the tinker and the priest, with the 'rural people' as a kind of unseen *punctum indifferens*, the dramatic tides move.

For the world of the ditch has its own peculiar troubles. All the tinkers know that Sarah's desire to get married is irrational, but the spring is a queer time, and the moon is changing, and that must account for her whim. The priest out of kindness, or pleasure at the prospect of an unexpected fee, agrees to marry them for half or less of the normal (we should remember, but need not detail, the elaborate system of fees and dues for every religious activity in an Irish parish). He drinks with them; and a Protestant (but not an Abbey) audience would catch the overtones of irony[1] in this. 'Isn't it a grand thing to see you sitting down, with no pride in you, and drinking a sup with the like of us, and we the poorest, wretched, starving creatures you'd see any place on earth?' For the priest is lonely, and full of self-pity; he is released by drink, the warm drunken friendliness of Mary, her scandalous innuendoes,[2] her assumed innocence, and the triple-shot of irony of:

> Stop till you say a prayer, your reverence; stop till you say a little prayer, I'm telling you, and I'll give you my blessing and the last sup from the jug.

It is Mary whom Synge draws most fully; many-sided, rich, Falstaffian, a poet with stories of great queens (who are yet women), that stirred Synge's imagination so greatly:

> I've a grand story of the great queens of Ireland, with white necks on them the like of Sarah Casey, and fine arms would hit you a slap the way Sarah Casey would hit you.[3]

It is she who has the richest imagery in her speech, the most picturesque flights of imagination. She has a subtlety of insight, a broad knowledge of the world, that makes Sarah seem naïve and bewildered. Yet Sarah too is capable of such subtle irony as this:

> (*Imploringly*). Marry us, your reverence, for the ten shillings in gold,

---

[1] Cf. Luke v. 30.
[2] e.g. the twice-repeated reference to 'whisper-talk' (flirtation).
[3] Cf. *Deirdre* . . . 'and queens will stick their tongues out at the rising moon'.

and we'll make you a grand can in the evening – a can would be fit to carry *water* for the holy man of God.[1]

In contrast to his talkative women-folk, Michael is gloomy, a little bewildered by their vanities and changing moods, that vary, like the weather, with the moon. He is prepared, stoically and stolidly, to go through with this whimsical marriage. For all other things he is a man of action; he reacts promptly and efficiently to the priest's threats.

This 'forlorn' play is to be seen, not as an isolated lapse of Synge's taste and skill, but as integral with his other works; exemplifying his theories of comedy, of diction, of imagery. In it we can see some of the often-handled themes. It concerns an unsatisfied woman, and her personality; as do *The Shadow*, *The Playboy*, perhaps even *Deirdre*. But her dissatisfaction is of a different kind. She is strong, healthy, still good-looking; she has borne children to her man. Her desire for marriage is irrational, a fact that is recognized gloomily by her husband and by her splendidly Rabelaisian mother-in-law; the suggestion that, unless they accede to her whim for marriage, she will go off with the handsome Jaunting Jim is no more than a make-weight, and the 'bad name' that she might earn from settled folk is clearly a flimsy pretext. Her frustration, like that of so many of Synge's women, finds its expression in her horror at the coming of old age and the passing of beauty; marriage may save her from the fate of Villon's old women.[2] The counter-image, in her mind (and always in Synge's), is that of the Queens, the polar opposites of the Beggars (who yet share all the distresses of womenhood with them), that have fired her imagination; then comes the countryside that lifts her speech into lyricism. We may see some symbolism in the wedding-ring, made by her man (again gloomily) from a piece of tin. It is something irrational and unwanted, yet magically sinister, in the tinkers' lives. Mary addresses the priest in the sack:

> It's sick and sorry we are to tease you; but what did you want meddling with the like of us, when it's a long time we are going our own ways – father and son, and his son after him, or mother and

---

[1] Is there a possible reference to the Woman of Samaria at the well?
[2] See *Translations*. Fausset (*Fortnightly Review*, cit.) stresses the point that such fears are peculiar to the Celtic races.

daughter, and her own daughter again; and it's little need we ever
had of going up into a church and swearing – I'm told there's
swearing in it – a word no man would believe, or with drawing rings
on our fingers, would be cutting our skins maybe when we'd be
taking the ass from the shafts, and pulling the straps the time
they'd be slippy with going around beneath the heavens in rains
falling.[1]

And it was a stroke of genius for Sarah to put the tin ring on the
priest's own finger, to remind him of his oath not to harm them.

The mother-in-law is even richer than Sarah in speech, with an
attitude towards her that varies between amazed tolerance and fear.
Mary's knowledge of the world is complete, her sensuality in drink
or speech abundant and unashamed. Both fulfil the traditional
comic rôle in abuse of each other or of the priest, with 'flyting
matches', like those of Pegeen and the Widow Quin, that are so
effective on the stage.

Much critical ink has been spilt on the character of the priest
himself. This is necessary for those who wish to show Synge as a
monster of sardonic anti-clericalism,[2] or to account for the priest's
deviations in some more subtle manner:

> The Priest is unlikable, not because he is a priest, but because
> he is not a true priest. He has officially renounced his Pagan
> instincts but he has not acquired the Christian virtues. He still has
> the old Pagan craving for the enjoyments of the flesh, but when he
> tries to satisfy this his pleasure is spoiled by the sense that he is
> sinning.[3]

I think the matter can be put much more simply. The priest is a
traditional comic figure, and a medieval audience would have
recognized him at once. In the eyes of the tinkers he is seen,
alternately, as a human being with troubles of his own, as a
representation of the wealthier classes (and as such liable to call in
the police) and as a figure exercising mysterious but time-honoured
powers over the supra-natural world. The lot of a parish priest, in a
remote country district, eighty or a hundred years ago, was in many
ways unenviable. His powers were considerable;[4] his wealth, from

[1] This is good observation, as always. Wet reins are most unpleasant things
to handle.
[2] e.g. Corkery, q.v.   [3] Price, op. cit., p. 130 et seq.
[4] I have talked with old people whose parents believed that the priest
would, if provoked, turn them, Circe-wise, into animals.

dues, 'stations' and other rites, might well be such as to ensure creature comforts, and in this respect he would be better off than the Protestant parson of whose daughter's gullibility the tinkers speak pityingly. His amusements, unless he shot or fished or hunted, would be few. The doctor, and perhaps a strong farmer or two, would be his only cronies. Hence the description:

> MICHAEL: It's often his reverence does be in there playing cards, or drinking a sup, or singing songs, until the dawn of day.
> SARAH: It's a big boast of a man with a long step on him and a trumpeting voice. It's his reverence, surely; and it's a great bargain we'll make now and he after drinking his glass.
> MICHAEL: There's your ring, Sarah Casey; but I'm thinking he'll walk by and not stop to speak with the like of us at all.

His first instinct is to have nothing to do with them, and he assumes naturally that the tinkers are only begging for money. But his self-pity, the drink in him, and the cajoling of the women make him unbend. His life is a hard one, and there are hints of the effects of celibacy:

> It's destroyed you must be hearing the sins of the rural people on a fine spring.

and Mary's comment is particularly sardonic in the light of this and of the confessions that he has heard:

> Leave me go, Mary Byrne; for I never met your like for hard abominations the score and two years I'm living in the place.
> MARY (*innocently*): Is that the truth?

He is big and heavily built – 'a big boast of a man'[1] – with his own troubles over the impending visit of the bishop, and the boredom of his life; so that he alternates between pathetic humanity, ecclesiastical dignity, and a fear of the tinkers which is intensified because he has allowed himself to relax with them. He offers the pair a shilling,[2] not out of charity, but to get rid of them. The imminence of the Bishop's visit, the appearance of the policemen on the road below, give a magnificent impetus to the last scene. But

---

[1] Perhaps this is in a way traditional: *v*. the description of the cleric in Donn Byrne's *Blind Raftery*.
[2] A shilling to a beggar, in 1905, would have been comparative wealth.

again it is necessary to point to certain aspects of the dialogue. The priest warns them against the enormity of striking him, in face of Michael's threat to beat him with the ass's reins:

> Is it lift your hand upon myself when the Lord God would blight your members if you'd touch me now? Go on from this. *He gives him a shove.*
> MICHAEL: Blight me, is it? Take it then, your reverence, and God help you so. *He runs at him with the reins.*

The point may be made more clearly if we remember the crimes for which Danny was assaulted and murdered by twenty-nine lads:

> He's left two pairs of female twins
> Beyond in Killacreest,
> *And twice in Crossmolina fair*
> *He's struck the parish priest.*[1]

The characterization of the priest made a performance in Ireland unthinkable; but Synge himself might have pointed to Chaucer's Monk and Friar, while setting them against the Poor Parson. This is traditional comedy with a farcical ending. It is excellent and consistent theatre. The Latin malediction is precisely what would rout the tinkers, who were unperturbed by the threat of being 'blighted' by straightforward words; and we may recall an earlier sentence of Mary's:

> And I'm thinking it should be great game to hear a scholar, the like of you, speaking Latin to the saints above.

Synge's delicate irony is never far to seek.

THE WELL OF THE SAINTS

'A couple of miles from the village we turned aside to look at an old ruined church of the Ceathair Aluinn (The Four Beautiful Persons), and a holy well near it that is famous for cures of blindness and epilepsy.'[2] This was the well on Inishmore that Martin Coneely showed to Synge; and indeed the Saint who bears the healing water has landed in Cashla Bay, west of Galway; no great voyage in fine weather, in a curragh. Holy Wells are common

---

[1] *v. P. & T.*   [2] *A.I.*, p. 20.

in Ireland, and we may think of many of them as re-dedicated from paganism by the Christian missionaries.[1] The time is 'a century or more ago'; the location is not given, but the setting that Synge has in mind is clearly Glendalough. The Saint is 'straying around saying prayers at the churches and high crosses, between this place and the hills'. This is the Sacred City of the Seven Churches, eight times plundered by Danes, Norsemen, Irish and Normans. Dramatic action makes it necessary to delay the Saint's appearance: 'he's gone up now through the thick woods to say a prayer at the Crosses of Grianan'. In fact he would have gone to the so-called Bed of Kevin, a cell on the far side of the lake; it is a difficult climb, so he leaves his cloak and bell behind: 'The lads told him no person could carry them things through the briers, and steep, slippy-feeling rocks he'll be climbing above, so he looked round then, and gave the water, and his big cloak, and his bell to the two of us.'

The source of the play is a fifteenth-century French farce, *Moralité de l'Aveugle et le Boiteux*, by Andrieu de la Vigne. Synge had come across it through the lectures of Petit de Julleville, which he had attended in Paris in 1895-6, and which de Julleville had discussed in his *Histoire du Théâtre en France*. From this Synge made notes, and copied fragments of dialogue, in his diary of 1903.[2] But whereas the original was based on a cripple who is carried by a blind man, until both are cured by passing a religious procession in which the remains of St Martin are displayed, Synge's beggars are man and wife, both blind. We may remember that Yeats used the Blind Beggar and the Lame Beggar in *The Cat and The Moon*, and that Blind Man and Fool are symbolic complementary aspects of personality in other plays; while a miraculous (but not holy) water occurs in *At the Hawk's Well*.

There are other source-resemblances in literature and in folklore, but it is not profitable to discuss them; except, perhaps to remember the miracles of the New Testament, and Oscar Wilde's story of the young man healed by Christ, who found no better use for his sight than to feed his lust; and Yeats' play *Calvary* in which Lazarus complains of the miracle that has torn him from the quiet

---

[1] *v.* Wood-Martin, *Traces of the Elder Faiths of Ireland*.
[2] Greene and Stephens, p. 134.

grave. The plot as it stands is wholly Synge's own, though Corkery has suggested a sort of inversion (which he finds typical of Synge) of a passage in Hyde's 'Love Songs of Connacht':

> Happy 'tis, thou blind, for thee
> That thou seest not our star;
> Could'st thou see as we now see
> Thou would'st be as we now are.[1]

It is a matter of some irony that in this play Synge comes nearest to the spirit of Ibsen; whom he had, with Zola, criticized for 'dealing with the reality of life in pallid and joyless words'. *The Well of the Saints* deals, at many levels, with the problems of human illusion and whether it be necessary for happiness; the shifts and turnings of characters confronted with the fact, and the failure of the fact; and their attempts to compromise with that failure, to make from it, by the creative imagination, a world which shall still be tolerable when the illusion is gone. It is yet another of Synge's perceptions of the tensions, the conflicts, between the idea, the dream, and the reality. For that purpose we have a timeless peasant setting,[2] its observed cruelty and humour, its sudden flashes of 'what is superb and wild in reality'. In the background moves the strange personality of the Saint; thin, stiff, angular, like a figure from an Italian primitive, yet with sufficient humanity to contribute those ironies and ambivalences that are part of Synge's world.

The plot is simple, the three acts carefully balanced. Martin Doul, in his blindness, has two illusions: that he and his wife Mary are a handsome couple, and that the visible world is full of wonder and delight. But it is not quite complete; through half-hints there emerges Martin's unsatisfied desire, an old man's longing for the young:

> It should be a fine, soft, rounded woman, I'm thinking, would have a voice the like of that.

With the gift of sight the double illusion, of husband and wife and each other's imagined beauty, is broken for ever. In desperation

---

[1] Corkery, op. cit., p. 155.
[2] Perhaps designed, like that of *Deirdre*, to distance the fable beyond criticism of its 'manners'.

Martin turns to the girl who had embodied, while he was blind, the qualities of the desired woman:

> . . . for it's grand hair you have, and soft skin, and eyes would make the saints, if they were dark awhile, and seeing again, fall down out of the sky. Hold up your head, Mary, the way I'll see it's richer I am than the great kings of the east.

The power and rhythm of the language, the casual glance at the Nativity, are in tone with the liturgical speech of the Saint that has gone before: it is counterpointed fiercely and brutally as Martin turns to Bride:

> For you've yellow hair, and white skin, and it's the smell of my own turf is rising from your shawl.

Martin and Molly Byrne are the most fully developed characters in the play. In contrast with the marriage bond that is so savagely tightened with the coming of sight, Molly remains the epitome of Martin's poetic imagination. She is the dream-woman, known by sound of voice and step, a symbol of the full-blooded life that old men seek to recapture –

> . . . and yet I'm told it's a grand thing to see a young girl walking the road.

Molly is vain, silly, provocative by turns. On both husband and wife she pours out her cruelty which is born out of vanity and fear, the fear and contempt of women for each other:

> Go up now and take her under the chin and be speaking the way you spoke to myself.

and of Martin:

> You're not saying a word, Mary. What is it you think of himself, with the fat legs on him, and the little neck like a ram?

She deflates Martin's poetry with her own special variety of giggling innuendo:

> MARTIN: It's a power of dirty days, and dark mornings, and shabby-looking fellows we do have to be looking on when we have our sight, God help us, but there's one fine thing we have, to be looking on a grand, white handsome girl the like of you . . . and every time I set my eyes on you I do be blessing the Saints, and

the holy water, and the power of the Lord Almighty in the heavens above.

MOLLY BYRNE: I've heard the priests say it isn't looking on a young girl would teach many to be saying their prayers.

Yet she is moved, or half-moved, by his poetry and 'fine bit of talk', as Nora of *The Shadow* was moved by the Tramp's. She invites him to continue his love-making, and as the poetic excitement grows he realizes the unique quality of what he has to offer. The brutality of the contrast, the Elizabethan image, is a perfect example of Synge's method:

I'm thinking by the mercy of God it's few sees anything but them is blind for a space. It's few sees the old women rotting for the grave, and it's few sees the like of yourself. *He bends over her.* Though it's shining you are, like a high lamp would drag in the ships out of the sea.[1]

She betrays him to Timmy the Smith, and again we may remember Dan's comment on the Tramp's lyricism, and perhaps Christy's wooing of Pegeen. So she taunts Martin Doul:

He's a bigger fool than that, Timmy. Look on him now, and tell me if that isn't a grand fellow to think he's only to open his mouth to have a fine woman, the like of me, running along by his heels.[2]

The stage direction that follows is worth noting:

(*Martin Doul recoils towards centre*, WITH HIS HAND TO HIS EYES; *Mary Doul is seen coming forward softly.*)

The married man is trapped in the age-old situation:

MARTIN DOUL *turns round, sees Mary Doul, whispers to Molly Byrne with imploring agony*: Let you not put shame on me, Molly, before herself and the smith. Let you not put shame on me and I after saying fine words to you, and dreaming . . . dreams . . . in the night.

The dreams in the night, and their delusion, are a stock subject, particularly at the turn of the nineteenth century; we may remember Ibsen, Hardy, Shaw.[3] In the breaking of the dream the

[1] For the image, see (e.g.) Shakespeare, Sonnet 116.
[2] Cf. Nora of *The Shadow*: 'but you've a fine bit of talk, stranger, and it's with yourself I'll go.'
[3] 'Every dream is a prophecy, every jest is an earnest in the womb of time.'

most common weapon is the physical reality, and Synge uses it brutally, in his characteristic fashion. The components of the dream are the sensuality of physical beauty, its imagined correlation with voice, dress, movement, smell. The senses of the blind are all sharpened to perceive these last; even the world of nature seems to offer the ideal:

> . . . I'm thinking it's a good right ourselves have to be sitting blind, hearing a soft wind turning round the little leaves of the spring and feeling the sun, and we not tormenting ourselves with the sight of the grey days, and the holy men, and the dirty feet is trampling the world.

The enlightened world outside them is full of earthiness, malignity, jealousy, and Synge uses it in counterpoint to the full. It is also a sexual world, restrained by custom only; we remember the freedom of the tinkers, and Martin would carry off Molly to lead the life of 'a tinker's doxy'.[1] And indeed Martin is not unlike 'The Wild Old Wicked Man' of Yeats. He is excited by the footsteps of Molly, by the very presence of the girls who mock him; and the fantasies of his blind desire are the springs of his poetry. This kind of poetry, the prodigal vows of the burning blood, are as old as literature; here, as in *The Shadow*, *The Playboy*, *Deirdre*, Synge makes his characters speak, offering no judgement of the value of what they say. There is only the steady remorseless shade-contrasts of his irony, so profound and subtle, that deny alike the romantic and the realist.

Perhaps the play is also a morality, a morality in which Synge's characteristic negative capability has joined with his irony to subtract all overt traces of the moral. In one sense we are confronted with the problem of appearances, that old Platonic dilemma of the Elizabethans; and it has been noted how strangely the restoration of sight to the married couple makes everyone anxiously concerned about how each one looks to others.[2] How does real or imagined appearance affect personality? Is soft white hair, a silky hand, a compensation for the old? What remains beneath 'The fading red and white, the body's quilt'?

But whatever consolation they may find in dreams they are

[1] *v*. the poem 'Queens'.
[2] e.g. Price, *Synge and Anglo-Irish Drama*, p. 159.

wrenched back to actuality by Synge's obsession with the unsparing ugliness of age:

> When the skin shrinks on your chin, Molly Byrne, there won't be the like of you for a shrunk hag in the four quarters of Ireland.

and

> In a short while you'll have a head on you as bald as an old turnip you'd see rolling round in the muck.

This is the lower plane of the morality. Above the characters is set the Saint. The critics have praised his simplicity, dignity, graciousness, the aura of holiness that surrounds him. Yet there is another side:

> SAINT *severely*: I never heard tell of any person wouldn't have great joy to be looking on the earth, and the image of the Lord thrown upon men.
> MARTIN DOUL *raising his voice*: Them is great sights, holy father . . . What was it I seen when I first opened my eyes but your own bleeding feet, and they cut with the stones? That was a great sight, maybe, of the image of God . . .

and again:

> What call has the like of you to be coming between married people – that you're not understanding at all – and be making a great mess with the holy water you have, and the length of your prayers?

This is the eternal protest of the common man against the right of the celibate to pronounce on love and marriage. The Saint is indeed the traditional ascetic; his bleeding feet and calloused knees witness it. Yet he has his own poetry:

> May the Lord who has given you sight send a little sense into your heads, the way it won't be on your two selves you'll be looking – on two pitiful sinners of the earth – but on the splendour of the Spirit of God, you'll see an odd time shining out through the big hills, and steep streams falling to the sea . . . [1]

He puts forward the conventional view of the goodness of virginity, drawing an amused comment from Mary Doul; his devotions have left him with 'a big head on you and a pitiful thin arm'.

[1] Cf. Yeats, 'Stream and Sun at Glendalough' (*C.P.*, p. 288),

> Through intricate motions ran
> Stream and gliding sun . . .

(Is there some contrast intended with the brute strength of Timmy the Smith?) Yet all the while he is being shaded with Synge's delicate irony, reinforced (as I think) by the whole ethos of the setting at Glendalough, with all its saintly associations.

His background is the crowd, eager for the entertainment of the miraculous healing, just as Mary and Martin fear that they may miss the hanging of the thief that might be causing all the stir. ('Come on till we watch.') They mock Martin in blindness or in sight; they are superstitious and obsequious before the Saint; there may even be a shadow of blasphemy when Molly dresses up Martin in the Saint's cloak. They are curious, cruel, brutal, like the peasant figures of a Breughel. 'But this too' (we remember the ending of *The Playboy*) 'was Synge's observation.'[1]

At the end the play returns on its circle. We began with the beggars and their queer cracked voices, who 'sit all the year in the rain falling'. Now Martin and Mary Doul will go southward, 'where the people will have kind voices maybe, and we won't know their black looks or villainy at all'. Their blindness will again evoke its own poetry, the imagined and remembered world that so many of Synge's characters make for themselves. Mary, like Nora of *The Shadow*, assents, though her woman's vision also is realistic; their paths will be wet and stony, 'with a north wind blowing behind'. There are deep rivers where – Timmy the Smith prophesies with gloomy satisfaction – the two of them will be drowned; and Synge's reticence gives no symbolism, as a lesser poet might have done, to sloughs or rivers or winds. Only what Martin creates by words will – for this verbal moment – remain; for here illusions can be recreated, and perhaps maintained, in the gallant security of blindness.

THE PLAYBOY OF THE WESTERN WORLD

I

The Playboy does not lend itself readily to classification; as we revolve it in our hands many facets take light and fire. In one mood we may suggest that it is sheer extravagant comedy, with elements

---

[1] *v. The Playboy*, p. 227: Notes, p. 301.

of strong farce in the 'resurrection' of Christy Mahon's father, and in the deflation of the boastful man, the revelation of a massive and mock-heroic lie. As such, it embodies the classic elements for reversal and recognition. Yet it is comedy that might have ended (for we are prepared from the first for a possible wedding) with Pegeen winning her Playboy and Old Mahon marrying the Widow Quin; comedy which at the end is edged, skilfully and unexpectedly, into a semi-tragedy. From another point of view we may call it 'free' comedy, in which moral issues are reversed, transcended or ignored in the desire for 'energy', though this view will be only part of the truth. It is helpful to quote Yeats:[1]

> In a country like Ireland, where personifications have taken the place of life, men have more hate than love, for the unhuman is nearly the same as the inhuman, but literature, which is a part of that charity that is the forgiveness of sins, will make us understand men however little they conform to our expectations. We will be more interested in heroic men than in heroic actions, and will have a little distrust for everything that can be called good or bad in itself with a very confident heart.

Again we may see *The Playboy* (carrying Yeats' thought a stage further) as a Dionysiac comedy, in which the instincts are, within Synge's conventions, given uninhibited play; this in keeping with his demand for what is 'superb and wild in reality'. So the Playboy himself becomes a country Don Juan, rejoicing in his new-found power to excite the admiration of women,[2] and the very growth of the language, 'richly flavoured as a nut or an apple', reflects his desire for 'an imagination that is fiery and magnificent and tender'.

We turn the play on its axis, and satire seems to predominate. It is a satire (but with more than a hint of approval) on the proverbial willingness of the West to give shelter to the malefactor and murderer, which goes back to the Elizabethan wars of conquest, the

---

[1] *Explorations* (1962), pp. 161-2. This was a frequent thought: cf. 'The Stare's Nest by My Window' (*C.P.*, p. 230)

> We had fed the heart on fantasies,
> The heart's grown brutal from the fare:
> *More substance in our enmities*
> *Than in our love . . .*

[2] We may remember Othello's reported wooing of Desdemona: 'Mark with what violence she loved the Moor but for bragging and telling her fantastical lies . . .'

shipwrecked sailors of the Armada, and beyond. Then the Playboy may become a comic Oedipus, 'the man who killed his da'; the mutual descriptions of each other by father and son give some point to the classic situation. There is satire in the pursuit of man by woman, the comic reversal of the conventional view; we may remember how Shakespeare and Shaw turned that theme to account, and the additional flavour lent to it by the romantically fostered idea of modest Irish womanhood. Indeed, we may carry the idea of the mock-heroic still further, and see in Christy Mahon an Odysseus, the wanderer cast up and seeking refuge; his triumph in the sports on the sea-shore a parody of the Greek games. We might then have a tragi-comic piece with the Widow Quin as Nausicaa, a chorus of girls, the village pub for a palace. But again we may see it, if we will, as tragedy. The Playboy finds his soul through a lie, the 'gallous story' of his parricide. Under the stimulus of heady admiration from men and women he grows in stature and in poetry. Detail is elaborated, the fatal blow struck by the potato-spade (we may note the irony)[1] becomes more final, more heroic.[2] He is indeed of the company of poets, 'fine fiery fellows with great rages when their temper's roused'. Under the shock of his father's reappearance (and the old man's account of his son's character has prepared the audience for this) he staggers, weakens and is finally reconciled; though with a new certainty of himself. He is 'master of all fights from now'. His father accepts the situation: 'Glory be to God!' (*with a broad smile*) 'I am crazy again.' The final 'turn' reminds us of the end of *The Shadow*: 'By the will of God, we'll have peace now for our drinks.' But it is Pegeen who is the heroine-victim. She has found her man, made him, won him in the teeth of opposition from her own sex. The marriage has been approved, in a superb drunken half-parody of the traditional blessing, by her father. From that marriage would come, because of Christy's heroic and virile virtues which have grown, mushroom-like, out of the tale of parricide, a band of 'little gallant swearers by the name of God'. At the end Pegeen's loss is absolute, beyond comfort, for

---

[1] There may even be an echo of a once-popular song, 'The Kerry Recruit': 'So I buttered me brogues, and shook hands with me spade.'

[2] Compare as stages in the narration: 'I just riz the loy and let fall the edge of it on the ridge of his skull'. '. . . the way they'd set their eyes upon a gallant orphan cleft his father with one blow to the breeches belt.'

she has lost her illusion of greatness in her man, and his body too; the complacent Shawn has seen the obstacle to his marriage removed.

> Oh my grief, I've lost him surely. I've lost the only Playboy of the Western World.

2

Synge intended that the play should run its course between antinomies. It is, for all its apparent simplicity of plot, a delicately balanced system of ironies, ambivalences, both of words and situation. We may quote his letter to the press after the storm of abuse which its production aroused:

> *The Playboy* is not a play with a 'purpose' in the modern sense of the word,

(he is thinking perhaps of Shaw, Brieux, and the then current misrepresentations of Ibsen as a didactic dramatist)

> – but, although parts of it are or are meant to be extravagant comedy, still a great deal that is in it and a great deal more that is behind it is perfectly serious when looked at in a certain light. This is often the case, I think, with comedy, and no one is quite sure today whether Shylock or Alceste should be played seriously or not. There are, it may be hinted, several sides to *The Playboy*.[1]

We may examine first the direct consequences of these 'several sides' of the play. Synge's conflict with outraged Irish morality had begun as early as 1903, when the portrait of Nora in *The Shadow* was felt to be a slur on Irish womanhood. But the week that followed the first production of *The Playboy* on 26 January 1907 was a continuous riot, with a hysteria that recalls the first production of Victor Hugo's *Hernani* (with its violation of the formal Alexandrine) or the reception of Ibsen's *Ghosts* in London. We may quote from Lady Gregory:

> There was a battle of a week. Every night protestors with their trumpets came and raised a din. Every night the police carried some of them off to the police courts. Every afternoon the paper gave reports of the trial before a magistrate who had not heard or read the play and who insisted on being given details of its incidents by the accused and by the police . . . There was a very large audience

---

[1] cit. Bourgeois, *J.M.S. and the Irish Theatre* (1913), p. 208.

on the first night . . . Synge was there, but Mr Yeats was giving a lecture in Scotland. The first act got its applause, and the second, though one felt that the audience were a little puzzled, a little shocked at the wild language. Near the end of the third act there was some hissing. We had sent a telegram to Mr Yeats after the end of the first act 'Play great success'; but at the end we sent another – 'Audience broke up in disorder at the word shift'.[1]

We may attempt first to set out the main causes of offence, however innocent they may appear to a modern audience. As a background it is well to remember the image of Romantic Ireland, sedulously fostered in the 90s: the Land of Saints, the country whose Literary Renaissance would save European culture. Ireland was the home of the most ancient Christian tradition; her women were models of chastity and purity. Against this are to be set the 'heroic' aspects of homicide, countless jests on the subject during the agrarian troubles,[2] the Phoenix Park murders, the raw material of the play itself:

An old man on the Aran Islands told me the very tale on which *The Playboy* is founded, beginning with the words: 'If any gentleman has done a crime we'll hide him. There was a gentleman that killed his father, and I had him in my own house six months till he got away to America.'[3]

As for the 'wild language', Lady Gregory and the actors[4] had indeed protested against its coarseness before the play was produced. But it was, at least overtly, an indelicacy rather than a blasphemy that triggered off the riot:

. . . a drift of chosen females, standing in their shifts itself, maybe, from this place to the eastern world.

The rancour of the mob centres on the fatal *shift*; in an access of outraged modesty, Victorian in character, but connected somehow

---

[1] *O.I.T.*, cit. Ellis-Fermor, p. 50.

[2] A shot fired in the dusk might provoke the hoary joke: 'There goes another landlord'; and there were times when one did not sit between the window and a lamp. See, e.g., Lady Gregory's *Journals*.

[3] Yeats, *Essays and Introductions*, pp. 337-8. Synge's own version is in *A.I.*, pp. 64-5, together with some interesting aspects of the morality of this action.

[4] 'Synge has just had an operation on his throat and has come through it all right. . . . When he woke out of the ether sleep his first words, to the great delight of the doctor, who knows his plays, were: "May God damn the English, they can't even swear without vulgarity." This tale delights the Company, who shudder at the bad language they have to speak in his plays' (Yeats, *Letters*, ed. Wade, p. 496). See also *O.I.T.*, p. 133.

with the idea that the very word was insulting to the womanhood of Ireland, whose chastity and purity had become a national myth, even as the saintliness of the island as a whole. It is probable that the audience, in their bewilderment at the more subtle ironies of the play, missed the full point of the phrase. The picture of Mayo maidens perceived in terms of a slave market, or a throng of Eastern houris, is made yet more fantastic in that the term *drift* is applied to a drove of heifers; and it is possible that they took the point of the *eastern* world (Leinster or Dublin) as opposed to the Western of Connemara or Mayo.

We may quote some of Yeats' account of the attacks on 'this wild, laughing thing':

> Picturesque, poetical, fantastical, a masterpiece of style and of music, the supreme work of our dialect theatre, his *Playboy* roused the populace to fury. We played it under police protection, seventy police in the theatre the last night, and five hundred, some newspaper said, keeping order in the streets outside. It is never played before any Irish audience for the first time without something or other being flung at the players. In New York a currant cake and a watch were flung, the owner of the watch claiming it at the stage-door afterwards. The Dublin audience has, however, long since accepted the play.[1]

And again:

> The Irish nationalists in America mobilized every force they could touch to boycott the [Abbey] plays throughout the Eastern States. The fight took much the same form everywhere, though it was fiercer in some towns than in others. It started in a prejudice, not the less violent for its ignorance and generally among the members of the Gaelic League, against the picture of Irish life and morals which the plays of the new school were said to give. The general prejudice was entangled with and sometimes manipulated by political prejudices of a far-reaching and almost infinitely complex kind. And mingled again with both was the religious prejudice of some sections at least of the Church.[2]

It seems to me likely that the offensive word was no more than a catalyst for the general but indeterminate unease caused by a number of other factors in the play; and these factors in this are themselves complicated by Synge's technique of producing, deliberately,

[1] *Autobiographies* (1955), p. 569. (This was written in 1925.)
[2] Ellis-Fermor, op. cit., p. 54.

an ebb and flow in the audience's response to character and situation.[1] The perception of ironies and ambivalences will, of course, vary with the type of audience, its age and its environment. It is worth noting, for example, that *The Playboy* was more popular in England, *The Shadow* in Ireland; and the Dublin audiences in 1907 might well have been particularly sensitive to anything provided by the 'Anglo-Irish Ascendancy' group of writers.[2] The more subtle, dispassionate and balanced the irony the less likely it is that the general pattern will be perceived, and the more probable that overt points of conventional distaste will be selected for attack. In *The Tinker's Wedding* Synge pleaded, unavailingly, for the recognition of a humour without malice. That of *The Playboy*, fantastic as it may be, was probably too close to observation to be taken lightly.

Synge's attitude to Ireland and to the Irish peasantry was highly ambivalent: insight combined with toleration, love without passion. We may think of broadly similar positions taken up by Swift, Shaw, Yeats. Love and understanding are not inseparable from a detached mockery. But the union of these may be so subtle, so fluctuating and yet so integral to the whole system of values in the play, that we may examine briefly some of the instances.

His irony is founded most often on incongruity, the perception of polar opposites;[3] and within the broad rhythm of the play's construction, the manipulation of character so that it rises and falls, retreats and advances in the sympathy of the audience, to form its characteristic patterns. The irony may go unperceived, or be furiously rejected, when one of the poles from which the current passes is felt by the audience to be unacceptable; whether as involving religion, womanhood, King Lear's 'nature', drunkenness, or aesthetic delicacy. (Curiously enough, the morbid, particularly

[1] For an account of this, see J. L. Styan, op. cit., p. 57 et seq.

[2] We may reflect, for example, on the affair of the Municipal Gallery and Lutyens' plans, and the bitter poems in Yeats' *Responsibilities*. Behind it again was the doctrinal controversy over *The Countess Cathleen*.

[3] These 'metaphysical' juxtapositions are everywhere, particularly when he wishes to emphasize the humanity of his characters: e.g. 'I've a grand story of the great queens of Ireland, with white necks on them the like of Sarah Casey, and fine arms would hit you a slap the way Sarah Casey would hit you.' 'At your age you should know there are nights when a king like Conchubor would spit upon his arm ring, and queens will stick their tongues out at the rising moon.'

THE PLAYBOY OF THE WESTERN WORLD

of the churchyard, seems to go unchallenged; the accessories or instruments of death have a perennial attraction for a peasantry.)

It was a lady novelist of the early nineteenth century who noted the proclivity of the Irish for swearing, and on those somewhat tenuous grounds asserted the Grecian origin of the Milesians. 'It is certain that the habit of confirming every assertion with an oath is as prevalent among the Irish as it was among the ancient, and is among the modern Greeks.'[1] In the Notes to these plays I have drawn attention to some instances of a pleasant and at best devotional practice in this respect. But rapid and violent verbal conjunction may give quite another aspect. Consider, for instance:

. . . or Marcus Quin, God rest him, got six months for maiming ewes –

('God rest him' is the normal pious expletive concerning the dead, but here a little incongruous with his crime)

– and he a great warrant to tell stories of holy Ireland . . .

– where the second clause links 'holy Ireland' with 'God rest him', and both combine ironically with the 'six months for maiming ewes'. But set against this triangle there are two background references: to the Moonlighters and the agrarian troubles with their horrible practice of maiming cattle, horses, sheep by hamstringing or cutting off their tails. The second is to the juxtaposition of 'holy Ireland', the kind of reference embodied in Yeats' poem whose title is the first three words:

Beautiful lofty things: O'Leary's noble head;
My father upon the Abbey stage, before him a raging crowd:
'This Land of Saints,' and then as the applause died out,
'Of plaster Saints;' his beautiful mischievous head thrown back.[2]

Something of the same metaphysical conjunction (which emerges only when distanced) is in Shawn's agonized cry 'Oh, Father Reilly and the saints of God, where will I hide myself today?' Sometimes we have a double counterpointing, when the romantic the religious and the realistic meet in a vortex characteristic of Synge's technique:

Amn't I after seeing the love-light of the star of knowledge shining from her brow, and hearing words would put you thinking on the

---

[1] Sydney Owenson, *The Wild Irish Girl.*
[2] *C.P.*, p. 348.

holy Brigid speaking to the infant saints, and now she'll be turning again, and speaking hard words to me, like an old woman with a spavindy ass she'd have, urging on a hill.

or,

There's poetry talk for a girl you'd see itching and scratching, and she with a stale stink of poteen on her from selling in the shop.

More subtle and less definable is Sara's speech as she tries on the boots:

There's a pair do fit me well, and I'll be keeping them for walking to the priest, when you'd be ashamed this place, going up winter and summer with nothing worth while to confess at all.

– when the ideas of confession and barefoot penance have a kind of subtle and uneasy association. It is the same with the convolutions of the plot. The Playboy's epic blow grows steadily in narration; but it is counterpointed and parodied by Pegeen's account of how the Widow Quin killed *her* man:

She hit himself with a worn pick, and the rusted poison did corrode his blood the way he never overed it, and died after. That was a sneaky kind of murder did win small glory with the boys itself.

and yet again Pegeen's

And to think of the coaxing glory we had given him, and he after doing nothing but hitting a soft blow and chasing northward in a sweat of fear.

There are the overt attacks on custom; the terrifying description of Kate Cassidy's wake is balanced against Michael's drunken blasphemy:

. . . aren't you a louty schemer to go burying your poor father unbeknownst when you'd a right to throw him on the crupper of a Kerry mule and drive him westwards, *like holy Joseph in the days gone by*, the way we would have given him a decent burial, and not have him rotting beyond, *and not a Christian drinking a smart drop to the glory of his soul?*[1]

Now the uneasiness set up in an audience is caused, not by the extravagance of these syntactical conjunctions, but because each of them is, *in itself*, perfectly natural and in common use, and is

---

[1] See Notes on the wake in *The Shadow*.

therefore elusive. It is Synge's art, which has something in common with Pope's, of suggesting value or its depreciation in this manner. Much the same is true of the plot, with its fantastical propositions. Does murder become heroic just because the blow is a good one, or because it and its context are narrated poetically? Granted that the police, together with the 'khaki cut-throats', are natural enemies of the community, embodying 'the treachery of the law', is it a moral act to shelter wrong-doers? Is a murderer likely to be a proper protector for Pegeen while the others are out? Is his reported valour a sufficient counterweight to the impropriety of his being left alone with her? If women are so easily won by poetical speech combined with inferred virility, what is the position of the conventional timid man as represented by Shawn Keogh?

Old Mahon boasting of his drink and lechery, his treatment in hospital, is in some sense a counterpart to the boasting of his son. They go off together, united in an utter reversal of relationship.

> Go with you, is it? I will then, like a gallant captain with his heathen slave.

and old Mahon's comment, that oblique and perhaps profound comment on metaphysics:

> Glory be to God! I am crazy again.

So Synge's art makes the characters and the themes advance and retreat from the audience. Outrageous statements become logical,[1] and the language of hyperbole makes them still more credible, in relation to the reality which is being questioned.

It is being questioned, of course, in the very title. A geographer could fix the scene of *The Playboy* with some accuracy. It is obviously in north-west Mayo, within sight of the sea-shore, and of the dominant mountain Nephin. It is not far from Belmullet and Castlebar. The Western World is the land lying westward of the Shannon; proverbial for its 'wildness' and poverty; isolated from the civilized East and South, and the dour virtues of the 'black North'. Perhaps there are connotations of the Holy Islands, the Country of the Sunset, St Brandon. Yet it is a *world*, fantastic,

---

[1] Perhaps this is the reason for the inclusion of *The Playboy* in the Surrealist Manifesto (Owen Quinn in *Envoy*).

romantic, brutal and sentimental, all at once. In the play Synge's own ambivalent attitude is fully apparent:

> I once said to John Synge, 'Do you write out of love or hate for Ireland?' and he replied, 'I have often asked myself that question . . .'[1]

Let us be frank about it. Synge's satiric view is constantly focused, with more or less directness, towards certain aspects of the peculiar blend of paganism and Roman Catholicism that he saw in the West. The pious ejaculations can, by juxtaposition and contrast, become loaded with ironies that demand both distance and an Anglo-Irish viewpoint to imagine their full implications. The unseen Father Reilly hovers in the background of *The Playboy* as the guardian of peasant morality, the supporter of the cowardly and feeble Shawn; whose comments on each situation are yet those of the ordinary man. Against settled and dull convention and a religion which can be made to appear superficial there are set Synge's tinkers, tramps, fishermen, publicans, in their actual or potential vitality. Yeats recognized the potential conflicts in a letter to Ricketts:

> I notice that when anybody here writes a play it always works out, whatever the ideas of the writer, into a cry for a more abundant and intense life. Synge and 'AE' the poet are staying here, and though they have come to their task from the opposite sides of the heavens they are both stirring the same pot – something of a witches' cauldron, I think.[2]

The Playboy exists as a work of art, and in a sense all comments on it are futile or irrelevant. The complexity that gives it life must be apprehended with all our senses. Its verbal harmonies and disharmonies are integral with its verbal rhythms and idiom, its characters with the waves and currents of the plot. We stand back from it, and we may remember Shaw:

> . . . the admirable comedies of Synge, who, having escaped from Ireland to France, drew mankind in the manner of Molière, and discreetly assured the public that this was merely the human nature of the Blasket Islands, and that, of course, civilized people never admired boastful criminals nor esteemed them according to the

---

[1] Yeats, *Letters*, ed. Wade, p. 618.
[2] ibid., p. 436.

atrocities they pretended to commit. The Playboy's real name was Synge; and the famous libel on Ireland (and who is Ireland that she should not be libelled as other countries are by their great comedians?) was the truth about the world.[1]

DEIRDRE OF THE SORROWS

I

Deirdre is Synge's last play. It was published posthumously, and we may regret, as with a more famous dramatist, that he did not oversee its final revision. The theme, one of the greatest of the love-stories in the Saga of Cuchulain, had been handled by Sir Samuel Ferguson in verse, and by Yeats and 'A.E.' as poetic drama. All had worked on the material provided by Hull, Standish O'Grady, Lady Gregory, and de Jubainville, at whose feet Synge had sat in Paris. The outline of the story is archetypal; a young and beautiful girl, destined to be the bride of an ageing king, elopes with a younger man, and after the magical seven years returns to her death, which brings with it the destruction of a city. It was for this reason that Yeats aligned it with the Trojan story:

> . . . Troy passed away in one high funeral gleam,
> and Usna's children died.[2]

The play was written in illness, in the course of a prolonged and frustrated love-affair, and in a state of depression to which *The Playboy* riots had contributed. In these circumstances it was natural that he should turn to the Saga. The subject matter ensured that it was far removed from popular disapprobation on grounds of religion, nationality or morals. Lady Gregory's *Cuchulain of Muirthemne* had overlaid the original with a veneer of the familiarized idiom that came to be called Kiltartanese. Yeats had produced, in 1907, a one-act poetic drama which concentrated on Deirdre to the exclusion of the other characters; using the technique of the heightened moment, the sheer intensity of emotion, with the ancillary resources of music and song.[3] 'A.E.''s was feeble to a

---

[1] G. B. Shaw, *The Matter with Ireland*, p. 84.
[2] 'The Rose of the World', *C.P.*, p. 41.
[3] The best analysis is by Professor Peter Ure: *Yeats the Playwright* (1963) especially Ch. III.

degree. Here was Synge's opportunity to test the prose-blade that he had forged on a subject that, for all its traditionalism, matched with a certain grimness his own horror of the grave, and that of the perennial Villon theme of the passing of love, the onset of old age. His own depression, his passionate awareness of his own situation, might find relief through the restatement of this theme; that offered full scope for a poet's sense of exaltation in high tragedy, for the ironies of which he was now master, and the counterpointing of brutality and violence with both.

2

It is necessary to illustrate the extent of Synge's commitment to the myth, and his departures from it. Conchubor was bidden to a feast at the house of Fedlimid, his story-teller. While the king and his train were enjoying the feast Fedlimid's wife was delivered of a daughter. Cathbad the Druid, who entered the feast-hall at that moment, recalled his own earlier prophecy:

> . . . I see by Druid signs that it is on account of a daughter belonging to you, that more blood will be shed than ever was shed in Ireland since time and race began. And great heroes and bright candles of the Gael will lose their lives because of her.[1]

When Deirdre is born, he renews the prophecy:

> Let Deirdre be her name; harm will come through her. She will be fair, comely, bright-haired; heroes will fight for her, and kings go seeking for her.

And then he took the child in his arms, and this is what he said:

> O Deirdre, on whose account many shall weep, on whose account many women shall be envious, there will be trouble on Ulster for your sake, O fair daughter of Fedlimid.
> Many will be jealous of your face, O flame of beauty; for your sake heroes shall go into exile. For your sake deeds of anger shall be done in Emain; there is harm in your face, for it will bring banishment and death on the sons of kings.

---

[1] Lady Gregory, *Cuchulain of Muirthemne*, p. 104.

In your fate, O beautiful child, are wounds, and ill-doings and the shedding of blood.

You will have a little grave apart to yourself; you will be a tale of wonder for ever, Deirdre.[1]

The warriors in the feast-hall wish to kill the child immediately; but Conchubor decides that she shall be put out to fosterage, so that one day she may become his own wife. He has a hut in a remote forest prepared for her; she is kept in the strictest isolation with her nurse, her 'fosterer', and a 'female satirist' called Lavarcham, daughter of Aedh. 'And there she lived until she was ripe for marriage, and she outwent in beauty the women of her time.'[2]

She tells Lavarcham (after she has seen a calf killed on a snowy day) that she would desire a husband who has 'the colour of the raven on his hair, the calf's blood on his cheeks, and the colour of the snow on his skin'.[3] Lavarcham replies that there is indeed such a man, Naisi, at the court of King Conchubor; and tells Naisi, who comes secretly to meet Deirdre. She declares her love for him, and begs him to take her away in flight. In spite of his fear of the king he consents. He flees with his two brothers, Ainnle and Ardan, and a hundred and fifty warriors, and the same number of women and greyhounds, to western Scotland. Conchubor attempts, by various devices, to prevent their flight. In Scotland they are maintained for a time by the king, and form an alliance with him. The king hears of Deirdre's beauty, and desires her for himself; in order to gain her he sends the brothers 'into every hard fight',[4] but without success. After various wanderings and battles the band settle, first by Loch Etive and then by Loch Ness; Deirdre and Naisi have two children, Gaiar and Aebgreine, who are sent off to be fostered by Manannán, King of the Sea.

After a lapse of time (the seven years of the play is only symbolic) Conchubor is at another feast, surrounded by his household and warriors. While boasting of his military strength he remarks that this is regrettably depleted by the absence of 'the

[1] ibid., pp. 105-6.
[2] Hull, E. M.., *The Cuchullin Saga*, p. 24: her account is more concise than Lady Gregory's.
[3] See Notes, p. 303.
[4] See, e.g., the story of David and Bathsheba.

three Lights of Valour of the Gael'; 'Naisi for valour and prowess was the making of an over-king of Ireland; by the might of his own arm hath he gained for himself a district and a half of Scotland.'[1]

So he plans to send messengers to Naisi to ask him to return. But he knows that Naisi is under a prohibition (*geasa*) to return into Ireland in peace, except when accompanied by one of three heroes: Cuchulain, Conall Cearneach (the Victorious) and Fergus mac Ross. Of each of these he inquires in turn what would happen if he, being the envoy who brought them back to Ulster, should find subsequently that they were destroyed. Cuchulain and Conall reply unequivocally that they would avenge this treachery with death and destruction upon anyone who should harm the Children of Usnach. Fergus alone replies in a different sense; were this to happen he would take revenge on any Ulsterman who would attack the Sons of Usnach, but gives his word that he would not attack Conchubor's own flesh and blood.

Fergus is therefore given and accepts the task of envoy, announces that he has undertaken the safe-conduct of the Children, and leaves for Loch Etive, taking with him only his two sons. Conchubor commands that on his return from the east Fergus is to go to the fortress of Borrach, son of Annte; but requires him to pledge his word that Deirdre and the Sons of Usnach are to go straight to Emain Macha, without stopping on the road. He arranges secretly with Borrach to provide a feast for Fergus, knowing that one of the latter's 'prohibitions' or tabus is that he must never refuse the offer of a feast.

Fergus comes to Naisi's fastness on Loch Etive. Deirdre has had a vision in the night, 'to wit, that three birds came to us out of Emain Macha; and in their bills three sips of honey; the sips of honey they left with us, but they took with them three sips of our blood'. She interprets the vision: 'Fergus hath come from our own native land with peace; for not sweeter is honey than [a false] message of peace; and the three sips of blood that have been taken from us, they are ye, who will go with him and will be beguiled.'[2]

But they go to greet Fergus, who confirms that Conchubor has

---

[1] Hull, p. 26.   [2] ibid., p. 29.

sent for them, and that he has entered into covenant for their safeguard. Deirdre tries to dissuade Naisi, for his lordship is greater in Scotland than that of Conchubor in Erin. But Fergus counters this in words which are echoed by Synge:

'Better than everything is one's native land,' saith Fergus: 'for poor is every excellence and prosperity to him who sees not his native land.' Deirdre is still reluctant, but Fergus reiterates his pledge, and Naisi agrees to return with him to Emain Macha. As Deirdre looks back to the coast of Scotland she utters her famous 'Farewell to Alba', parts of which Synge wove into the play,[1] and of which Sir Samuel Ferguson and Dora Sigerson had already made poems.

They arrive at the fortress of Borrach, who immediately invites Fergus to his feast. Fergus rages; he cannot refuse because of his *geasa*, nor can he break his promise to Conchubor to send Deirdre and the Sons of Usnach direct to Emain. He compromises by sending them on, but with his own two sons as escort and pledges, while he keeps his obligation to go to the feast. Deirdre pleads with them to go together to the island of Cuilenn,[2] between Ireland and Scotland, and there wait till Fergus' feast is ended. Ilann, Fergus' son, will not hear of this. He is confident in their own armed strength, and in the pledge of Fergus.

'Now is woe come upon us by means of that plighted word of Fergus,' said Deirdre, 'when he forsook us for a feast.' She utters another lamentation; Naisi reproves her for her vehemence. When they reach Slieve Fuadh, Deirdre has a vision and a dream: 'I beheld each of you without a head, and Ilann the Fair headless also, but Buinne the Ruthless with his own head upon him, and his assistance not with us.' In another vision she sees a cloud of blood above Naisi's head. She counsels him to go to Dundealgan, where Cuchulain dwells; and either to wait there till Fergus comes, or to go to Emain under the protection of Cuchulain. Naisi says that this would show cowardice, and they go forward to Emain. When they are within sight of it, Deirdre gives further advice: that if they are invited into King Conchubor's palace he intends them no harm, but if he sends them to the Red Branch House he means treachery. This is where they are sent; Conchubor supplied them with food,

[1] *v.* Notes, pp. 307–8.   [2] Hull suggests that this is Rathlin Island.

drink and attendants, but they are too weary to eat. Naisi and Deirdre call for a chess-board, and begin to play.

Meanwhile Conchubor sends Lavarcham to the Red Branch House to report to him 'whether her own form and shape remain on Deirdre'. She finds them playing at chess, and greets them with love and despair, for she knows that Conchubor has planned a deed of treachery. She tells them to close the doors and windows and to fight manfully if they are attacked. With that she returns to Conchubor to tell him that Deirdre's beauty has indeed passed. The king does not believe her, and sends one Trendorn, whose father had been killed by Naisi, to spy upon them. He approaches the house in fear, but finds one window unclosed through negligence. Through it he watches Deirdre and Naisi at their game. Deirdre signals his presence to Naisi, who throws a chess-man and cuts out one of his eyes. Trendorn returns to Conchubor, and reports: 'The woman whose form and feature are loveliest in the world is there, and Naisi would be king of the world if she were left to him.' This is the signal for the attack on the Red Branch House. At first Buinne makes a devastating sortie and kills many of the attackers, who attempt to set fire to the House, but he is then won over by a bribe from Conchubor. Ilann, however, continues loyal. Conchubor sends on Fiacha against Ilann; Ilann gets the better of him, and Fiacha's shield 'roars' to show the greatness of his need. The Three Great Waves of Ireland[1] respond; Conall Cearneach in Dundrum Bay hears the war on the wave of Rury, decides that Conchubor is in danger, and goes up to Emain. He kills Ilann with a spear thrust from behind. In death, Ilann tells him of Conchubor's treachery; Conall is shocked, and kills Fiacha.

There follows a three days' battle against Conchubor's men, with Naisi, Ardan and Ainnle inflicting great slaughter upon the besiegers. The three warriors make a sortie, with Deirdre between them, and inflict such losses upon the men of Ulster that Conchubor calls on Cathbad the Druid for magical help. Cathbad sets a 'great-waved sea' along the field in front of the Sons of Usnach, so that Naisi has to lift Deirdre in his arms above the flood.

Though the Children are now weaponless in the Druid sea, none of the men of Ulster dare kill them; but among Conchubor's men

[1] Hull, p. 42.

is Maire Red-hand, the son of the King of Norway, whose father and two brothers Naisi had slain. He claims his revenge: the three brothers stretch out their necks on one block, and are beheaded at a single blow. Deirdre meets Cuchulain (who has also been warned of trouble by a Wave) and he takes her under his protection. 'Then came Cuchulain and Deirdre to where the Children of Usnach lay and Deirdre dishevelled her hair, and began to drink Naisi's blood, and the colour of (burning) embers came into her cheeks, and she sang thus.'[1]

In one version, 'Deirdre flung herself upon Naisi in the tomb, and gave three kisses to Naisi, and died forthwith.' Cathbad the Druid curses Emain. Fergus arrives a day too late, gives battle to Conchubor's men, and burns Emain. In another version, Deirdre is kept for a year in the household of Conchubor, in deep dejection and lament, resisting all Conchubor's attempts to soothe her. He then asks her whom she hates most: 'Thou thyself, and Eogan, son of Durtheacht.' So Conchubor gives her to Eogan for a year. As she is driving off in his chariot, Conchubor cries out in jest 'Ah, Deirdre, it is the glance of an ewe between two rams, that you cast between me and Eogan!'

'When Deirdre heard that, she started up, and gave a leap out of the chariot, and struck her head against the rocks that were before her, and dashed her skull to pieces, so that her brain fell suddenly out. And thus came to pass the death of Deirdre.'[2]

3

It has been necessary to set out the saga-plot at some length; partly to convey something of the atmosphere of the original, partly in order to see what Synge used and what he rejected. In contrast to Yeats he rejected the magical elements of the fable, and the scene of Deirdre and Naisi playing chess. He has followed the outline of events that bring Fergus to Glen Laoi, and the hostility to the sons of Usnach; though it is not clear just why Fergus comes too late to help them, and we miss the subtlety of Conchubor's love-crazed intrigues.

[1] ibid., p. 53: q.v. for her final lament. [2] Hull, p. 45 et seq.

On the epic level it is a tragedy of fate, of a star-crossed girl, of a compulsive closing of the net that drives Deirdre to fulfil the doom that was prophesied at her birth. Here Synge keeps to the high-road of his fable; introducing only his invented character of Owen, the 'grotesque', whom (according to Yeats)[1] he had intended to bring in also in Act I. Nor did he succeed in his intention 'to weave . . . a grotesque peasant element throughout the play',[2] and we may question Yeats' suggestion that he would thereby have made *Deirdre* into 'a world-famous masterpiece'; for he himself has called it – all but the last Act – 'a Master's unfinished work, monotonous and melancholy'.[3] It seems likely that much of the economy, concentration and unity of tone would have been lost. As it stands, the play reveals a considerable depth and subtlety of characterization.

We can, at the outset, indicate some of the dominant themes that had been Synge's concern in other plays. There is the wrong of the marriage planned by the High King, between youth and age, which is in part the subject of *The Shadow*. There is Synge's lyric delight in the countryside, made credible and apposite by Deirdre's pastoral upbringing, and the lovers' idyllic life in Alban; the experience of country, birds and beasts, sea and mountain in *vécu*, even to the often-remembered detail of the stepping-stones flooded by the rain. There is the problem of the endurance of love, to be staled by mere custom, old age; or by its dissolution, at the siege of the Red Branch House, before the stronger claim of the warriors to loyalty in arms. There is the complex of motives that makes Deirdre return, to fall, clear-eyed, before Conchubor's treachery; for the Atê that overshadows her may be averted till this last moment of choice. And since many critics have felt this to be a flaw in the play,[4] it may be well to consider why she makes her choice.

First there is the compulsion of Synge's perennial theme of age and the passing of beauty. Fergus and Owen repeat it; they are, in some sense, the Tempters. The idyllic love of Deirdre and Naisi

[1] *Autobiographies* (1955), p. 487. Owen's original seems to be Trendorn: *v. supra*.
[2] ibid., p. 441.
[3] *Essays and Introductions* (1961), p. 239. Lady Gregory says that he had thought of 'cutting it down into two longish acts' (*O.I.T.*, p. 137).
[4] *v.* e.g. the discussion by Styan, op. cit., p. 258, et seq.

has lasted seven years. Conchubor's emissary arrives at a critical time:

> DEIRDRE: There are as many ways to wither love as there are stars in a night of Samhain; but there is no way to keep life, or love with it, a short space only . . .
> NAISI *giving in*: You're right, maybe. It should be a poor thing to see great lovers and they sleepy and old.

All but Naisi know that the High King's oaths and sureties are useless. Within the closing net of her foretold doom, Deirdre makes her choice. She must fulfil the prophecy, and be rewarded by fame. How she confronts death, the complexity of fear for love's passing, her pride, and her own woman's profound sense of her dramatic part, is Synge's problem and vision. Beside her the others are sketches only. Naisi comes to life, briefly, in the quarrel. His brothers are no more than shadows. Owen is no doubt a part of the 'peasant element' that Synge had projected; but he is also the Tempter, the Malcontent, the Thersites-figure who deflates heroism. He brings alive an evil past, to accelerate the plot with a kind of fierce momentum; for his father had made love to Lavarcham and was killed by Naisi, so that his horrifying suicide shadows the main action, and suggests (through the pouring out of the gold) a Judas-theme. It is he who hints at 'plots and tricks, and spies were well-paid for their play'. His violent raving precipitates the quarrel among the sons of Usnach. Among all the characters only Lavarcham, the archetypal Nurse-Confidante (for all that she is much more, being a 'female satirist') takes the normal view of growing old; for she, like the Shepherd in *A Winter's Tale*, is

> the weather-beaten conduit of many kings' reigns.

Old age, the passing of love, the isolation of the woods of Cuán, the subtle suggestion of Fergus that she is wasting her royal destiny;

> Wouldn't it be a poor story if a queen the like of you should have no thought but to be scraping up her hours dallying in the sunshine with the sons of kings?

Yeats found in the third Act of *Deirdre* an example of what he called 'tragic reverie'. 'Tragic art, passionate art, the drowner of dykes, the confounder of understanding, moves us by setting us to reverie, by alluring us almost to the intensity of trance. The persons upon the stage . . . greaten till they are humanity itself. We feel our minds expand convulsively or spread out slowly.'[1] In his essay on 'The Tragic Theatre'[2] he selects Deirdre's

> . . . isn't it a poor thing we should miss the safety of the grave, and we trampling its edge?

to exemplify this 'reverie of passion that mounts and mounts till grief itself has carried her beyond grief into pure contemplation'. It is this aspect of Deirdre that has fired Synge's imagination; remembering his own 'Queens', and Villon's, and the lines of Nashe that Yeats was so fond of quoting:

> Brightness falls from the air;
> Queens have died young and fair;
> Dust hath closed Helen's eye.

Again and again she asserts her own royal state: 'It was not by a low birth I made kings uneasy.' If she returns to Emain she will fulfil the prophecy, confirm and establish a great love-story that will be told to the end of time. Her pride will be spared the humiliation of love and beauty that pass, and the dreariness of a domestic peace in the woods that she now sees as a projection of her own adolescent happiness; which will leave her, in middle age, a nonentity. Again we may think of Cleopatra:

> Bravest at the last,
> She levell'd at our purpose, and, being royal,
> Took her own way.[3]

It is in keeping both with her character and with the rhythms of the tragic pattern that her full resolution is not confirmed, her speech pressed up to its lyric height, before Naisi's death. Until this scene with Conchubor her speech has been mainly elegiac in tone. (Again we may think of Cleopatra's interview with Caesar.) She tries to pacify the king. She appeals wildly to Naisi not to leave her in order to join her brothers in their epic last fight. Then between them comes the double-wedge of irony, which Synge had made new in the story; that a fighting hero must put battle-loyalty before

---

[1] Preface to *Plays for an Irish Theatre* (1911), pp. ix–x. I am indebted for this reference to Professor Ure. *v.* also *The Harvest of Tragedy*, Ch. 17.

[2] *Essays and Introductions*, p. 239.

[3] v. ii. 332.

love, and that, when he is torn between this and his love, he will
curse (as Antony does) both love and woman:

> They'll not get a death that's cruel, and they with men alone.
> It's women that have loved are cruel only; and if I went on living
> this day I'd be putting a curse on the lot of them. . . .
> DEIRDRE *bitterly*: I'm well pleased there's no one in this place to
> make a story that Naisi was a laughing-stock the night he died.

It is at this point we are given the essence of the tragedy. Deirdre
has returned to Emain, partly out of pride in the fulfilment of the
destiny that was foretold for her, partly so that Naisi's love should
not grow weary and old. At the moment of testing she fails Naisi.
He goes to his death with a 'hard word' from her lips, bitterness in
his eyes.

> There'd not be many'd make a story, for that mockery is in your eyes
> will spot the face of Emain with a plague of pitted graves.

(So it might have been with Antony and Cleopatra after the first
battle when her galleys fled.) Naisi goes out to his death.
Conchubor approaches Deirdre. Her wild lament is the more bitter
because she now recognizes that she has betrayed Naisi. Her words
become more and more frantic:

> It's the way pity has me this night, when I think of Naisi, that I could
> set my teeth into the heart of a king.

All Conchubor's pleading for their future life in Emain drives her
to clutch more tightly the thoughts of her seven years with Naisi.
Lavarcham recognizes her hysteria, tries to coax her away, playing
up so pitiably to her mood of grief and to the actress in her:

> If it is that way you'd be, come till I find you a sunny place where
> you'll be a great wonder they'll call the queen of sorrows; and you'll
> begin taking a pride to be sitting up pausing and dreaming when the
> summer comes.

Fergus arrives too late, and confronts Conchubor. The two
heroes, and the backcloth of the burning city, give to her, as to
Cleopatra, resolution and a calmer poetry. With her great speech
that begins 'I see the flames of Emain starting upward in the dark
night' she begins to fulfil her own dramatic destiny, the doom of her
story; her exaltation of mood gathers into it the remembrance of
sensuous love. Her bitterness, and Naisi's, the moment of betrayal,

is forgotten. The tragic action is pitiful, but its epic endurance is her reward: it is yet

a thing will be a joy and triumph to the ends of life and time.

And if we are to believe what Yeats has written of the ending, this exaltation is won out of experience:

It was only at the last in his unfinished *Deirdre of the Sorrows* that his mood changed. He knew some twelve months ago that he was dying, though he told no one about it but his betrothed, and he gave all his thought to this play, that he might finish it. Sometimes he would despond and say that he could not, and then his betrothed would act it for him in his sick-room, and give him heart to write again. And now by a strange chance, for he began the play before the last failing of his health, his persons awake to no disillusionment but to death only, and as if his soul already thirsted for the fiery fountains there is nothing grotesque, but beauty only.

After Deirdre's death there is, in miniature, the classic resolution of tension by simplicity of speech. It is worth quoting.

LAVARCHAM: I have a little hut where you can rest, Conchubor; there is a great dew falling.
CONCHUBOR *with the voice of an old man*: Take me with you. I'm hard set to see the way before me.
OLD WOMAN: This way, Conchubor. *They go out*.
LAVARCHAM *beside the grave*: Deirdre is dead, and Naisi is dead; and if the oaks and stars could die for sorrow, it's a dark sky and a hard and naked earth we'd have this night in Emain.

Is it hubris to think that if Synge had lived to oversee the play he might have dropped Lavarcham's final speech, so that we might have thought of the ending as we think of *King Lear* or *The Cenci*?

[1] *Essays and Introductions*, pp. 309-10.

III
THE PLAYS

In the Shadow of the Glen

———

PERSONS IN THE PLAY

DAN BURKE, farmer and herd

NORA BURKE, his wife

MICHAEL DARA, a young herd

A TRAMP

*Scene: the last cottage at the head of a long glen
in County Wicklow*

Cottage kitchen; turf fire on the right; a bed near it against the wall, with a body lying on it covered with a sheet. A door is at the other end of the room, with a low table near it, and stools, or wooden chairs. There are a couple of glasses on the table, and a bottle of whisky, as if for a wake, with two cups, a tea-pot, and a home-made cake. There is another small door near the bed. Nora Burke is moving about the room, settling a few things, and lighting candles on the table, looking now and then at the bed with an uneasy look. Someone knocks softly at the door. She takes up a stocking with money from the table and puts it in her pocket. Then she opens the door.

TRAMP *outside*: Good evening to you, lady of the house.

NORA: Good evening kindly, stranger; it's a wild night, God help you, to be out in the rain falling.

TRAMP: It is, surely, and I walking to Brittas from the Aughrim fair.

NORA: Is it walking on your feet, stranger?

TRAMP: On my two feet, lady of the house, and when I saw the light below I thought may be if you'd a sup of new milk and a quiet, decent corner where a man could sleep . . . *He looks in past her and sees the dead man.* The Lord have mercy on us all!

NORA: It doesn't matter anyway, stranger; come in out of the rain.

TRAMP *coming in slowly and going towards the bed*: Is it departed he is?

NORA: It is, stranger. He's after dying on me, God forgive him, and there I am now with a hundred sheep beyond on the hills, and no turf drawn for the winter.

TRAMP *looking closely at the dead man*: It's a queer look is on him for a man that's dead.

NORA *half humorously*: He was always queer, stranger; and I suppose them that's queer and they living men, will be queer bodies after.

TRAMP: Isn't it a great wonder you're letting him lie there, and he not tidied, or laid out itself?

NORA *coming to the bed*: I was afeard, stranger, for he put a black curse on me this morning if I'd touch his body the time he'd die sudden, or let any one touch it except his sister only, and it's ten miles away she lives, in the big glen over the hill.

TRAMP *looking at her and nodding slowly*: It's a queer story he wouldn't let his own wife touch him, and he dying quiet in his bed.

NORA: He was an old man, and an odd man, stranger, and it's always up on the hills he was, thinking thoughts in the dark mist. . . . *She pulls back a bit of the sheet.* Lay your hand on him now, and tell me if it's cold he is surely.

TRAMP: Is it getting the curse on me you'd be, woman of the house? I wouldn't lay my hand on him for the Lough Nahanagan and it filled with gold.

NORA *looking uneasily at the body*: Maybe cold would be no sign of death with the like of him, for he was always cold, every day since I knew him . . . and every night, stranger . . . (*she covers up his face and comes away from the bed*); but I'm thinking it's dead he is surely, for he's complaining a while back of a pain in his heart, and this morning, the time he was going off to Brittas for three days or four, he was taken with a sharp turn. Then he went into his bed, and he was saying it was destroyed he was, the time the shadow was going up through the glen, and when the sun set on the bog beyond he made a great lep, and let a great cry out of him, and stiffened himself out the like of a dead sheep.

TRAMP *crosses himself*: God rest his soul.

NORA *pouring him out a glass of whisky*: Maybe that would do you better than the milk of the sweetest cow in County Wicklow.

TRAMP: The Almighty God reward you and may it be to your good health. *He drinks.*

NORA *giving him a pipe and tobacco*: I've no pipes saving his own, stranger, but they're sweet pipes to smoke.

TRAMP: Thank you kindly, lady of the house.

NORA: Sit down now, stranger, and be taking your rest.

TRAMP *filling a pipe and looking about the room*: I've walked a great way through the world, lady of the house, and seen great wonders, but I never seen a wake till this day with fine spirits, and good tobacco, and the best pipes, and no one to taste them but a woman only.

NORA: Didn't you hear me say it was only after dying on me he was when the sun went down, and how would I got out into the glen

83

and tell the neighbours, and I a lone woman with no house near me?

TRAMP *drinking*: There's no offence, lady of the house?

NORA: No offence in life, stranger. How would the like of you, passing in the dark night, know the lonesome way I was with no house near me at all?

TRAMP *sitting down*: I knew rightly. *He lights his pipe, so that there is a sharp light beneath his haggard face.* And I was thinking, and I coming in through the door, that it's many a lone woman would be afeard of the like of me in the dark night, in a place wouldn't be as lonesome as this place, where there aren't two living souls would see the little light you have shining from the glass.

NORA *slowly*: I'm thinking many would be afeard, but I never knew what way I'd be afeard of beggar or bishop or any man of you at all. . . . *She looks towards the window and lowers her voice.* It's other things than the like of you, stranger, would make a person afeard.

TRAMP *looking round with a half shudder*: It is surely, God help us all!

NORA *looking at him for a moment with curiosity*: You're saying that, stranger, as if you were easy afeard.

TRAMP *speaking mournfully*: Is it myself, lady of the house, that does be walking round in the long nights, and crossing the hills when the fog is on them, the time a little stick would seem as big as your arm, and a rabbit as big as a bay horse, and a stack of turf as big as a towering church in the city of Dublin? If myself was easy afeard, I'm telling you, it's long ago I'd have been locked into the Richmond Asylum, or maybe have run up into the back hills with nothing on me but an old shirt, and been eaten by the crows the like of Patch Darcy – the Lord have mercy on him – in the year that's gone.

NORA *with interest*: You knew Darcy?

TRAMP: Wasn't I the last one heard his living voice in the whole world?

NORA: There were great stories of what was heard at that time, but would any one believe the things they do be saying in the glen?

TRAMP: It was no lie, lady of the house. . . . I was passing below on a dark night the like of this night, and the sheep were lying under the ditch and every one of them coughing and choking like an old man, with the great rain and the fog. Then I heard a thing talking – queer talk, you wouldn't believe it at all, and you out of your dream – and 'Merciful God,' says I, 'if I begin hearing the like of that voice out of the thick mist, I'm destroyed surely.' Then I run and I run till I was below in Rathvanna. I got drunk that night, I got drunk in the morning, and drunk the day after – I was coming from the races beyond – and the third day they found Darcy. . . . Then I knew it was himself I was after hearing, and I wasn't afeard any more.

NORA *speaking sorrowfully and slowly*: God spare Darcy; he'd always look in here and he passing up or passing down, and it's very lonesome I was after him a long while (*she looks over at the bed and lowers her voice, speaking very slowly*), and then I got happy again – if it's ever happy we are, stranger – for I got used to being lonesome. *A short pause; then she stands up*. Was there any one on the last bit of the road, stranger, and you coming from Aughrim?

TRAMP: There was a young man with a drift of mountain ewes, and he running after them this way and that.

NORA *with a half smile*: Far down, stranger?

TRAMP: A piece only.

Nora fills the kettle and puts it on the fire.

NORA: Maybe, if you're not easy afeard, you'd stay here a short while alone with himself.

TRAMP: I would surely. A man that's dead can do no hurt.

NORA *speaking with a sort of constraint*: I'm going a little back to the west, stranger, for himself would go there one night and another and whistle at that place, and then the young man you're after seeing – a kind of a farmer has come up from the sea to live in a cottage beyond – would walk round to see if there was a thing we'd have to be done, and I'm wanting him this night, the way he can go down into the glen when the sun goes up and tell the people that himself is dead.

TRAMP *looking at the body in the sheet*: It's myself will go for him, lady of the house, and let you not be destroying yourself with the great rain.

NORA: You wouldn't find your way, stranger, for there's a small path only, and it running up between two sluigs where an ass and cart would be drowned. *She puts a shawl over her head.* Let you be making yourself easy, and saying a prayer for his soul, and it's not long I'll be coming again.

TRAMP *moving uneasily*: Maybe if you'd a piece of a grey thread and a sharp needle – there's great safety in a needle, lady of the house – I'd be putting a little stitch here and there in my old coat, the time I'll be praying for his soul, and it going up naked to the saints of God.

NORA *takes a needle and thread from the front of her dress and gives it to him*: There's the needle, stranger, and I'm thinking you won't be lonesome, and you used to the back hills, for isn't a dead man itself more company than to be sitting alone, and hearing the winds crying, and you not knowing on what thing your mind would stay?

TRAMP *slowly*: It's true, surely, and the Lord have mercy on us all!

Nora goes out. The tramp begins stitching one of the tags in his coat, saying the 'De Profundis' under his breath. In an instant the sheet is drawn slowly down, and Dan Burke looks out. The tramp moves uneasily, then looks up, and springs to his feet with a movement of terror.

DAN *with a hoarse voice*: Don't be afeard, stranger; a man that's dead can do no hurt.

TRAMP *trembling*: I meant no harm, your honour; and won't you leave me easy to be saying a little prayer for your soul?

A long whistle is heard outside.

DAN *sitting up in his bed and speaking fiercely*: Ah, the devil mend her. . . . Do you hear that, stranger? Did ever you hear another woman could whistle the like of that with two fingers in her mouth? *He looks at the table hurriedly.* I'm destroyed with the drouth, and let you bring me a drop quickly before herself will come back.

TRAMP *doubtfully*: Is it not dead you are?

DAN: How would I be dead, and I as dry as a baked bone, stranger?

TRAMP *pouring out the whisky*: What will herself say if she smells the stuff on you, for I'm think it's not for nothing you're letting on to be dead?

DAN: It is not, stranger; but she won't be coming near me at all, and it's not long now I'll be letting on, for I've a cramp in my back, and my hip's asleep on me, and there's been the devil's own fly itching my nose. It's near dead I was wanting to sneeze, and you blathering about the rain, and Darcy (*bitterly*) – the devil choke him – and the towering church. *Crying out impatiently*. Give me that whisky. Would you have herself come back before I taste a drop at all?

Tramp gives him the glass.

After drinking. Go over now to that cupboard, and bring me a black stick you'll see in the west corner by the wall.

TRAMP *taking a stick from the cupboard*: Is it that, your honour?

DAN: It is, stranger; it's a long time I'm keeping that stick, for I've a bad wife in the house.

TRAMP *with a queer look*: Is it herself, master of the house, and she a grand woman to talk?

DAN: It's herself, surely, it's a bad wife she is – a bad wife for an old man, and I'm getting old, God help me, though I've an arm to me still. *He takes the stick in his hand*. Let you wait now a short while, and it's a great sight you'll see in this room in two hours or three. *He stops to listen*. Is that somebody above?

TRAMP *listening*: There's a voice speaking on the path.

DAN: Put that stick here in the bed and smooth the sheet the way it was lying. *He covers himself up hastily*. Be falling to sleep now, and don't let on you know anything, or I'll be having your life. I wouldn't have told you at all but it's destroyed with the drouth I was.

TRAMP *covering his head*: Have no fear, master of the house. What is it I know of the like of you that I'd be saying a word or putting out my hand to stay you at all? *He goes back to the fire, sits down on a stool with his back to the bed, and goes on stitching his coat.*

DAN *under the sheet, querulously*: Stranger!

TRAMP *quickly*: Whisht! whisht! Be quiet, I'm telling you; they're coming now at the door.

Nora comes in with Michael Dara, a tall, innocent young man, behind her.

NORA: I wasn't long at all, stranger, for I met himself on the path.

TRAMP: You were middling long, lady of the house.

NORA: There was no sign from himself?

TRAMP: No sign at all, lady of the house.

NORA *to Michael*: Go over now and pull down the sheet, and look on himself, Michael Dara, and you'll see it's the truth I'm telling you.

MICHAEL: I will not, Nora; I do be afeard of the dead.

He sits down on a stool next the table, facing the tramp. Nora puts the kettle on a lower hook of the pot-hooks, and piles turf under it.

NORA *turning to the tramp*: Will you drink a cup of tea with myself and the young man, stranger, or (*speaking more persuasively*) will you go into the little room and stretch yourself a short while on the bed? I'm thinking it's destroyed you are walking the length of that way in the great rain.

TRAMP: Is it go away and leave you, and you having a wake, lady of the house? I will not, surely. *He takes a drink from his glass, which he has beside him.* And it's none of your tea I'm asking either.

He goes on stitching. Nora makes the tea.

MICHAEL *after looking at the tramp rather scornfully for a moment*: That's a poor coat you have, God help you, and I'm thinking it's a poor tailor you are with it.

TRAMP: If it's a poor tailor I am, I'm thinking it's a poor herd does be running backward and forward after a little handful of ewes, the way I seen yourself running this day, young fellow, and you coming from the fair.

Nora comes back to the table.

NORA *to Michael, in a low voice*: Let you not mind him at all, Michael Dara; he has a drop taken, and it's soon he'll be falling asleep.

MICHAEL: It's no lie he's telling; I was destroyed, surely. They were that wilful they were running off into one man's bit of oats, and another man's bit of hay, and tumbling into the red

88

bog till it's more like a pack of old goats than sheep they were.
. . . Mountain ewes is a queer breed, Nora Burke, and I not
used to them at all.

NORA *settling the tea-things*: There's no one can drive a mountain
ewe but the men do be reared in the Glenmalure, I've heard
them say, and above by Rathvanna, and the Glen Imaal – men
the like of Patch Darcy, God spare his soul, who would walk
through five hundred sheep and miss one of them, and he not
reckoning them at all.

MICHAEL *uneasily*: Is it the man went queer in his head the year
that's gone?

NORA: It is, surely.

TRAMP *plaintively*: That was a great man, young fellow – a great
man, I'm telling you. There was never a lamb from his own
ewes he wouldn't know before it was marked, and he'd run
from this to the city of Dublin and never catch for his breath.

NORA *turning round quickly*: He was a great man surely, stranger;
and isn't it a grand thing when you hear a living man saying a
good word of a dead man, and he mad dying?

TRAMP: It's the truth I'm saying, God spare his soul.

*He puts the needle under the collar of his coat, and settles himself to sleep
in the chimney corner. Nora sits down at the table: Nora and Michael's
backs are turned to the bed.*

MICHAEL *looking at her with a queer look*: I heard tell this day, Nora
Burke, that it was on the path below Patch Darcy would be
passing up and passing down, and I heard them say he'd never
pass it night or morning without speaking with yourself.

NORA *in a low voice*: It was no lie you heard, Michael Dara.

MICHAEL: I'm thinking it's a power of men you're after knowing
if it's in a lonesome place you live itself.

NORA *giving him his tea*: It's in a lonesome place you do have to be
talking with someone, and looking for someone, in the evening
of the day, and if it's a power of men I'm after knowing they
were fine men, for I was a hard child to please, and a hard girl
to please (*she looks at him a little sternly*), and it's a hard woman
I am to please this day, Michael Dara, and it's no lie I'm telling
you.

MICHAEL *looking over to see that the tramp is asleep, and then pointing to the dead man*: Was it a hard woman to please you were when you took himself for your man?

NORA: What way would I live, and I an old woman, if I didn't marry a man with a bit of a farm, and cows on it, and sheep on the back hills?

MICHAEL *considering*: That's true, Nora, and maybe it's no fool you were, for there's good grazing on it, if it is a lonesome place, and I'm thinking it's a good sum he's left behind.

NORA *taking the stocking with the money from her pocket, and putting it on the table*: I do be thinking in the long nights it was a big fool I was that time, Michael Dara; for what good is a bit of a farm with cows on it, and sheep on the back hills, when you do be sitting looking out from a door the like of that door, and seeing nothing but the mists rolling down the bog, and the mists again and they rolling up the bog, and hearing nothing but the wind crying out in the bits of broken trees were left from the great storm, and the streams roaring with the rain.

MICHAEL *looking at her uneasily*: What is it ails you this night, Nora Burke? I've heard tell it's the like of that talk you do hear from men, and they after being a great while on the back hills.

NORA *putting out the money on the table*: It's a bad night, and a wild night, Michael Dara, and isn't it a great while I am at the foot of the back hills, sitting up here boiling food for himself, and food for the brood sow, and baking a cake when the night falls? *She puts up the money listlessly in little piles on the table.* Isn't it a long while I am sitting here in the winter and the summer, and the fine spring, with the young growing behind me and the old passing, saying to myself one time to look on Mary Brien, who wasn't that height (*holding out her hand*) and I a fine girl growing up, and there she is now with two children, and another coming on her in three months or four. *She pauses.*

MICHAEL *moving over three of the piles*: That's three pounds we have now, Nora Burke.

NORA *continuing in the same voice*: And saying to myself another time, to look on Peggy Cavanagh, who had the lightest hand at milking a cow that wouldn't be easy, or turning a cake, and there she is now walking round on the roads, or sitting in a dirty old house, with no teeth in her mouth, and no sense, and no more hair than you'd see on a bit of hill and they after burning the furze from it.

MICHAEL: That's five pounds and ten notes, a good sum, surely! . . . It's not that way you'll be talking when you marry a young man, Nora Burke, and they were saying in the fair my lambs were the best lambs, and I got a grand price, for I'm no fool now at making a bargain when my lambs are good.

NORA: What was it you got?

MICHAEL: Twenty pounds for the lot, Nora Burke. . . . We'd do right to wait now till himself will be quiet awhile in the Seven Churches, and then you'll marry me in the chapel of Rathvanna, and I'll bring the sheep up on the bit of a hill you have on the back mountain, and we won't have anything we'd be afeard to let our minds on when the mist is down.

NORA *pouring him out some whisky*: Why would I marry you, Mike Dara? You'll be getting old and I'll be getting old, and in a little while, I'm telling you, you'll be sitting up in your bed – the way himself was sitting – with a shake in your face, and your teeth falling, and the white hair sticking out round you like an old bush where sheep do be leaping a gap.

Dan Burke sits up noiselessly from under the sheet, with his hand to his face. His white hair is sticking out round his head. Nora goes on slowly without hearing him.

It's a pitiful thing to be getting old, but it's a queer thing surely. It's a queer thing to see an old man sitting up there in his bed with no teeth in him, and a rough word in his mouth, and his chin the way it would take the bark from the edge of an oak board you'd have building a door. . . . God forgive me, Michael Dara, we'll all be getting old, but it's a queer thing surely.

MICHAEL: It's too lonesome you are from living a long time with an old man, Nora, and you're talking again like a herd that would be coming down from the thick mist (*he puts his arm round her*), but it's a fine life you'll have now with a young man – a fine life, surely. . . .

Dan sneezes violently. Michael tries to get to the door, but before he can do so Dan jumps out of the bed in queer white clothes, with the stick in his hand, and goes over and puts his back against it.

Son of God deliver us! *Crosses himself, and goes backward across the room.*

DAN *holding up his hand at him*: Now you'll not marry her the time I'm rotting below in the Seven Churches, and you'll see the thing I'll give you will follow you on the back mountains when the wind is high.

MICHAEL *to Nora*: Get me out of it, Nora, for the love of God. He always did what you bid him, and I'm thinking he would do it now.

NORA *looking at the tramp*: Is it dead he is or living?

DAN *turning towards her*: It's little you care if it's dead or living I am; but there'll be an end now of your fine times, and all the talk you have of young men and old men, and of the mist coming up or going down. *He opens the door.* You'll walk out now from that door, Nora Burke; and it's not to-morrow, or the next day, or any day of your life, that you'll put in your foot through it again.

TRAMP *standing up*: It's a hard thing you're saying for an old man, master of the house; and what would the like of her do if you put her out on the roads?

DAN: Let her walk round the like of Peggy Cavanagh below, and be begging money at the cross-roads, or selling songs to the men. *To Nora.* Walk out now, Nora Burke, and it's soon you'll be getting old with that life, I'm telling you; it's soon your teeth'll be falling and your head'll be the like of a bush where sheep do be leaping a gap.

He pauses; Nora looks round at Michael.

MICHAEL *timidly*: There's a fine Union below in Rathdrum.

DAN: The like of her would never go there. . . . It's lonesome roads she'll be going and hiding herself away till the end will come, and they find her stretched like a dead sheep with the frost on her, or the big spiders maybe, and they putting their webs on her, in the butt of a ditch.

NORA *angrily*: What way will yourself be that day, Daniel Burke? What way will you be that day and you lying down a long while in your grave? For it's bad you are living, and it's bad you'll be when you're dead. *She looks at him a moment fiercely, then half turns away and speaks plaintively again.* Yet, if it is itself, Daniel Burke, who can help it at all, and let you be getting up into your bed, and not be taking your death with the wind blowing on you, and the rain with it, and you half in your skin.

DAN: It's proud and happy you'd be if I was getting my death the day I was shut of yourself. *Pointing to the door.* Let you walk out through that door, I'm telling you, and let you not be passing this way if it's hungry you are, or wanting a bed.

TRAMP *pointing to Michael*: Maybe himself would take her.

NORA: What would he do with me now?

TRAMP: Give you the half of a dry bed, and good food in your mouth.

DAN: Is it a fool you think him, stranger; or is it a fool you were born yourself? Let her walk out of that door, and let you go along with her, stranger – if it's raining itself – for it's too much talk you have surely.

TRAMP *going over to Nora*: We'll be going now, lady of the house; the rain is falling, but the air is kind, and maybe it'll be a grand morning, by the grace of God.

NORA: What good is a grand morning when I'm destroyed surely, and I going out to get my death walking the roads?

TRAMP: You'll not be getting your death with myself, lady of the house, and I knowing all the ways a man can put food in his mouth. . . . We'll be going now, I'm telling you, and the time you'll be feeling the cold, and the frost, and the great rain, and the sun again, and the south wind blowing in the glens, you'll not be sitting up on a wet ditch, the way you're after sitting in this place, making yourself old with looking on each day, and it passing you by. You'll be saying one time: 'It's a grand evening, by the grace of God,' and another time, 'It's a wild night, God help us; but it'll pass, surely.' You'll be saying . . .

DAN *goes over to them, crying out impatiently*: Go out of that door, I'm telling you, and do your blathering below in the glen.

Nora gathers a few things into her shawl.

TRAMP *at the door*: Come along with me now, lady of the house, and it's not my blather you'll be hearing only, but you'll be hearing the herons crying out over the black lakes, and you'll be hearing the grouse and the owls with them, and the larks and the big thrushes when the days are warm; and it's not from the like of them you'll be hearing a tale of getting old like Peggy Cavanagh, and losing the hair off you, and the light of your eyes, but it's fine songs you'll be hearing when the sun goes up, and there'll be no old fellow wheezing, the like of a sick sheep, close to your ear.

NORA: I'm thinking it's myself will be wheezing that time with lying down under the heavens when the night is cold; but you've a fine bit of talk, stranger, and it's with yourself I'll go. *She goes towards the door, then turns to Dan.* You think it's a grand thing you're after doing with your letting on to be dead, but what is it at all? What way would a woman live in a lonesome place the like of this place, and she not making a talk with the men passing? And what way will yourself live from this day, with none to care you? What is it you'll have now but a black life, Daniel Burke; and it's not long, I'm telling you, till you'll be lying again under that sheet, and you dead surely.

She goes out with the tramp. Michael is slinking after them, but Dan stops him.

DAN: Sit down now and take a little taste of the stuff, Michael Dara. There's a great drouth on me, and the night is young.

MICHAEL *coming back to the table*: And it's very dry I am, surely, with the fear of death you put on me, and I after driving mountain ewes since the turn of the day.

DAN *throwing away his stick*: I was thinking to strike you, Michael Dara; but you're a quiet man, God help you, and I don't mind you at all. *He pours out two glasses of whisky, and gives one to Michael.* Your good health, Michael Dara.

MICHAEL: God reward you, Daniel Burke, and may you have a long life and a quiet life, and good health with it.

They drink.

CURTAIN

Riders to the Sea

———

Cottage kitchen, with nets, oilskins, spinning-wheel, some new boards standing by the wall, etc. Cathleen, a girl of about twenty, finishes kneading cake, and puts it down in the pot-oven by the fire; then wipes her hands, and begins to spin at the wheel. Nora, a young girl, puts her head in at the door.

NORA *in a low voice*: Where is she?

CATHLEEN: She's lying down, God help her, and maybe sleeping, if she's able.

Nora comes in softly, and takes a bundle from under her shawl.

    Spinning the wheel rapidly. What is it you have?

NORA: The young priest is after bringing them. It's a shirt and a plain stocking were got off a drowned man in Donegal.

Cathleen stops her wheel with a sudden movement, and leans out to listen.

    We're to find out if it's Michael's they are, some time herself will be down looking by the sea.

CATHLEEN: How would they be Michael's, Nora? How would he go the length of that way to the far north?

NORA: The young priest says he's known the like of it. 'If it's Michael's they are,' says he, 'you can tell herself he's got a clean burial, by the grace of God; and if they're not his, let no one say a word about them, for she'll be getting her death,' says he, 'with crying and lamenting.'

The door which Nora half closed is blown open by a gust of wind.

CATHLEEN *looking out anxiously*: Did you ask him would he stop Bartley going this day with the horses to the Galway fair?

NORA: 'I won't stop him,' says he; 'but let you not be afraid. Herself does be saying prayers half through the night, and the Almighty God won't leave her destitute,' says he, 'with no son living.'

CATHLEEN: Is the sea bad by the white rocks, Nora?

NORA: Middling bad, God help us. There's a great roaring in the west, and it's worse it'll be getting when the tide's turned to the wind. *She goes over to the table with the bundle.* Shall I open it now?

CATHLEEN: Maybe she'd wake up on us, and come in before we'd done. *Coming to the table.* It's a long time we'll be, and the two of us crying.

NORA *goes to the inner door and listens*: She's moving about on the bed. She'll be coming in a minute.

CATHLEEN: Give me the ladder, and I'll put them up in the turf loft, the way she won't know of them at all, and maybe when the tide turns she'll be going down to see would he be floating from the east.

They put the ladder against the gable of the chimney; Cathleen goes up a few steps and hides the bundle in the turf loft. Maurya comes from the inner room.

MAURYA *looking up at Cathleen and speaking querulously*: Isn't it turf enough you have for this day and evening?

CATHLEEN: There's a cake baking at the fire for a short space (*throwing down the turf*), and Bartley will want it when the tide turns if he goes to Connemara.

Nora picks up the turf and puts it round the pot-oven.

MAURYA *sitting down on a stool at the fire*: He won't go this day with the wind rising from the south and west. He won't go this day, for the young priest will stop him surely.

NORA: He'll not stop him, mother; and I heard Eamon Simon and Stephen Pheety and Colum Shawn saying he would go.

MAURYA: Where is he itself?

NORA: He went down to see would there be another boat sailing in the week, and I'm thinking it won't be long till he's here now, for the tide's turning at the green head, and the hooker's tacking from the east.

CATHLEEN: I hear someone passing the big stones.

NORA *looking out*: He's coming now, and he in a hurry.

BARTLEY *comes in and looks round the room. Speaking sadly and quietly*: Where is the bit of new rope, Cathleen, was bought in Connemara?

CATHLEEN *coming down*: Give it to him, Nora; it's on a nail by the white boards. I hung it up this morning, for the pig with the black feet was eating it.

97

NORA *giving him a rope*: Is that it, Bartley?

MAURYA: You'd do right to leave that rope, Bartley, hanging by the boards. *Bartley takes the rope.* It will be wanting in this place, I'm telling you, if Michael is washed up to-morrow morning, or the next morning, or any morning in the week; for it's a deep grave we'll make him, by the grace of God.

BARTLEY *beginning to work with the rope*: I've no halter the way I can ride down on the mare, and I must go now quickly. This is the one boat going for two weeks or beyond it, and the fair will be a good fair for horses, I heard them saying below.

MAURYA: It's a hard thing they'll be saying below if the body is washed up and there's no man in it to make the coffin, and I after giving a big price for the finest white boards you'd find in Connemara. *She looks round at the boards.*

BARTLEY: How would it be washed up, and we after looking each day for nine days, and a strong wind blowing a while back from the west and south?

MAURYA: If it isn't found itself, that wind is raising the sea, and there was a star up against the moon, and it rising in the night. If it was a hundred horses, or a thousand horses you had itself, what is the price of a thousand horses against a son where there is one son only?

BARTLEY *working at the halter, to Cathleen*: Let you go down each day, and see the sheep aren't jumping in on the rye, and if the jobber comes you can sell the pig with the black feet if there is a good price going.

MAURYA: How would the like of her get a good price for a pig?

BARTLEY *to Cathleen*: If the west winds holds with the last bit of the moon let you and Nora get up weed enough for another cock for the kelp. It's hard set we'll be from this day with no one in it but one man to work.

MAURYA: It's hard set we'll be surely the day you're drowned with the rest. What way will I live and the girls with me, and I an old woman looking for the grave?

Bartley lays down the halter, takes off his old coat, and puts on a newer one of the same flannel.

BARTLEY *to Nora*: Is she coming to the pier?

NORA *looking out*: She's passing the green head and letting fall her sails.

BARTLEY *getting his purse and tobacco*: I'll have half an hour to go down, and you'll see me coming again in two days, or in three days, or maybe in four days if the wind is bad.

MAURYA *turning round to the fire, and putting her shawl over her head*: Isn't it a hard and cruel man won't hear a word from an old woman, and she holding him from the sea?

CATHLEEN: It's the life of a young man to be going to the sea, and who would listen to an old woman with one thing and she saying it over?

BARTLEY *taking the halter*: I must go now quickly. I'll ride down on the red mare, and the grey pony 'ill run behind me. . . . The blessing of God on you.

He goes out.

MAURYA *crying out as he is in the door*: He's gone now, God spare us, and we'll not see him again. He's gone now, and when the black night is falling I'll have no son left me in the world.

CATHLEEN: Why wouldn't you give him your blessing and he looking round in the door? Isn't it sorrow enough is on every one in this house without your sending him out with an unlucky word behind him, and a hard word in his ear?

Maurya takes up the tongs and begins raking the fire aimlessly without looking round.

NORA *turning towards her*: You're taking away the turf from the cake.

CATHLEEN *crying out*: The Son of God forgive us, Nora, we're after forgetting his bit of bread. *She comes over to the fire.*

NORA: And it's destroyed he'll be going till dark night, and he after eating nothing since the sun went up.

CATHLEEN *turning the cake out of the oven*: It's destroyed he'll be surely. There's no sense left on any person in a house where an old woman will be talking for ever.

Maurya sways herself on her stool.

Cutting off some of the bread and rolling it in a cloth; to Maurya. Let you go down now to the spring well and give him this and he passing. You'll see him then and the dark word will be broken, and you can say 'God speed you,' the way he'll be easy in his mind.

MAURYA *taking the bread*: Will I be in it as soon as himself?

CATHLEEN: If you go now quickly.

MAURYA *standing up unsteadily*: It's hard set I am to walk.

CATHLEEN *looking at her anxiously*: Give her the stick, Nora, or maybe she'll slip on the big stones.

NORA: What stick?

CATHLEEN: The stick Michael brought from Connemara.

MAURYA *taking a stick Nora gives her*: In the big world the old people do be leaving things after them for their sons and children, but in this place it is the young men do be leaving things behind for them that do be old.

She goes out slowly. Nora goes over to the ladder.

CATHLEEN: Wait, Nora, maybe she'd turn back quickly. She's that sorry, God help her, you wouldn't know the thing she'd do.

NORA: Is she gone round by the bush?

CATHLEEN *looking out*: She's gone now. Throw it down quickly, for the Lord knows when she'll be out of it again.

NORA *getting the bundle from the loft*: The young priest said he'd be passing to-morrow, and we might go down and speak to him below if it's Michael's they are surely.

CATHLEEN *taking the bundle*: Did he say what way they were found?

NORA *coming down*: 'There were two men,' said he, 'and they rowing round with poteen before the cocks crowed, and the oar of one of them caught the body, and they passing the black cliffs of the north.'

CATHLEEN *trying to open the bundle*: Give me a knife, Nora; the string's perished with the salt water, and there's a black knot on it you wouldn't loosen in a week.

NORA *giving her a knife*: I've heard tell it was a long way to Donegal.

CATHLEEN *cutting the string*: It is surely. There was a man in here a while ago – the man sold us that knife – and he said if you set off walking from the rocks beyond, it would be in seven days you'd be in Donegal.

NORA: And what time would a man take, and he floating?

Cathleen opens the bundle and takes out a bit of a shirt and a stocking. They look at them eagerly.

CATHLEEN *in a low voice*: The Lord spare us, Nora! isn't it a queer hard thing to say if it's his they are surely?

NORA: I'll get his shirt off the hook the way we can put the one flannel on the other. *She looks through some clothes hanging in the corner.* It's not with them, Cathleen, and where will be it?

CATHLEEN: I'm thinking Bartley put it on him in the morning, for his own shirt was heavy with the salt in it. *Pointing to the corner.* There's a bit of a sleeve was of the same stuff. Give me that and it will do.

Nora brings it to her and they compare the flannel.

It's the same stuff, Nora; but if it is itself, aren't there great rolls of it in the shops of Galway, and isn't it many another man may have a shirt of it as well as Michael himself?

NORA *who has taken up the stocking and counted the stitches, crying out*: It's Michael, Cathleen, it's Michael; God spare his soul, and what will herself say when she hears this story, and Bartley on the sea?

CATHLEEN *taking the stocking*: It's a plain stocking.

NORA: It's the second one of the third pair I knitted, and I put up three-score stitches, and I dropped four of them.

CATHLEEN *counts the stitches*: It's that number is in it. *Crying out.* Ah, Nora, isn't it a bitter thing to think of him floating that way to the far north, and no one to keen him but the black hags that do be flying on the sea?

NORA *swinging herself half round, and throwing out her arms on the clothes*: And isn't it a pitiful thing when there is nothing left of a man who was a great rower and fisher but a bit of an old shirt and a plain stocking?

CATHLEEN *after an instant*: Tell me is herself coming, Nora? I hear a little sound on the path.

NORA *looking out*: She is, Cathleen. She's coming up to the door.

CATHLEEN: Put these things away before she'll come in. Maybe it's easier she'll be after giving her blessing to Bartley, and we won't let on we've heard anything the time he's on the sea.

NORA *helping Cathleen to close the bundle*: We'll put them here in the corner.

They put them into a hole in the chimney corner. Cathleen goes back to the spinning-wheel.

Will she see it was crying I was?

CATHLEEN: Keep your back to the door the way the light'll not be on you.

Nora sits down at the chimney corner, with her back to the door. Maurya comes in very slowly, without looking at the girls, and goes over to her stool at the other side of the fire. The cloth with the bread is still in her hand. The girls look at each other, and Nora points to the bundle of bread.

After spinning for a moment. You didn't give him his bit of bread?

Maurya begins to keen softly, without turning round.

Did you see him riding down?

Maurya goes on keening.

A little impatiently. God forgive you; isn't it a better thing to raise your voice and tell what you seen, than to be making lamentation for a thing that's done? Did you see Bartley, I'm saying to you?

MAURYA *with a weak voice*: My heart's broken from this day.

CATHLEEN *as before*: Did you see Bartley?

MAURYA: I seen the fearfullest thing.

CATHLEEN *leaves her wheel and looks out*: Give forgive you; he's riding the mare now over the green head, and the grey pony behind him.

MAURYA *starts so that her shawl falls back from her head and shows her white tossed hair. With a frightened voice*: The grey pony behind him. . . .

CATHLEEN *coming to the fire*: What is it ails you at all?

MAURYA *speaking very slowly*: I've seen the fearfullest thing any person has seen since the day Bride Dara seen the dead man with the child in his arms.

CATHLEEN *and* NORA: Uah.

They crouch down in front of the old woman at the fire.

NORA: Tell us what it is you seen.

MAURYA: I went down to the spring well, and I stood there saying a prayer to myself. Then Bartley came along, and he riding on the red mare with the grey pony behind him. *She puts up her hands, as if to hide something from her eyes.* The Son of God spare us, Nora!

CATHLEEN: What is it you seen?

MAURYA: I seen Michael himself.

CATHLEEN *speaking softly*: You did not, mother. It wasn't Michael you seen, for his body is after being found in the far north, and he's got a clean burial, by the grace of God.

MAURYA *a little defiantly*: I'm after seeing him this day, and he riding and galloping. Bartley came first on the red mare, and I tried to say 'God speed you,' but something choked the words in my throat. He went by quickly; and 'The blessing of God on you,' says he, and I could say nothing. I looked up then, and I crying, at the grey pony, and there was Michael upon it – with fine clothes on him, and new shoes on his feet.

CATHLEEN *begins to keen*: It's destroyed we are from this day. It's destroyed, surely.

NORA: Didn't the young priest say the Almighty God won't leave her destitute with no son living?

MAURYA *in a low voice, but clearly*: It's little the like of him knows of the sea. . . . Bartley will be lost now, and let you call in Eamon and make me a good coffin out of the white boards, for I won't live after them. I've had a husband, and a husband's father, and six sons in this house – six fine men, though it was a hard birth I had with every one of them and they coming into the world – and some of them were found and some of them were not found, but they're gone now the lot of them. . . . There were Stephen and Shawn were lost in the great wind, and found after in the Bay of Gregory of the Golden Mouth, and carried up the two of them on one plank, and in by that door.

She pauses for a moment; the girls start as if they heard something through the door that is half open behind them.

NORA *in a whisper*: Did you hear that, Cathleen? Did you hear a noise in the north-east?

CATHLEEN *in a whisper*: There's someone after crying out by the seashore.

MAURYA *continues without hearing anything*: There was Sheamus and his father, and his own father again, were lost in a dark night, and not a stick or sign was seen of them when the sun went up. There was Patch after was drowned out of a curragh that turned over. I was sitting here with Bartley, and he a baby lying on my two knees, and I seen two women, and three women, and four women coming in, and they crossing themselves and not saying a word. I looked out then, and there were men coming after them, and they holding a thing in the half of a red sail, and water dripping out of it – it was a dry day, Nora – and leaving a track to the door.

She pauses with her hand stretched out towards the door. It opens softly and old women begin to come in, crossing themselves on the threshold, and kneeling down in front of the stage with red petticoats over their heads.

> *Half in a dream, to Cathleen.* Is it Patch, or Michael, or what is it at all?

CATHLEEN: Michael is after being found in the far north, and when he is found there how could he be here in this place?

MAURYA: There does be a power of young men floating round in the sea, and what way would they know if it was Michael they had, or another man like him, for when a man is nine days in the sea, and the wind blowing, it's hard set his own mother would be to say what man was in it.

CATHLEEN: It's Michael, God spare him, for they're after sending us a bit of his clothes from the far north.

She reaches out and hands Maurya the clothes that belonged to Michael. Maurya stands up slowly, and takes them in her hands. Nora looks out.

NORA: They're carrying a thing among them, and there's water dripping out of it and leaving a track by the big stones.

CATHLEEN *in a whisper to the women who have come in*: Is it Bartley it is?

ONE OF THE WOMEN: It is, surely, God rest his soul.

Two younger women come in and pull out the table. Then men carry in the body of Bartley, laid on a plank, with a bit of a sail over it, and lay it on the table.

CATHLEEN *to the women as they are doing so*: What way was he drowned?

ONE OF THE WOMEN: The grey pony knocked him over into the sea, and he was washed out where there is a great surf on the white rocks.

Maurya has gone over and knelt down at the head of the table. The women are keening softly and swaying themselves with a slow movement. Cathleen and Nora kneel at the other end of the table. The men kneel near the door.

MAURYA *raising her head and speaking as if she did not see the people around her*: They're all gone now, and there isn't anything more the sea can do to me. . . . I'll have no call now to be up crying and praying when the wind breaks from the south, and you can hear the surf is in the east, and the surf is in the west, making a great stir with the two noises, and they hitting one on the other. I'll have no call now to be going down and getting Holy Water in the dark nights after Samhain, and I won't care what way the sea is when the other women will be keening. *To Nora.* Give me the Holy Water, Nora; there's a small sup still on the dresser.

Nora gives it to her.

> *Drops Michael's clothes across Bartley's feet, and sprinkles the Holy Water over him.* It isn't that I haven't prayed for you, Bartley, to the Almighty God. It isn't that I haven't said prayers in the dark night till you wouldn't know what I'd be saying; but it's a great rest I'll have now, and it's time, surely. It's a great rest I'll have now, and great sleeping in the long nights after Samhain, if it's only a bit of wet flour we do have to eat, and maybe a fish that would be stinking. *She kneels down again, crossing herself, and saying prayers under her breath.*

CATHLEEN *to an old man*: Maybe yourself and Eamon would make a coffin when the sun rises. We have fine white boards herself bought, God help her, thinking Michael would be found, and I have a new cake you can eat while you'll be working.

THE OLD MAN *looking at the boards*: Are there nails with them?

CATHLEEN: There are not, Colum; we didn't think of the nails.

ANOTHER MAN: It's a great wonder she wouldn't think of the nails, and all the coffins she's seen made already.

CATHLEEN: It's getting old she is, and broken.

Maurya stands up again very slowly and spreads out the pieces of Michael's clothes beside the body, sprinkling them with the last of the Holy Water.

NORA *in a whisper to Cathleen*: She's quiet now and easy; but the day Michael was drowned you could hear her crying out from this to the spring well. It's fonder she was of Michael, and would any one have thought that?

CATHLEEN *slowly and clearly*: An old woman will be soon tired with anything she will do, and isn't it nine days herself is after crying and keening, and making great sorrow in the house?

MAURYA *puts the empty cup mouth downwards on the table, and lays her hands together on Bartley's feet*: They're all together this time, and the end is come. May the Almighty God have mercy on Bartley's soul, and on Michael's soul, and on the souls of Sheamus and Patch, and Stephen and Shawn (*bending her head*); and may He have mercy on my soul, Nora, and on the soul of every one is left living in the world.

She pauses, and the keen rises a little more loudly from the women, then sinks away.

Continuing. Michael has a clean burial in the far north, by the grace of the Almighty God. Bartley will have a fine coffin out of the white boards, and a deep grave surely. What more can we want than that? No man at all can be living for ever, and we must be satisfied.

She kneels down again and the curtain falls slowly.

The Tinker's Wedding

PERSONS IN THE PLAY

MICHAEL BYRNE, a tinker

MARY BYRNE, an old woman, his mother

SARAH CASEY, a young tinker woman

A PRIEST

Scene: a village roadside after nightfall

Preface

The drama is made serious – in the French sense of the word – not by the degree in which it is taken up with problems that are serious in themselves, but by the degree in which it gives the nourishment, not very easy to define, on which our imaginations live. We should not go to the theatre as we go to a chemist's or a dram-shop, but as we go to a dinner where the food we need is taken with pleasure and excitement. This was nearly always so in Spain and England and France when the drama was at its richest – the infancy and decay of the drama tend to be didactic – but in these days the playhouse is too often stocked with the drugs of many seedy problems, or with the absinthe or vermouth of the last musical comedy.

The drama, like the symphony, does not teach or prove anything. Analysts with their problems, and teachers with their systems, are soon as old-fashioned as the pharmacopoeia of Galen – look at Ibsen and the Germans – but the best plays of Ben Jonson and Molière can no more go out of fashion than the blackberries on the hedges.

Of the things which nourish the imagination humour is one of the most needful, and it is dangerous to limit or destroy it. Baudelaire calls laughter the greatest sign of the Satanic element in man; and where a country loses its humour, as some towns in Ireland are doing, there will be morbidity of mind, as Baudelaire's mind was morbid.

In the greater part of Ireland, however, the whole people, from the tinkers to the clergy, have still a life, and view of life, that are rich and genial and humorous. I do not think that these country people, who have so much humour themselves, will mind being laughed at without malice, as the people in every country have been laughed at in their own comedies.

J. M. S.

2nd December 1907

NOTE: *The Tinker's Wedding* was first written a few years ago, about the time I was working at *Riders to the Sea* and *In the Shadow of the Glen*. I have re-written it since.

ACT ONE

A village roadside after nightfall. A fire of sticks is burning near the ditch a little to the right. Michael is working beside it. In the background, on the left, a sort of tent and ragged clothes drying on the hedge. On the right a chapel gate.

SARAH CASEY *coming in on right, eagerly*: We'll see his reverence this place, Michael Byrne, and he passing backward to his house to-night.

MICHAEL *grimly*: That'll be a sacred and a sainted joy!

SARAH *sharply*: It'll be small joy for yourself if you aren't ready with my wedding ring. *She goes over to him.* Is it near done this time, or what way is it at all?

MICHAEL: A poor way only, Sarah Casey, for it's the divil's job making a ring, and you'll be having my hands destroyed in a short while the way I'll not be able to make a tin can at all maybe at the dawn of day.

SARAH *sitting down beside him and throwing sticks on the fire*: If it's the divil's job, let you mind it, and leave your speeches that would choke a fool.

MICHAEL *slowly and glumly*: And it's you'll go talking of fools, Sarah Casey, when no man did ever hear a lying story even of your like unto this mortal day. You to be going beside me a great while, and rearing a lot of them, and then to be setting off with your talk of getting married, and your driving me to it, and I not asking it at all.

Sarah turns her back to him and arranges something in the ditch.

Angrily: Can't you speak a word when I'm asking what is it ails you since the moon did change?

SARAH *musingly*: I'm thinking there isn't anything ails me, Michael Byrne; but the springtime is a queer time, and it's queer thoughts maybe I do think at whiles.

MICHAEL: It's hard set you'd be to think queerer than welcome, Sarah Casey; but what will you gain dragging me to the priest this night, I'm saying, when it's new thoughts you'll be thinking at the dawn of day?

SARAH *teasingly*: It's at the dawn of day I do be thinking I'd have a right to be going off to the rich tinkers do be travelling from Tibradden to the Tara Hill; for it'd be a fine life to be driving with young Jaunting Jim, where there wouldn't be any big hills to break the back of you, with walking up and walking down.

MICHAEL *with dismay*: It's the like of that you do be thinking!

SARAH: The like of that, Michael Byrne, when there is a bit of sun in it, and a kind air, and a great smell coming from the thorn-trees is above your head.

MICHAEL *looks at her for a moment with horror and then hands her the ring*: Will that fit you now?

SARAH *trying it on*: It's making it tight you are, and the edges sharp on the tin.

MICHAEL *looking at it carefully*: It's the fat of your own finger, Sarah Casey; and isn't it a mad thing I'm saying again that you'd be asking marriage of me, or making a talk of going away from me, and you thriving and getting your good health by the grace of the Almighty God?

SARAH *giving it back to him*: Fix it now, and it'll do, if you're wary you don't squeeze it again.

MICHAEL *moodily, working again*: It's easy saying be wary; there's many things easy said, Sarah Casey, you'd wonder a fool even would be saying at all. *He starts violently.* The divil mend you, I'm scalded again!

SARAH *scornfully*: If you are, it's a clumsy man you are this night, Michael Byrne (*raising her voice*); and let you make haste now, or herself will be coming with the porter.

MICHAEL *defiantly, raising his voice*: Let me make haste? I'll be making haste maybe to hit you a great clout; for I'm thinking it's the like of that you want. I'm thinking on the day I got you above at Rathvanna, and the way you began crying out and we coming down off the hill, crying out and saying 'I'll go back to my ma'; and I'm thinking on the way I came behind you that time, and hit you a great clout in the lug, and how quiet and easy it was you came along with me from that hour to this present day.

SARAH *standing up and throwing all her sticks into the fire*: And a big fool I was, too, maybe; but we'll be seeing Jaunting Jim to-morrow in Ballinaclash, and he after getting a great price for his white foal in the horse fair of Wicklow, the way it'll be a great sight to see him squandering his share of gold, and he with a grand eye for a fine horse, and a grand eye for a woman.

MICHAEL *working again with impatience*: The divil do him good with the two of them.

SARAH *kicking up the ashes with her foot*: Ah, he's a great lad, I'm telling you, and it's proud and happy I'll be to see him, and he the first one called me the Beauty of Ballinacree, a fine name for a woman.

MICHAEL *with contempt*: It's the like of that name they do be putting on the horses they have below racing in Arklow. It's easy pleased you are, Sarah Casey, easy pleased with a big word, or the liar speaks it.

SARAH: Liar!

MICHAEL: Liar, surely.

SARAH *indignantly*: Liar, is it? Didn't you ever hear tell of the peelers followed me ten miles along the Glen Malure, and they talking love to me in the dark night; or of the children you'll meet coming from school and they saying one to the other: 'It's this day we seen Sarah Casey, the Beauty of Ballinacree, a great sight, surely.'

MICHAEL: God help the lot of them.

SARAH: It's yourself you'll be calling God to help, in two weeks or three, when you'll be waking up in the dark night and thinking you see me coming with the sun on me, and I driving a high cart with Jaunting Jim going behind. It's lonesome and cold you'll be feeling the ditch where you'll be lying down that night, I'm telling you, and you hearing the old woman making a great noise in her sleep, and the bats squeaking in the trees.

MICHAEL: Whisht. I hear someone coming the road.

SARAH *looking out right*: It's someone coming forward from the doctor's door.

MICHAEL: It's often his reverence does be in there playing cards, or drinking a sup, or singing songs, until the dawn of day.

SARAH: It's a big boast of a man with a long step on him and a trumpeting voice. It's his reverence, surely; and if you have the ring down, it's a great bargain we'll make now and he after drinking his glass.

MICHAEL *going to her and giving her the ring*: There's your ring, Sarah Casey; but I'm thinking he'll walk by and not stop to speak with the like of us at all.

SARAH *tidying herself, in great excitement*: Let you be sitting here and keeping a great blaze, the way he can look on my face; and let you seem to be working, for it's great love the like of him have to talk of work.

MICHAEL *moodily, sitting down and beginning to work at a tin can*: Great love, surely.

SARAH *eagerly*: Make a great blaze now, Michael Byrne.

The Priest comes in on right; she comes forward in front of him.

In a very plausible voice. Good evening, your reverence. It's a grand fine night, by the grace of God.

PRIEST: The Lord have mercy on us! What kind of a living woman is it that you are at all?

SARAH: It's Sarah Casey I am, your reverence, the Beauty of Ballinacree, and it's Michael Byrne is below in the ditch.

PRIEST: A holy pair surely! Let you get out of my way. *He tries to pass by.*

SARAH *keeping in front of him*: We are wanting a little word with your reverence.

PRIEST: I haven't a halfpenny at all. Leave the road, I'm saying.

SARAH: It isn't a halfpenny we're asking, holy father; but we were thinking maybe we'd have a right to be getting married; and we were thinking it's yourself would marry us for not a halfpenny at all; for you're a kind man, your reverence, a kind man with the poor.

PRIEST *with astonishment*: Is it marry you for nothing at all?

SARAH: It is, your reverence; and we were thinking maybe you'd give us a little small bit of silver to pay for the ring.

PRIEST *loudly*: Let you hold your tongue; let you be quiet, Sarah Casey. I've no silver at all for the like of you; and if you want to be married, let you pay your pound. I'd do it for a pound only, and that's making it a sight cheaper than I'd make it for one of my own pairs is living here in the place.

SARAH: Where would the like of us get a pound, your reverence?

PRIEST: Wouldn't you easy get it with your selling asses, and making cans, and your stealing east and west in Wicklow and Wexford and the county Meath? *He tries to pass her.* Let you leave the road, and not be plaguing me more.

SARAH *pleadingly, taking money from her pocket*: Wouldn't you have a little mercy on us, your reverence? *Holding out money.* Wouldn't you marry us for a half a sovereign, and it a nice shiny one with a view on it of the living king's mamma?

PRIEST: If it's ten shillings you have, let you get ten more the same way, and I'll marry you then.

SARAH *whining*: It's two years we are getting that bit, your reverence, with our pence and our halfpence and an odd threepenny bit; and if you don't marry us now, himself and the old woman, who has a great drouth, will be drinking it to-morrow in the fair (*she puts her apron to her eyes, half sobbing*), and then I won't be married any time, and I'll be saying till I'm an old woman: 'It's a cruel and a wicked thing to be bred poor.'

PRIEST *turning up towards the fire*: Let you not be crying, Sarah Casey. It's a queer woman you are to be crying at the like of that and you your whole life walking the roads.

SARAH *sobbing*: It's two years we are getting the gold, your reverence, and now you won't marry us for that bit, and we hard-working poor people do be making cans in the dark night, and blinding our eyes with the black smoke from the bits of twigs we do be burning.

An old woman is heard singing tipsily on the left.

PRIEST *looking at the can Michael is making*: When will you have that can done, Michael Byrne?

MICHAEL: In a short space only, your reverence, for I'm putting the last dab of solder on the rim.

PRIEST: Let you get a crown along with the ten shillings and the gallon can, Sarah Casey, and I will wed you so.

MARY *suddenly shouting behind, tipsily*: Larry was a fine lad, I'm saying; Larry was a fine lad, Sarah Casey –

MICHAEL: Whisht, now, the two of you. There's my mother coming, and she'd have us destroyed if she heard the like of that talk the time she's been drinking her fill.

Mary *comes in singing:*

> And when he asked him what way he'd die,
>   And he hanging unrepented,
> 'Begob,' says Larry, 'that's all in my eye,
>   By the clergy first invented.'

SARAH: Give me the jug now, or you'll have it spilt in the ditch.

MARY *holding the jug with both her hands, in a stilted voice*: Let you leave me easy, Sarah Casey. I won't spill it, I'm saying. God help you; are you thinking it's frothing full to the brim it is at this hour of the night, and I after carrying it in my two hands a long step from Jemmy Neill's?

MICHAEL *anxiously*: Is there a sup left at all?

SARAH *looking into the jug*: A little small sup only, I'm thinking.

MARY *sees the Priest, and holds out jug towards him*: God save your reverence. I'm after bringing down a smart drop; and let you drink it up now, for it's a middling drouthy man you are at all times, God forgive you, and this night is cruel dry.

She tries to go towards him. Sarah holds her back.

PRIEST *waving her away*: Let you not be falling to the flames. Keep off, I'm saying.

MARY *persuasively*: Let you not be shy of us, your reverence. Aren't we all sinners, God help us! Drink a sup now, I'm telling you; and we won't let on a word about it till the Judgment Day. *She takes up a tin mug, pours some porter into it, and gives it to him. Singing, and holding the jug in her hand.*

> A lonesome ditch in Ballygan
> The day you're beating a tenpenny can;
> A lonesome bank in Ballyduff
> The time . . .

She breaks off. It's a bad, wicked song, Sarah Casey; and let you put me down now in the ditch, and I won't sing it till himself will be gone; for it's bad enough he is, I'm thinking, without ourselves making him worse.

SARAH *putting her down, to the Priest, half laughing*: Don't mind her at all, your reverence. She's no shame the time she's a drop taking; and if it was the Holy Father from Rome was in it, she'd

give him a little sup out of her mug, and say the same as she'd
say to yourself.

MARY *to the Priest*: Let you drink it up, holy father. Let you drink
it up, I'm saying, and not be letting on you wouldn't do the like
of it, and you with a stack of pint bottles above reaching the sky.

PRIEST *with resignation*: Well, here's to your good health and God
forgive us all. *He drinks*.

MARY: That's right now, your reverence, and the blessing of God
be on you. Isn't it a grand thing to see you sitting down, with
no pride in you, and drinking a sup with the like of us, and we
the poorest, wretched, starving creatures you'd see any place
on the earth?

PRIEST: If it's starving you are itself, I'm thinking it's well for the
like of you that do be drinking when there's drouth on you, and
lying down to sleep when your legs are stiff. *He sighs gloomily*.
What would you do if it was the like of myself you were, saying
Mass with your mouth dry, and running east and west for a sick
call maybe, and hearing the rural people again and they saying
their sins?

MARY *with compassion*: It's destroyed you must be hearing the sins
of the rural people on a fine spring.

PRIEST *with despondency*: It's a hard life, I'm telling you, a hard life,
Mary Byrne; and there's the bishop coming in the morning,
and he an old man, would have you destroyed if he seen a thing
at all.

MARY *with great sympathy*: It'd break my heart to hear you talking
and sighing the like of that, your reverence. *She pats him on the
knee*. Let you rouse up now, if it's a poor, single man you are
itself, and I'll be singing you songs unto the dawn of day.

PRIEST *interrupting her*: What is it I want with your songs when it'd
be better for the like of you, that'll soon die, to be down on your
two knees saying prayers to the Almighty God?

MARY: If it's prayer I want, you'd have a right to say one yourself
holy father; for we don't have them at all, and I've heard tell a
power of times it's that you're for. Say one now, your
reverence; for I've heard a power of queer things and I walking
the world, but there's one thing I never heard any time, and
that's a real priest saying a prayer.

PRIEST: The Lord protect us!

MARY: It's no lie, holy father. I often heard the rural people making a queer noise and they going to rest; but who'd mind the like of them? And I'm thinking it should be great game to hear a scholar, the like of you, speaking Latin to the saints above.

PRIEST *scandalized*: Stop your talking, Mary Byrne; you're an old, flagrant heathen, and I'll stay no more with the lot of you. *He rises.*

MARY *catching hold of him*: Stop till you say a prayer, your reverence; stop till you say a little prayer, I'm telling you, and I'll give you my blessing and the last sup from the jug.

PRIEST *breaking away*: Leave me go, Mary Byrne; for I never met your like for hard abominations the score and two years I'm living in the place.

MARY *innocently*: Is that the truth?

PRIEST: It is, then, and God have mercy on your soul.

The Priest goes towards the left, and Sarah follows him.

SARAH *in a low voice*: And what time will you do the thing I'm asking, holy father? for I'm thinking you'll do it surely, and not have me growing into an old, wicked heathen like herself.

MARY *calling out shrilly*: Let you be walking back here, Sarah Casey, and not be talking whisper-talk with the like of him in the face of the Almighty God.

SARAH *to the Priest*: Do you hear her now, your reverence? Isn't it true, surely, she's an old, flagrant heathen, would destroy the world?

PRIEST *to Sarah, moving off*: Well, I'll be coming down early to the chapel, and let you come to me a while after you see me passing, and bring the bit of gold along with you, and the tin can. I'll marry you for them two, though it's a pitiful sum; for I wouldn't be easy in my soul if I left you growing into an old, wicked heathen the like of her.

SARAH *following him out*: The blessing of the Almighty God be on you, holy father, and that He may reward and watch you from this present day.

MARY *nudging Michael*: Did you see that, Michael Byrne? Didn't you hear me telling you she's flighty a while back since the change of the moon? With her fussing for marriage, and she making whisper-talk with one man or another man along by the road.

MICHAEL: Whisht now, or she'll knock the head of you the time she comes back.

MARY: Ah, it's a bad, wicked way the world is this night, if there's a fine air in it itself. You'd never have seen me, and I a young woman, making whisper-talk with the like of him, and he the fearfullest old fellow you'd see any place walking the world.

Sarah comes back quickly.

Calling out to her. What is it you're after whispering above with himself?

SARAH *exultingly*: Lie down, and leave us in peace. *She whispers with Michael.*

MARY *poking out her pipe with a straw, sings*:

She'd whisper with one, and she'd whisper with two –

She breaks off coughing. My singing voice is gone for this night, Sarah Casey. *She lights her pipe.* But if it's flighty you are itself, you're a grand, handsome woman, the glory of tinkers, the pride of Wicklow, the Beauty of Ballinacree. I wouldn't have you lying down and you lonesome to sleep this night in a dark ditch when the spring is coming in the trees; so let you sit down there by the big bough, and I'll be telling you the finest story you'd hear any place from Dundalk to Ballinacree, with great queens in it, making themselves matches from the start to the end, and they with shiny silks on them the length of the day, and white shifts for the night.

MICHAEL *standing up with the tin can in his hand*: Let you go asleep, and not have us destroyed.

MARY *lying back sleepily*: Don't mind him, Sarah Casey. Sit down now, and I'll be telling you a story would be fit to tell a woman the like of you in the springtime of the year.

SARAH *taking the can from Michael, and tying it up in a piece of sacking*: That'll not be rusting now in the dews of night. I'll put it up in the ditch the way it will be handy in the morning; and now we've that done, Michael Byrne, I'll go along with you and welcome for Tim Flaherty's hens. *She puts the can in the ditch.*

MARY *sleepily*: I've a grand story of the great queens of Ireland, with white necks on them the like of Sarah Casey, and fine arms would hit you a slap the way Sarah Casey would hit you.

SARAH *beckoning on the left*: Come along now, Michael, while she's falling asleep.

He goes towards left. Mary sees that they are going, starts up suddenly, and turns over on her hands and knees.

MARY *piteously*: Where is it you're going? Let you walk back here, and not be leaving me lonesome when the night is fine.

SARAH: Don't be waking the world with your talk when we're going up through the back wood to get two of Tim Flaherty's hens are roosting in the ash-tree above at the well.

MARY: And it's leaving me lone you are? Come back here, Sarah Casey. Come back here, I'm saying; or if it's off you must go, leave me the two little coppers you have, the way I can walk up in a short while, and get another pint for my sleep.

SARAH: It's too much you have taken. Let you stretch yourself out and take a long sleep; for isn't that the best thing any woman can do, and she an old drinking heathen like yourself?

She and Michael go out left.

MARY *standing up slowly*: It's gone they are and I with my feet that weak under me you'd knock me down with a rush; and my head with a noise in it the like of what you'd hear in a stream and it running between two rocks and rain falling. *She goes over to the ditch where the can is tied in sacking, and takes it down.* What good am I this night, God help me? What good are the grand stories I have when it's few would listen to an old woman, few but a girl maybe would be in great fear the time her hour was come, or a little child wouldn't be sleeping with the hunger on a cold night? *She takes the can from the sacking, and fits in three empty bottles and straw in its place, and ties them up.* Maybe the two of them have a good right to be walking out the little short while they'd be young; but if they have itself they'll not keep Mary Byrne from her full pint when the night's fine, and there's a dry moon in the sky. *She takes up the can, and puts the package back in the ditch.* Jemmy Neill's a decent lad; and he'll give me a good drop for the

can; and maybe if I keep near the peelers to-morrow for the first
bit of the fair, herself won't strike me at all; and if she does itself,
what's a little stroke on your head beside sitting lonesome on a
fine night, hearing the dogs barking, and the bats squeaking, and
you saying over, it's a short while only till you die.

She goes out singing 'The night before Larry was stretched.'

CURTAIN

ACT TWO

*The same scene as before. Early morning. Sarah is washing her face in
an old bucket; then plaits her hair. Michael is tidying himself also. Mary
Byrne is asleep against the ditch.*

SARAH *to Michael, with pleased excitement*: Go over, now, to the
bundle beyond, and you'll find a kind of red handkerchief to
put upon your neck, and a green one for myself.
MICHAEL *getting them*: You're after spending more money on the
like of them. Well, it's a power we're losing this time, and we
not gaining a thing at all. *With the handkerchief.* Is it them two?
SARAH: It is, Michael. *She takes one of them.* Let you tackle that one
round under your chin; and let you not forget to take your hat
from your head when we go up into the church. I asked Biddy
Flynn below, that's after marrying her second man, and she
told me it's the like of that they do.

Mary yawns, and turns over in her sleep.

With anxiety. There she is waking up on us, and I thinking we'd
have the job done before she'd know of it at all.
MICHAEL: She'll be crying out now, and making game of us, and
saying it's fools we are surely.
SARAH: I'll send her to her sleep again, or get her out of it one way
or another; for it'd be a bad case to have a divil's scholar the like
of her turning the priest against us maybe with her godless talk.

MARY *waking up, and looking at them with curiosity, blandly*: That's fine things you have on you, Sarah Casey; and it's a great stir you're making this day, washing your face. I'm that used to the hammer, I wouldn't hear it at all; but washing is a rare thing, and you're after waking me up, and I having a great sleep in the sun. *She looks around cautiously at the bundle in which she has hidden the bottles.*

SARAH *coaxingly*: Let you stretch out again for a sleep, Mary Byrne; for it'll be a middling time yet before we go to the fair.

MARY *with suspicion*: That's a sweet tongue you have, Sarah Casey; but if sleep's a grand thing, it's a grand thing to be waking up a day the like of this, when there's a warm sun in it, and a kind air, and you'll hear the cuckoos singing and crying out on the top of the hills.

SARAH: If it's that gay you are, you'd have a right to walk down and see would you get a few halfpence from the rich men do be driving early to the fair.

MARY: When rich men do be driving early it's queer tempers they have, the Lord forgive them; the way it's little but bad words and swearing out you'd get from them all.

SARAH *losing her temper and breaking out fiercely*: Then if you'll neither beg nor sleep, let you walk off from this place where you're not wanted, and not have us waiting for you maybe at the turn of day.

MARY *rather uneasy, turning to Michael*: God help our spirits, Michael; there she is again rousing cranky from the break of dawn. Oh! isn't she a terror since the moon did change? *She gets up slowly.* And I'd best be going forward to sell the gallon can. *She goes over and takes up the bundle.*

SARAH *crying out angrily*: Leave that down, Mary Byrne. Oh! aren't you the scorn of women to think that you'd have that drouth and roguery on you that you'd go drinking the can and the dew not dried from the grass?

MARY *in a feigned tone of pacification with the bundle still in her hand*: It's not a drouth but a heartburn I have this day, Sarah Casey, so I'm going down to cool my gullet at the blessed well; and I'll sell the can to the parson's daughter below, a harmless poor creature would fill your hand with shillings for a brace of lies.

SARAH: Leave down the tin can, Mary Byrne, for I hear the drouth upon your tongue to-day.

MARY: There's not a drink-house from this place to the fair, Sarah Casey; the way you'll find me below with the full price, and not a farthing gone. *She turns to go off left.*

SARAH *jumping up, and picking up the hammer threateningly*: Put down that can, I'm saying.

MARY *looking at her for a moment in terror, and putting down the bundle in the ditch*: Is it raving mad you're going, Sarah Casey, and you the pride of women to destroy the world?

SARAH *going up to her, and giving her a push off left*: I'll show you if it's raving mad I am. Go on from this place, I'm saying, and be wary now.

MARY *turning back after her*: If I go, I'll be telling old and young you're a weathered heathen savage, Sarah Casey, the one did put down a head of the parson's cabbage to boil in the pot with your clothes (*the Priest comes in behind her, on the left, and listens*), and quenched the flaming candles on the throne of God the time your shadow fell within the pillars of the chapel door.

Sarah turns on her, and she springs round nearly into the Priest's arms. When she sees him, she claps her shawl over her mouth, and goes up towards the ditch, laughing to herself.

PRIEST *going to Sarah, half terrified at the language that he has heard*: Well, aren't you a fearful lot? I'm thinking it's only humbug you were making at the fall of night, and you won't need me at all.

SARAH *with anger still in her voice*: Humbug is it! Would you be turning back upon your spoken promise in the face of God?

PRIEST *dubiously*: I'm thinking you were never christened, Sarah Casey; and it would be a queer job to go dealing Christian sacraments unto the like of you. *Persuasively, feeling in his pocket.* So it would be best, maybe, I'd give you a shilling for to drink my health, and let you walk on, and not trouble me at all.

SARAH: That's your talking, is it? If you don't stand to your spoken word, holy father, I'll make my own complaint to the mitred bishop in the face of all.

PRIEST: You'd do that!

SARAH: I would surely, holy father, if I walked to the city of Dublin with blood and blisters on my naked feet.

PRIEST *uneasily scratching his ear*: I wish this day was done, Sarah Casey; for I'm thinking it's a risky thing getting mixed in any matters with the like of you.

SARAH: Be hasty then, and you'll have us done with before you'd think at all.

PRIEST *giving in*: Well, maybe it's right you are, and let you come up to the chapel when you see me looking from the door. *He goes up into the chapel*.

SARAH *calling after him*: We will, and God preserve you, holy father.

MARY *coming down to them, speaking with amazement and consternation, but without anger*: Going to the chapel! It's at marriage you're fooling again, maybe?

Sarah turns her back on her.

It was for that you were washing your face, and you after sending me for porter at the fall of night the way I'd drink a good half from the jug? *Going round in front of Sarah*. Is it at marriage you're fooling again?

SARAH *triumphantly*: It is, Mary Byrne. I'll be married now in a short while; and from this day there will no one have a right to call me a dirty name, and I selling cans in Wicklow or Wexford or the city of Dublin itself.

MARY *turning to Michael*: And it's yourself is wedding her, Michael Byrne?

MICHAEL *gloomily*: It is, God spare us.

MARY *looks at Sarah for a moment, and then bursts out into a laugh of derision*: Well, she's a tight, hardy girl, and it's no lie; but I never knew till this day it was a black born fool I had for a son. You'll breed asses, I've heard them say, and poaching dogs, and horses'd go licking the wind, but it's a hard thing, God help me, to breed sense in a son.

MICHAEL *gloomily*: If I didn't marry her, she'd be walking off to Jaunting Jim maybe at the fall of night; and it's well yourself knows there isn't the like of her for getting money and selling songs to the men.

MARY: And you're thinking it's paying gold to his reverence would make a woman stop when she's a mind to go?

SARAH *angrily*: Let you not be destroying us with your talk when I've as good a right to a decent marriage as any speckled female does be sleeping in the black hovels above, would choke a mule.

MARY *soothingly*: It's as good a right you have, surely, Sarah Casey, but what good will it do? Is it putting that ring on your finger will keep you from getting an aged woman and losing the fine face you have, or be easing your pains; when it's the grand ladies to be married in silk dresses, with rings of gold, that do pass any woman with their share of torment in the hour of birth, and do be paying the doctors in the city of Dublin a great price at that time, the like of what you'd pay for a good ass and a cart? *She sits down.*

SARAH *puzzled*: Is that the truth?

MARY *pleased with the point she has made*: Wouldn't any know it's the truth? Ah, it's few short years you are yet in the world, Sarah Casey, and it's little or nothing at all maybe you know about it.

SARAH *vehement but uneasy*: What is it yourself knows of the fine ladies when they wouldn't let the like of you go near to them at all?

MARY: If you do be drinking a little sup in one town and another town, it's soon you get great knowledge and a great sight into the world. You'll see men there, and women there, sitting up on the ends of barrels in the dark night, and they making great talk would soon have the like of you, Sarah Casey, as wise as a March hare.

MICHAEL *to Sarah*: That's the truth she's saying, and maybe, if you've sense in you at all you'd have a right still to leave your fooling, and not be wasting our gold.

SARAH *decisively*: If it's wise or fool I am, I've made a good bargain, and I'll stand to it now.

MARY: What is it he's making you give?

MICHAEL: The ten shillings in gold, and the tin can is above tied in the sack.

MARY *looking at the bundle with surprise and dread*: The bit of gold and the tin can, is it?

123

MICHAEL: The half a sovereign and the gallon can.

MARY *scrambling to her feet quickly*: Well, I think I'll be walking off the road to the fair the way you won't be destroying me going too fast on the hills. *She goes a few steps towards the left, then turns and speaks to Sarah very persuasively.* Let you not take the can from the sack, Sarah Casey; for the people is coming above would be making game of you, and pointing their fingers if they seen you do the like of that. Let you leave it safe in the bag, I'm saying, Sarah darling. It's that way will be best. *She goes towards left, and pauses for a moment, looking about her with embarrassment.*

MICHAEL *in a low voice*: What ails her at all?

SARAH *anxiously*: It's real wicked she does be when you hear her speaking as easy as that.

MARY *to herself*: I'd be safer in the chapel, I'm thinking; for if she caught me after on the road, maybe she would kill me then. *She comes hobbling back towards the right.*

SARAH: Where is it you're going? It isn't that way we'll be walking to the fair.

MARY: I'm going up into the chapel to give you my blessing and hear the priest saying his prayers. It's a lonesome road is running below to Grianan, and a woman would never know the things might happen her and she walking single in a lonesome place.

As she reaches the chapel gate, the Priest comes to it in his surplice.

PRIEST *crying out*: Come along now. Is it the whole day you'd keep me here saying my prayers, and I getting my death with not a bit in my stomach, and my breakfast in ruins, and the Lord Bishop maybe driving on the road to-day?

SARAH: We're coming now, holy father.

PRIEST: Give me the bit of gold into my hand.

SARAH: It's here, holy father.

She gives it to him. Michael takes the bundle from the ditch and brings it over, standing a little behind Sarah. He feels the bundle and looks at Mary with a meaning look.

PRIEST *looking at the gold*: It's a good one, I'm thinking, wherever you got it. And where is the can?

SARAH *taking the bundle*: We have it here in a bit of clean sack, your reverence. We tied it up in the inside of that to keep it from rusting in the dews of night, and let you not open it now or you'll have the people making game of us and telling the story on us, east and west to the butt of the hills.

PRIEST *taking the bundle*: Give it here into my hand, Sarah Casey. What is it any person would think of a tinker making a can? *He begins opening the bundle.*

SARAH: It's a fine can, your reverence; for if it's poor, simple people we are, it's fine cans we can make, and himself, God help him, is a great man surely at the trade.

Priest open the bundle; the three empty bottles fall out.

Glory to the saints of joy!

PRIEST: Did ever any man see the like of that? To think you'd be putting deceit on me, and telling lies to me, and I going to marry you for a little sum wouldn't marry a child.

SARAH *crestfallen and astonished*: It's the divil did it, your reverence, and I wouldn't tell you a lie. *Raising her hands.* May the Lord Almighty strike me dead if the divil isn't after hooshing the tin can from the bag.

PRIEST *vehemently*: Go along now, and don't be swearing your lies. Go along now, and let you not be thinking I'm big fool enough to believe the like of that when it's after selling it you are, or making a swap for drink of it, maybe, in the darkness of the night.

MARY *in a peacemaking voice, putting her hand on the Priest's left arm*: She wouldn't do the like of that, your reverence, when she hasn't a decent standing drouth on her at all; and she setting great store on her marriage the way you'd have a right to be taking her easy, and not minding the can. What differ would an empty can make with a fine, rich, hardy man the like of you?

SARAH *imploringly*: Marry us, your reverence, for the ten shillings in gold, and we'll make you a grand can in the evening – a can would be fit to carry water for the holy man of God. Marry us now and I'll be saying fine prayers for you, morning and night, if it'd be raining itself and it'd be in two black pools I'd be setting my knees.

PRIEST *loudly*: It's a wicked, thieving, lying, scheming lot you are, the pack of you. Let you walk off now and take every stinking rag you have there from the ditch.

MARY *putting her shawl over her head*: Marry her, your reverence, for the love of God, for there'll be queer doings below if you send her off the like of that and she swearing crazy on the road.

SARAH *angrily*: It's the truth she's saying; for it's herself, I'm thinking, is after swapping the tin can for a pint, the time she was raging mad with the drouth, and ourselves above walking the hill.

MARY *crying out with indignation*: Have you no shame, Sarah Casey, to tell lies unto a holy man?

SARAH *to Mary, working herself into a rage*: It's making game of me you'd be, and putting a fool's head on me in the face of the world; but if you were thinking to be mighty cute walking off, or going up to hide in the church, I've got you this time, and you'll not run from me now. *She seizes one of the bottles.*

MARY *hiding behind the Priest*: Keep her off, your reverence; keep her off, for the love of the Almighty God. What at all would the Lord Bishop say if he found me here lying with my head broken across, or the two of yous maybe digging a bloody grave for me at the door of the church?

PRIEST (*waving Sarah off*): Go along, Sarah Casey. Would you be doing murder at my feet? Go along from me now, and wasn't I a big fool to have to do with you when it's nothing but distraction and torment I get from the kindness of my heart?

SARAH *shouting*: I've bet a power of strong lads east and west through the world, and are you thinking I'd turn back from a priest? Leave the road now, or maybe I would strike yourself.

PRIEST: You would not, Sarah Casey. I've no fear for the lot of you; but let you walk off, I'm saying, and not be coming where you've no business, and screeching tumult and murder at the doorway of the church.

SARAH: I'll not go a step till I have her head broke, or till I'm wed with himself. If you want to get shut of us, let you marry us now, for I'm thinking the ten shillings in gold is a good price for the like of you, and you near burst with the fat.

PRIEST: I wouldn't have you coming in on me and soiling my church; for there's nothing at all, I'm thinking, would keep the like of you from hell. *He throws down the ten shillings on the ground.* Gather up your gold now, and begone from my sight, for if ever I set an eye on you again you'll hear me telling the peelers who it was stole the black ass belonging to Philly O'Cullen, and whose hay it is the grey ass does be eating.

SARAH: You'd do that?

PRIEST: I would surely.

SARAH: If you do, you'll be getting all the tinkers from Wicklow and Wexford, and the county Meath, to put up block tin in the place of glass to shield your windows where you do be looking out and blinking at the girls. It's hard set you'll be that time, I'm telling you, to fill the depth of your belly the long days of Lent; for we wouldn't leave a laying pullet in your yard at all.

PRIEST *losing his temper finally*: Go on, now, or I'll send the Lords of Justice a dated story of your villainies – burning, stealing, robbing, raping to this mortal day. Go on now, I'm saying, if you'd run from Kilmainham or the rope itself.

MICHAEL *taking off his coat*: Is it run from the like of you, holy father? Go up to your own shanty, or I'll beat you with the ass's reins till the world would hear you roaring from this place to the coast of Clare.

PRIEST: Is it lift your hand upon myself when the Lord would blight your members if you'd touch me now? Go on from this. *He gives him a shove.*

MICHAEL: Blight me, is it? Take it then, your reverence, and God help you so. *He runs at him with the reins.*

PRIEST *runs up to ditch, crying out*: There are the peelers passing, by the grace of God. Hey, below!

MARY *clapping her hand over his mouth*: Knock him down on the road; they didn't hear him at all.

Michael pulls him down.

SARAH: Gag his jaws.

MARY: Stuff the sacking in his teeth.

They gag him with the sack that had the can in it.

SARAH: Tie the bag around his head, and if the peelers come, we'll put him head first in the bog-hole is beyond the ditch.

They tie him up in some sacking.

MICHAEL *to Mary*: Keep him quiet, and the rags tight on him for fear he'd screech. *He goes back to their camp.* Hurry with the things, Sarah Casey. The peelers aren't coming this way, and maybe we'll get off from them now.

They bundle the things together in wild haste, the Priest wriggling and struggling about on the ground, with old Mary trying to keep him quiet.

MARY *patting his head*: Be quiet, your reverence. What is it ails you, with your wrigglings now? Is it choking maybe? *She puts her hand under the sack, and feels his mouth, patting him on the back.* It's only letting on you are, holy father, for your nose is blowing back and forward as easy as an east wind on an April day. *In a soothing voice.* There now, holy father, let you stay easy, I'm telling you, and learn a little sense and patience, the way you'll not be so airy again going to rob poor sinners of their scraps of gold. *He gets quieter.* That's a good boy you are now, your reverence, and let you not be uneasy, for we wouldn't hurt you at all. It's sick and sorry we are to tease you; but what did you want meddling with the like of us, when it's a long time we are going our own ways – father and son, and his son after him, or mother and daughter, and her own daughter again; and it's little need we ever had of going up into a church and swearing – I'm told there's swearing with it – a word no man would believe, or with drawing rings on our fingers, would be cutting our skins maybe when we'd be taking the ass from the shafts, and pulling the straps the time they'd be slippy with going around beneath the heavens in rains falling.

MICHAEL *who has finished bundling up the things, comes over with Sarah*: We're fixed now; and I have a mind to run him in a bog-hole the way he'll not be tattling to the peelers of our games to-day.

SARAH: You'd have a right too, I'm thinking.

MARY *soothingly*: Let you not be rough with him, Sarah Casey, and he after drinking his sup of porter with us at the fall of night. Maybe he'd swear a mighty oath he wouldn't harm us, and then we'd safer loose him; for if we went to drown him, they'd maybe hang the batch of us, man and child and woman, and the ass itself.

MICHAEL: What would he care for an oath?

MARY: Don't you know his like do live in terror of the wrath of
God? *Putting her mouth to the Priest's ear in the sacking.* Would
you swear an oath, holy father, to leave us in our freedom, and
not talk at all? *Priest nods in sacking.* Didn't I tell you? Look at
the poor fellow nodding his head off in the bias of the sacks.
Strip them off from him, and he'll be easy now.

MICHAEL *as if speaking to a horse*: Hold up, holy father.

*He pulls the sacking off, and shows the Priest with his hair on end. They
free his mouth.*

MARY: Hold him till he swears.

PRIEST *in a faint voice*: I swear, surely. If you let me go in peace,
I'll not inform against you or say a thing at all, and may God
forgive me for giving heed unto your like to-day.

SARAH *puts the ring on his finger*: There's the ring, holy father, to
keep you minding of your oath until the end of time; for my
heart's scalded with your fooling; and it'll be a long day till I go
making talk of marriage or the like of that.

MARY *complacently, standing up slowly*: She's vexed now, your
reverence; and let you not mind her at all, for she's right, surely,
and it's little need we ever had of the like of you to get us our
bit to eat, and our bit to drink, and our time of love when we
were young men and women, and were fine to look at.

MICHAEL: Hurry on now. He's a great man to have kept us from
fooling our gold; and we'll have a great time drinking that bit
with the trampers on the green of Clash.

They gather up their things. The Priest stands up.

PRIEST *lifting up his hand*: I've sworn not to call the hand of man
upon your crimes to-day; but I haven't sworn I wouldn't call
the fire of heaven from the hand of the Almighty God. *He begins
saying a Latin malediction in a loud ecclesiastical voice.*

MARY: There's an old villain.

ALL *together*: Run, run. Run for your lives.

They rush out, leaving the Priest master of the situation.

CURTAIN

The Well of the Saints

PERSONS IN THE PLAY

MARTIN DOUL, weather-beaten blind beggar

MARY DOUL, his wife, weather-beaten, ugly woman, blind also, nearly fifty

TIMMY, a middle-aged almost elderly, but vigorous smith

MOLLY BYRNE, fine-looking girl with fair hair

BRIDE, another handsome girl

MAT SIMON

THE SAINT, a wandering friar

OTHER GIRLS AND MEN

Scene: Some lonely mountainous district in the east of Ireland one or more centuries ago

ACT ONE

Roadside with big stones, etc., on the right; low loose wall at back with gap near centre; at left, ruined doorway of church with bushes beside it. Martin Doul and Mary Doul grope in on left and pass over to stones on right, where they sit.

MARY DOUL: What place are we now, Martin Doul?

MARTIN DOUL: Passing the gap.

MARY DOUL *raising her head*: The length of that! Well, the sun's coming warm this day if it's late autumn itself.

MARTIN DOUL *putting out his hands in sun*: What way wouldn't it be warm and it getting high up in the south? You were that length plaiting your yellow hair you have the morning lost on us, and the people are after passing to the fair of Clash.

MARY DOUL: It isn't going to the fair, the time they do be driving their cattle and they with a litter of pigs maybe squealing in their carts, they'd give us a thing at all. *She sits down.* It's well you know that, but you must be talking.

MARTIN DOUL *sitting down beside her and beginning to shred rushes she gives him*: If I didn't talk I'd be destroyed in a short while listening to the clack you do be making, for you've a queer cracked voice, the Lord have mercy on you, if it's fine to look on you are itself.

MARY DOUL: Who wouldn't have a cracked voice sitting out all the year in the rain falling? It's a bad life for the voice, Martin Doul, though I've heard tell there isn't anything like the wet south wind does be blowing upon us for keeping a white beautiful skin – the like of my skin – on your neck and on your brows, and there isn't anything at all like a fine skin for putting splendour on a woman.

MARTIN DOUL *teasingly, but with good humour*: I do be thinking odd times we don't know rightly what way you have your splendour, or asking myself, maybe, if you have it at all, for the time I was a young lad, and had fine sight, it was the ones with sweet voices were the best in face.

MARY DOUL: Let you not be making the like of that talk when you've heard Timmy the smith, and Mat Simon, and Patch

132

Ruadh, and a power besides saying fine things of my face, and you know rightly it was 'the beautiful dark woman' they did call me in Ballinatone.

MARTIN DOUL *as before*: If it was itself I heard Molly Byrne saying at the fall of night it was little more than a fright you were.

MARY DOUL *sharply*: She was jealous, God forgive her, because Timmy the smith was after praising my hair –

MARTIN DOUL *with mock irony*: Jealous!

MARY DOUL: Ay, jealous, Martin Doul; and if she wasn't itself, the young and silly do be always making game of them that's dark, and they'd think it a fine thing if they had us deceived, the way we wouldn't know we were so fine-looking at all. *She puts her hand to her face with a complacent gesture.*

MARTIN DOUL *a little plaintively*: I do be thinking in the long nights it'd be a grand thing if we could see ourselves for one hour, or a minute itself, the way we'd know surely we were the finest man and the finest woman of the seven counties of the east – (*bitterly*) and then the seeing rabble below might be destroying their souls telling bad lies, and we'd never heed a thing they'd say.

MARY DOUL: If you weren't a big fool you wouldn't heed them this hour, Martin Doul, for they're a bad lot those that have their sight, and they do have great joy, the time they do be seeing a grand thing, to let on they don't see it at all, and to be telling fool's lies, the like of what Molly Byrne was telling to yourself.

MARTIN DOUL: If it's lies she does be telling she's a sweet, beautiful voice you'd never tire to be hearing, if it was only the pig she'd be calling, or crying out in the long grass, maybe, after her hens. *Speaking pensively.* It should be a fine, soft, rounded woman, I'm thinking, would have a voice the like of that.

MARY DOUL *sharply again, scandalized*: Let you not be minding if it's flat or rounded she is; for she's a flighty, foolish woman you'll hear when you're off a long way, and she making a great noise and laughing at the well.

MARTIN DOUL: Isn't laughing a nice thing the time a woman's young?

MARY DOUL *bitterly*: A nice thing is it? A nice thing to hear a woman making a loud braying laugh the like of that? Ah, she's a great one for drawing the men, and you'll hear Timmy himself, the time he does be sitting in his forge, getting mighty fussy if she'll come walking from Grianan, the way you'll hear his breath going, and he wringing his hands.

MARTIN DOUL *slightly piqued*: I've heard him say a power of times it's nothing at all she is when you see her at the side of you, and yet I never heard any man's breath getting uneasy the time he'd be looking on yourself.

MARY DOUL: I'm not the like of the girls do be running round on the roads, swinging their legs, and they with their necks out looking on the man. . . . Ah, there's a power of villainy walking the world, Martin Doul, among them that do be gadding around, with their gaping eyes, and their sweet words, and they with no sense in them at all.

MARTIN DOUL *sadly*: It's the truth, maybe, and yet I'm told it's a grand thing to see a young girl walking the road.

MARY DOUL: You'd be as bad as the rest of them if you had your sight, and I did well, surely, not to marry a seeing man – it's scores would have had me and welcome – for the seeing is a queer lot, and you'd never know the thing they'd do. *A moment's pause.*

MARTIN DOUL *listening*: There's someone coming on the road.

MARY DOUL: Let you put the pith away out of their sight, or they'll be picking it out with the spying eyes they have, and saying it's rich we are, and not sparing us a thing at all.

They bundle away the rushes. Timmy the smith comes in on left.

MARTIN DOUL *with a begging voice*: Leave a bit of silver for blind Martin, your honour. Leave a bit of silver, or a penny copper itself, and we'll be praying the Lord to bless you and you going the way.

TIMMY *stopping before them*: And you letting on a while back you knew my step! *He sits down.*

MARTIN DOUL *with his natural voice*: I know it when Molly Byrne's walking in front, or when she's two perches maybe, lagging behind; but it's a few times I've heard you walking up the like of that, as if you'd met a thing wasn't right and you coming on the road.

TIMMY *hot and breathless, wiping his face*: You've good ears, God bless you, if you're a liar itself; for I'm after walking up in great haste from hearing wonders in the fair.

MARTIN DOUL *rather contemptuously*: You're always hearing queer wonderful things, and the lot of them nothing at all; but I'm thinking, this time, it's a strange thing surely you'd be walking up before the turn of day, and not waiting below to look on them lepping, or dancing, or playing shows on the green of Clash.

TIMMY *huffed*: I was coming to tell you it's in this place there'd be a bigger wonder done in a short while (*Martin Doul stops working*) than was ever done on the green of Clash, or the width of Leinster itself; but you're thinking, maybe, you're too cute a little fellow to be minding me at all.

MARTIN DOUL *amused, but incredulous*: There'll be wonders in this place, is it?

TIMMY: Here at the crossing of the roads.

MARTIN DOUL: I never heard tell of anything to happen in this place since the night they killed the old fellow going home with his gold, the Lord have mercy on him, and threw down his corpse into the bog. Let them not be doing the like of that this night, for it's ourselves have a right to the crossing roads, and we don't want any of your bad tricks, or your wonders either, for it's wonder enough we are ourselves.

TIMMY: If I'd a mind I'd be telling you of a real wonder this day, and the way you'll be having a great joy, maybe, you're not thinking on at all.

MARTIN DOUL *interested*: Are they putting up a still behind in the rocks? It'd be a grand thing if I'd a sup handy the way I wouldn't be destroying myself groping up across the bogs in the rain falling.

TIMMY *still moodily*: It's not a still they're bringing, or the like of it either.

MARY DOUL *persuasively, to Timmy*: Maybe they're hanging a thief, above at the bit of a tree. I'm told it's a great sight to see a man hanging by his neck; but what joy would that be to ourselves, and we not seeing it at all?

TIMMY *more pleasantly*: They're hanging no one this day, Mary Doul, and yet, with the help of God, you'll see a power hanged before you die.

MARY DOUL: Well, you've queer humbugging talk. . . . What way would I see a power hanged, and I a dark woman since the seventh year of my age?

TIMMY: Did you ever hear tell of a place across a bit of the sea, where there is an island, and the grave of the four beautiful saints?

MARY DOUL: I've heard people have walked round from the west and they speaking of that.

TIMMY *impressively*: There's a green ferny well, I'm told, behind of that place, and if you put a drop of the water out of it on the eyes of a blind man, you'll make him see as well as any person is walking the world.

MARTIN DOUL *with excitement*: Is that the truth, Timmy? I'm thinking you're telling a lie.

TIMMY *gruffly*: That's the truth, Martin Doul, and you may believe it now, for you're after believing a power of things weren't as likely at all.

MARY DOUL: Maybe we could send a young lad to bring us the water. I could wash a naggin bottle in the morning, and I'm thinking Patch Ruadh would go for it, if we gave him a good drink, and the bit of money we have hid in the thatch.

TIMMY: It'd be no good to be sending a sinful man the like of ourselves, for I'm told the holiness of the water does be getting soiled with the villainy of your heart, the time you'd be carrying it, and you looking round on the girls, maybe, or drinking a small sup at a still.

MARTIN DOUL *with disappointment*: It'd be a long terrible way to be walking ourselves, and I'm thinking that's a wonder will bring small joy to us at all.

TIMMY *turning on him impatiently*: What is it you want with your walking? It's as deaf as blind you're growing if you're not after hearing me say it's in this place the wonder would be done.

MARTIN DOUL *with a flash of anger*: If it is can't you open the big slobbering mouth you have and say what way it'll be done, and not be making blather till the fall of night.

TIMMY *jumping up*: I'll be going on now (*Mary Doul rises*), and not wasting time talking civil talk with the like of you.

MARY DOUL *standing up, disguising her impatience*: Let you come here to me, Timmy, and not be minding him at all.

Timmy stops, and she gropes up to him and takes him by the coat.

You're not huffy with myself, and let you tell me the whole story and don't be fooling me more. . . . Is it yourself has brought us the water?

TIMMY: It is not, surely.

MARY DOUL: Then tell us your wonder, Timmy. . . . What person'll bring it at all?

TIMMY *relenting*: It's a fine holy man will bring it, a saint of the Almighty God.

MARY DOUL *overawed*: A saint is it?

TIMMY: Ay, a fine saint, who's going round through the churches of Ireland, with a long cloak on him, and naked feet, for he's brought a sup of the water slung at his side, and, with the like of him, any little drop is enough to cure the dying, or to make the blind see as clear as the grey hawks do be high up, on a still day, sailing the sky.

MARTIN DOUL *feeling for his stick*: What place is he, Timmy? I'll be walking to him now.

TIMMY: Let you stay quiet, Martin. He's straying around saying prayers at the churches and high crosses, between this place and the hills, and he with a great crowd going behind – for it's fine prayers he does be saying, and fasting with it, till he's as thin as one of the empty rushes you have there on your knee; then he'll be coming after to this place to cure the two of you – we're after telling him the way you are – and to say his prayers in the church.

MARTIN DOUL *turning suddenly to Mary Doul*: And we'll be seeing ourselves this day. Oh, glory be to God, is it true surely?

MARY DOUL *very pleased, to Timmy*: Maybe I'd have time to walk down and get the big shawl I have below, for I do look my best, I've heard them say, when I'm dressed up with that thing on my head.

TIMMY: You'd have time surely.

MARTIN DOUL *listening*: Whisht now. . . . I hear people again coming by the stream.

TIMMY *looking out left, puzzled*: It's the young girls I left walking after the Saint. . . . They're coming now (*goes up to entrance*) carrying things in their hands, and they walking as easy as you'd see a child walk who'd have a dozen eggs hid in her bib.

MARTIN DOUL *listening*: That's Molly Byrne, I'm thinking.

Molly Byrne and Bride come on left and cross to Martin Doul, carrying water can, Saint's bell, and cloak.

MOLLY *volubly*: God bless you, Martin. I've holy water here, from the grave of the four saints of the west, will have you cured in a short while and seeing like ourselves –

TIMMY *crosses to Molly, interrupting her*: He's heard that, God help you! But where at all is the Saint, and what way is he after trusting the holy water with the likes of you?

MOLLY BYRNE: He was afeard to go a far way with the clouds is coming beyond, so he's gone up now through the thick woods to say a prayer at the crosses of Grianan, and he's coming on this road to the church.

TIMMY *still astonished*: And he's after leaving the holy water with the two of you? It's a wonder, surely. *Comes down left a little.*

MOLLY BYRNE: The lads told him no person could carry them things through the briers, and steep, slippy-feeling rocks he'll be climbing above, so he looked round then, and gave the water and his big cloak, and his bell to the two of us, for young girls, says he, are the cleanest holy people you'd see walking the world.

Mary Doul goes near seat.

MARY DOUL *sits down, laughing to herself*: Well, the Saint's a simple fellow, and it's no lie.

MARTIN DOUL *leaning forward, holding out his hands*: Let you give me the water in my hand, Molly Byrne, the way I'll know you have it surely.

MOLLY BYRNE *giving it to him*: Wonders is queer things, and maybe it'd cure you, and you holding it alone.

MARTIN DOUL *looking round*: It does not, Molly. I'm not seeing at all. *He shakes the can.* There's a small sup only. Well, isn't it a great wonder the little trifling thing would bring seeing to the blind, and be showing us the big women and the young girls, and all the fine things is walking the world. *He feels for Mary Doul and gives her the can.*

MARY DOUL *shaking it*: Well, glory be to God –

MARTIN DOUL *pointing to Bride*: And what is it herself has, making sounds in her hand?

BRIDE *crossing to Martin Doul*: It's the Saint's bell; you'll hear him ringing out the time he'll be going up some place, to be saying his prayers.

Martin Doul holds out his hands; she gives it to him.

MARTIN DOUL *ringing it*: It's a sweet, beautiful sound.

MARY DOUL: You'd know, I'm thinking, by the little silvery voice of it, a fasting holy man was after carrying it a great way at his side.

Bride crosses a little right behind Martin Doul.

MOLLY BYRNE *unfolding Saint's cloak*: Let you stand up now, Martin Doul, till I put his big cloak on you.

Martin Doul rises, comes forward, centre a little.

The way we'd see how you'd look, and you a saint of the Almighty God.

MARTIN DOUL *standing up, a little diffidently*: I've heard the priests a power of times making great talk and praises of the beauty of the saints.

Molly Byrne slips cloak round him.

TIMMY *uneasily*: You'd have a right to be leaving him alone, Molly. What would the Saint say if he seen you making game with his cloak?

MOLLY BYRNE *recklessly*: How would he see us, and he saying prayers in the wood? *She turns Martin Doul round.* Isn't that a fine, holy-looking saint, Timmy the smith? *Laughing foolishly.* There's a grand, handsome fellow, Mary Doul; and if you seen him now you'd be as proud, I'm thinking, as the archangels below, fell out with the Almighty God.

MARY DOUL *with quiet confidence going to Martin Doul and feeling his cloak*: It's proud we'll be this day, surely.

Martin Doul is still ringing.

MOLLY BYRNE *to Martin Doul*: Would you think well to be all your life walking round the like of that, Martin Doul, and you bell-ringing with the saints of God?

MARY DOUL *turning on her fiercely*: How would he be bell-ringing with the saints of God and he wedded with myself?

MARTIN DOUL: It's the truth she's saying, and if bell-ringing is a fine life, yet I'm thinking, maybe, it's better I am wedded with the beautiful dark woman of Ballinatone.

MOLLY BYRNE *scornfully*: You're thinking that, God help you; but it's little you know of her at all.

MARTIN DOUL: It's little surely, and I'm destroyed this day waiting to look upon her face.

TIMMY *awkwardly*: It's well you know the way she is; for the like of you do have great knowledge in the feeling of your hands.

MARTIN DOUL *still feeling the cloak*: We do, maybe. Yet it's little I know of faces, or of fine beautiful cloaks, for it's few cloaks I've had my hand to, and few faces (*plaintively*); for the young girls is mighty shy, Timmy the smith, and it isn't much they heed me, though they do be saying I'm a handsome man.

MARY DOUL *mockingly, with good humour*: Isn't it a queer thing the voice he puts on him, when you hear him talking of the skinny-looking girls, and he married with a woman he's heard called the wonder of the western world?

TIMMY *pityingly*: The two of you will see a great wonder this day, and it's no lie.

MARTIN DOUL: I've heard tell her yellow hair, and her white skin, and her big eyes are a wonder, surely –

BRIDE *who has looked out left*: Here's the Saint coming from the selvage of the wood. . . . Strip the cloak from him, Molly, or he'll be seeing it now.

MOLLY BYRNE *hastily to Bride*: Take the bell and put herself by the stones. *To Martin Doul.* Will you hold your head up till I loosen the cloak? *She pulls off the cloak and throws it over her arm. Then she pushes Martin Doul over and stands him beside*

Mary Doul. Stand there now, quiet, and let you not be saying a word.

She and Bride stand a little on their left, demurely, with bell, etc., in their hands.

MARTIN DOUL *nervously arranging his clothes*: Will he mind the way we are, and not tidied or washed cleanly at all?

MOLLY BYRNE: He'll not see what way you are. . . . He'd walk by the finest woman in Ireland, I'm thinking, and not trouble to raise his two eyes to look upon her face. . . . Whisht!

The Saint comes left, with crowd.

SAINT: Are these the two poor people?

TIMMY *officiously*: They are, holy father; they do be always sitting here at the crossing of the roads, asking a bit of copper from them that do pass, or stripping rushes for lights, and they not mournful at all, but talking out straight with a full voice, and making game with them that likes it.

SAINT *to Martin Doul and Mary Doul*: It's a hard life you've had not seeing sun or moon, or the holy priests itself praying to the Lord, but it's the like of you who are brave in a bad time will make a fine use of the gift of sight the Almighty God will bring to you to-day. *He takes his cloak and puts it about him.* It's on a bare starving rock that there's the grave of the four beauties of God, the way it's little wonder, I'm thinking, if it's with bare starving people the water should be used. *He takes the water and bell and slings them round his shoulders.* So it's to the like of yourselves I do be going, who are wrinkled and poor, a thing rich men would hardly look at at all, but would throw a coin to or a crust of bread.

MARTIN DOUL *moving uneasily*: When they look on herself, who is a fine woman –

TIMMY *shaking him*: Whisht now, and be listening to the Saint.

SAINT *looks at them a moment, continues*: If it's raggy and dirty you are itself, I'm saying, the Almighty God isn't at all like the rich men of Ireland; and, with the power of the water I'm after bringing in a little curragh into Cashla Bay, He'll have pity on you, and put sight into your eyes.

MARTIN DOUL *taking off his hat*: I'm ready now, holy father –

SAINT *taking him by the hand*: I'll cure you first, and then I'll come for your wife. We'll go up now into the church, for I must say a prayer to the Lord. *To Mary Doul, as he moves off.* And let you be making your mind still and saying praises in your heart, for it's a great wonderful thing when the power of the Lord of the world is brought down upon your like.

PEOPLE *pressing after him*: Come on till we watch.

BRIDE: Come, Timmy.

SAINT *waving them back*: Stay back where you are, for I'm not wanting a big crowd making whispers in the church. Stay back there, I'm saying, and you'd do well to be thinking on the way sin has brought blindness to the world, and to be saying a prayer for your own sakes against false prophets and heathens, and the words of women and smiths, and all knowledge that would soil the soul or the body of a man.

People shrink back. He goes into church. Mary Doul gropes half-way towards the door and kneels near path. People form a group at right.

TIMMY: Isn't it a fine, beautiful voice he has, and he a fine, brave man if it wasn't for the fasting?

BRIDE: Did you watch him moving his hands?

MOLLY BYRNE: It'd be a fine thing if someone in this place could pray the like of him, for I'm thinking the water from our own blessed well would do rightly if a man knew the way to be saying prayers, and then there'd be no call to be bringing water from that wild place, where, I'm told, there are no decent houses, or fine-looking people at all.

BRIDE *who is looking in at door from right*: Look at the great trembling Martin has shaking him, and he on his knees.

TIMMY *anxiously*: God help him. . . . What will he be doing when he sees his wife this day? I'm thinking it was bad work we did when we let on she was fine-looking, and not a wrinkled, wizened hag the way she is.

MAT SIMON: Why would he be vexed, and we after giving him great joy and pride, the time he was dark?

MOLLY BYRNE *sitting down in Mary Doul's seat and tidying her hair*: If it's vexed he is itself, he'll have other things now to think on as well as his wife; and what does any man care for a wife, when it's two weeks, or three, he is looking on her face?

MAT SIMON: That's the truth now, Molly, and it's more joy dark Martin got from the lies we told of that hag is kneeling by the path than your own man will get from you, day or night, and he living at your side.

MOLLY BYRNE *defiantly*: Let you not be talking, Mat Simon, for it's not yourself will be my man, though you'd be crowing and singing fine songs if you'd that hope in you at all.

TIMMY *shocked, to Molly Byrne*: Let you not be raising your voice when the Saint's above at his prayers.

BRIDE *crying out*: Whisht. . . . Whisht. . . . I'm thinking he's cured.

MARTIN DOUL *crying out in the church*: Oh, glory be to God. . . .

SAINT *solemnly*:

> Laus Patri sit et Filio cum Spiritu Paraclito
> Qui suae dono gratiae misertus est Hiberniae. . . .

MARTIN DOUL *ecstatically*: Oh, glory be to God, I see now surely. . . . I see the walls of the church, and the green bits of ferns in them, and yourself, holy father, and the great width of the sky.

He runs out half foolish with joy, and comes past Mary Doul as she scrambles to her feet, drawing a little away from her as he goes by.

TIMMY *to the others*: He doesn't know her at all.

The Saint comes out behind Martin Doul, and leads Mary Doul into the church. Martin Doul comes on to the people. The men are between him and the girls; he verifies his position with his stick.

MARTIN DOUL *crying out joyfully*: That's Timmy, I know Timmy by the black of his head. . . . That's Mat Simon, I know Mat by the length of his legs. . . . That should be Patch Ruadh, with the gamy eyes in him, and the fiery hair. *He sees Molly Byrne on Mary Doul's seat, and his voice changes completely.* Oh, it was no lie they told me, Mary Doul. Oh, glory to God and the seven saints I didn't die and not see you at all. The blessing of God on the water, and the feet carried it round through the land. The blessing of God on this day, and them that brought me the Saint, for it's grand hair you have (*she lowers her head a little*

143

confused), and soft skin, and eyes would make the saints, if they were dark awhile, and seeing again, fall down out of the sky. *He goes nearer to her.* Hold up your head, Mary, the way I'll see it's richer I am than the great kings of the east. Hold up your head, I'm saying, for it's soon you'll be seeing me, and I not a bad one at all. *He touches her and she starts up.*

MOLLY BYRNE: Let you keep away from me, and not be soiling my chin.

People laugh loudly.

MARTIN DOUL *bewildered*: It's Molly's voice you have.

MOLLY BYRNE: Why wouldn't I have my own voice? Do you think I'm a ghost?

MARTIN DOUL: Which of you all is herself? *He goes up to Bride.* Is it you is Mary Doul? I'm thinking you're more the like of what they said. *Peering at her.* For you've yellow hair, and white skin, and it's the smell of my own turf is rising from your shawl. *He catches her shawl.*

BRIDE *pulling away her shawl*: I'm not your wife, and let you get out of my way.

The people laugh again.

MARTIN DOUL *with misgiving, to another girl*: Is it yourself it is? You're not so fine-looking, but I'm thinking you'd do, with the grand nose you have, and your nice hands and your feet.

GIRL *scornfully*: I never seen any person that took me for blind, and a seeing woman, I'm thinking, would never wed the like of you.

She turns away, and the people laugh once more, drawing back a little and leaving him on their left.

PEOPLE *jeeringly*: Try again, Martin, try again, and you'll be finding her yet.

MARTIN DOUL *passionately*: Where is it you have her hidden away? Isn't it a black shame for a drove of pitiful beasts the like of you to be making game of me, and putting a fool's head on me the grand day of my life? Ah, you're thinking you're a fine lot, with your giggling, weeping eyes, a fine lot to be making game of myself and the woman I've heard called the great wonder of the west.

During this speech, which he gives with his back towards the church, Mary Doul has come out with her sight cured, and come down towards the right with a silly simpering smile, till she is a little behind Martin Doul.

MARY DOUL *when he pauses*: Which of you is Martin Doul?

MARTIN DOUL *wheeling round*: It's her voice surely.

They stare at each other blankly.

MOLLY BYRNE *to Martin Doul*: Go up now and take her under the chin and be speaking the way you spoke to myself.

MARTIN DOUL *in a low voice, with intensity*: If I speak now, I'll speak hard to the two of you –

MOLLY BYRNE *to Mary Doul*: You're not saying a word, Mary. What is it you think of himself, with the fat legs on him, and the little neck like a ram?

MARY DOUL: I'm thinking it's a poor thing when the Lord God gives you sight and puts the like of that man in your way.

MARTIN DOUL: It's on your two knees you should be thanking the Lord God you're not looking on yourself, for if it was yourself you seen you'd be running round in a short while like the old screeching madwoman is running round in the glen.

MARY DOUL *beginning to realize herself*: If I'm not so fine as some of them said, I have my hair, and big eyes, and my white skin –

MARTIN DOUL *breaking out into a passionate cry*: Your hair and your big eyes, is it? . . . I'm telling you there isn't a wisp on any grey mare on the ridge of the world isn't finer than the dirty twist on your head. There isn't two eyes in any starving sow isn't finer than the eyes you were calling blue like the sea.

MARY DOUL *interrupting him*: It's the devil cured you this day with your talking of sows; it's the devil cured you this day, I'm saying, and drove you crazy with lies.

MARTIN DOUL: Isn't it yourself is after playing lies on me, ten years in the day and in the night; but what is that to you now the Lord God has given eyes to me, the way I see you an old, wizendy hag, was never fit to rear a child to me itself.

MARY DOUL: I wouldn't rear a crumpled whelp the like of you. It's many a woman is married with finer than yourself should be praising God if she's no child, and isn't loading the earth with things would make the heavens lonesome above, and they scaring the larks, and the crows, and the angels passing in the sky.

MARTIN DOUL: Go on now to be seeking a lonesome place where the earth can hide you away; go on now, I'm saying, or you'll be having men and women with their knees bled, and they screaming to God for a holy water would darken their sight, for there's no man but would liefer be blind a hundred years or a thousand itself, than to be looking on your like.

MARY DOUL *raising her stick*: Maybe if I hit you a strong blow you'd be blind again, and having what you want –

The Saint is seen in church door with his head bent in prayer.

MARTIN DOUL *raising his stick and driving Mary Doul back towards left*: Let you keep off from me now if you wouldn't have me strike out the little handful of brains you have about on the road.

He is going to strike her, but Timmy catches him by the arm.

TIMMY: Have you no shame to be making a great row, and the Saint above saying his prayers?

MARTIN DOUL: What is it I care for the like of him? *Struggling to free himself*. Let me hit her one good one, for the love of the Almighty God, and I'll be quiet after till I die.

TIMMY *shaking him*: Will you whisht, I'm saying.

SAINT *coming forward, centre*: Are their minds troubled with joy, or is their sight uncertain, the way it does often be the day a person is restored?

TIMMY: It's too certain their sight is, holy father; and they're after making a great fight, because they're a pair of pitiful shows.

SAINT *coming between them*: May the Lord who has given you sight send a little sense into your heads, the way it won't be on your two selves you'll be looking – on two pitiful sinners of the earth – but on the splendour of the Spirit of God, you'll see an odd time shining out through the big hills, and steep streams falling to the sea. For if it's on the like of that you do be thinking, you'll not be minding the faces of men, but you'll be saying prayers and great praises, till you'll be living the way the great saints do be living, with little but old sacks, and skin covering their bones. *To Timmy.* Leave him go now, you're seeing he's quiet again. *He frees Martin Doul.* And let you (*he turns to Mary Doul*) not be raising your voice, a bad thing in a woman; but let the lot of you, who have seen the power of the Lord, be thinking on it in the dark night, and be saying to yourselves it's great pity and love He has for the poor, starving people of Ireland. *He gathers his cloak about him.* And now the Lord send blessing to you all, for I am going on to Annagolan, where there is a deaf woman, and to Laragh, where there are two men without sense, and to Glenassil, where there are children blind from their birth; and then I'm going to sleep this night in the bed of the holy Kevin, and to be praising God, and asking great blessing on you all. *He bends his head.*

CURTAIN

ACT TWO

Village roadside, on left the door of a forge, with broken wheels, etc., lying about. A well near centre, with board above it, and room to pass behind it. Martin Doul is sitting near forge, cutting sticks.

TIMMY *heard hammering inside forge, then calls*: Let you make haste out there. . . . I'll be putting up new fires at the turn of day, and you haven't the half of them cut yet.

MARTIN DOUL *gloomily*: It's destroyed I'll be whacking your old thorns till the turn of day, and I with no food in my stomach would keep the life in a pig. *He turns towards the door.* Let you come out here and cut them yourself if you want them cut, for there's an hour every day when a man has a right to his rest.

TIMMY *coming out with a hammer, impatiently*: Do you want me to be driving you off again to be walking the roads? There you are now, and I giving you your food, and a corner to sleep, and money with it; and, to hear the talk of you, you'd think I was after beating you, or stealing your gold.

MARTIN DOUL: You'd do it handy, maybe, if I'd gold to steal.

TIMMY *throws down hammer, picks up some of the sticks already cut, and throws them into door*: There's no fear of your having gold – a lazy, basking fool the like of you.

MARTIN DOUL: No fear, maybe, and I here with yourself; for it's more I got a while since, and I sitting blinded in Grianan, than I get in this place, working hard, and destroying myself, the length of the day.

TIMMY *stopping with amazement*: Working hard? *He goes over to him*. I'll teach you to work hard, Martin Doul. Strip off your coat now, and put a tuck in your sleeves, and cut the lot of them, while I'd rake the ashes from the forge, or I'll not put up with you another hour itself.

MARTIN DOUL *horrified*: Would you have me getting my death sitting out in the black wintry air with no coat on me at all?

TIMMY *with authority*: Strip it off now, or walk down upon the road.

MARTIN DOUL *bitterly*: Oh, God help me! *He begins taking off his coat*. I've heard tell you stripped the sheet from your wife and you putting her down into the grave, and there isn't the like of you for plucking your living ducks, the short days, and leaving them running round in their skins, in the great rains and the cold. *He tucks up his sleeves*. Ah, I've heard a power of queer things of yourself, and there isn't one of them I'll not believe from this day, and be telling to the boys.

TIMMY *pulling over a big stick*: Let you cut that now, and give me rest from your talk, for I'm not heeding you at all.

MARTIN DOUL *taking stick*: That's a hard, terrible stick, Timmy; and isn't it a poor thing to be cutting strong timber the like of that, when it's cold the bark is, and slippy with the frost of the air?

TIMMY *gathering up another armful of sticks*: What way wouldn't it be cold, and it freezing since the moon was changed? *He goes into forge*.

MARTIN DOUL *querulously, as he cuts slowly*: What way, indeed, Timmy? For it's a raw, beastly day we do have each day, till I do be thinking it's well for the blind don't be seeing them grey clouds driving on the hill, and don't be looking on people with their noses red, the like of your nose, and their eyes weeping and watering, the like of your eyes, God help you, Timmy the smith.

TIMMY *seen blinking in the doorway*: Is it turning now you are against your sight?

MARTIN DOUL *very miserably*: It's a hard thing for a man to have his sight, and he living near to the like of you (*he cuts a stick and throws it away*), or wed with a wife (*cuts a stick*); and I do be thinking it should be a hard thing for the Almighty God to be looking on the world, bad days, and on men the like of yourself walking around on it, and they slipping each way in the muck.

TIMMY *with pot-hooks which he taps on anvil*: You'd have a right to be minding, Martin Doul, for it's a power the Saint cured lose their sight after a while. Mary Doul's dimming again, I've heard them say; and I'm thinking the Lord, if He hears you making that talk, will have little pity left for you at all.

MARTIN DOUL: There's not a bit of fear of me losing my sight, and if it's a dark day itself it's too well I see every wicked wrinkle you have round by your eye.

TIMMY *looking at him sharply*: The day's not dark since the clouds broke in the east.

MARTIN DOUL: Let you not be tormenting yourself trying to make me afeard. You told me a power of bad lies the time I was blind, and it's right now for you to stop, and be taking your rest,

Mary Doul comes in unnoticed on right with a sack filled with green-stuff on her arm.

for it's little ease or quiet any person would get if the big fools of Ireland weren't weary at times. *He looks up and sees Mary Doul.* Oh, glory be to God, she's coming again. *He begins to work busily with his back to her.*

TIMMY *amused, to Mary Doul, as she is going by without looking at them*: Look on him now, Mary Doul. You'd be a great one for keeping him steady at his work, for he's after idling and blathering to this hour from the dawn of day.

MARY DOUL *stiffly*: Of what is it you're speaking, Timmy the smith?

TIMMY *laughing*: Of himself, surely. Look on him there, and he with the shirt on him ripping from his back. You'd have a right to come round this night, I'm thinking, and put a stitch into his clothes, for it's long enough you are not speaking one to the other.

MARY DOUL: Let the two of you not torment me at all.

She goes out left with her head in the air.

MARTIN DOUL *stops work and looks after her*: Well, isn't it a queer thing she can't keep herself two days without looking on my face?

TIMMY *jeeringly*: Looking on your face is it? And she after going by with her head turned the way you'd see a priest going where there'd be a drunken man in the side ditch talking with a girl.

Martin Doul gets up and goes to corner of forge, and looks out left.

Come back here and don't mind her at all. Come back here, I'm saying, you've no call to be spying behind her since she went off and left you, in place of breaking her heart, trying to keep you in the decency of clothes and food.

MARTIN DOUL *crying out indignantly*: You know rightly, Timmy, it was myself drove her away.

TIMMY: That's a lie you're telling, yet it's little I care which one of you was driving the other, and let you walk back here, I'm saying, to your work.

MARTIN DOUL *turning round*: I'm coming, surely. *He stops and looks out right, going a step or two towards centre.*

TIMMY: On what is it you're gaping, Martin Doul?

MARTIN DOUL: There's a person walking above. . . . It's Molly Byrne, I'm thinking, coming down with her can.

TIMMY: If she is itself let you not be idling this day, or minding her at all, and let you hurry with them sticks, for I'll want you in a short while to be blowing in the forge. *He throws down pot-hooks.*

MARTIN DOUL *crying out*: Is it roasting me now you'd be? *Turns back and sees pot-hooks; he takes them up.* Pot-hooks? Is it over them you've been inside sneezing and sweating since the dawn of day?

TIMMY *resting himself on anvil, with satisfaction*: I'm making a power of things you do have when you're settling with a wife,

Martin Doul; for I heard tell last night the Saint'll be passing again in a short while, and I'd have him wed Molly with myself. . . . He'd do it, I've heard them say, for not a penny at all.

MARTIN DOUL *lays down hooks and looks at him steadily*: Molly'll be saying great praises now to the Almighty God and He giving her a fine, stout, hardy man the like of you.

TIMMY uneasily: And why wouldn't she, if she's a fine woman itself?

MARTIN DOUL *looking up right*: Why wouldn't she, indeed, Timmy? . . . The Almighty God's made a fine match in the two of you, for if you went marrying a woman was the like of yourself you'd be having the fearfullest little children, I'm thinking, was ever seen in the world.

TIMMY *seriously offended*: God forgive you! if you're an ugly man to be looking at, I'm thinking your tongue's worse than your view.

MARTIN DOUL *hurt also*: Isn't it destroyed with the cold I am, and if I'm ugly itself I never seen any one the like of you for dreepiness this day, Timmy the smith, and I'm thinking now herself's coming above you'd have a right to step up into your old shanty, and give a rub to your face, and not be sitting there with your bleary eyes, and your big nose, the like of an old scarecrow stuck down upon the road.

TIMMY *looking up the road uneasily*: She's no call to mind what way I look, and I after building a house with four rooms in it above on the hill. *He stands up.* But it's a queer thing the way yourself and Mary Doul are after setting every person in this place, and up beyond to Rathvanna, talking of nothing, and thinking of nothing, but the way they do be looking in the face. *Going towards forge.* It's the devil's work you're after doing with your talk of fine looks, and I'd do right, maybe, to step in and wash the blackness from my eyes.

He goes into forge. Martin Doul rubs his face furtively with the tail of his coat. Molly Byrne comes on right with a water can, and begins to fill it at the well.

MARTIN DOUL: God save you, Molly Byrne.
MOLLY BYRNE *indifferently*: God save you.

MARTIN DOUL: That's a dark, gloomy day, and the Lord have mercy on us all.

MOLLY BYRNE: Middling dark.

MARTIN DOUL: It's a power of dirty days, and dark mornings, and shabby-looking fellows (*he makes a gesture over his shoulder*) we do have to be looking on when we have our sight, God help us, but there's one fine thing we have, to be looking on a grand, white, handsome girl, the like of you . . . and every time I set my eyes on you I do be blessing the saints, and the holy water, and the power of the Lord Almighty in the heavens above.

MOLLY BYRNE: I've heard the priests say it isn't looking on a young girl would teach many to be saying their prayers. *Bailing water into her can with a cup.*

MARTIN DOUL: It isn't many have been the way I was, hearing your voice speaking, and not seeing you at all.

MOLLY BYRNE: That should have been a queer time for an old, wicked, coaxing fool to be sitting there with your eyes shut, and not seeing a sight of a girl or woman passing the road.

MARTIN DOUL: If it was a queer time itself it was great joy and pride I had the time I'd hear your voice speaking and you passing to Grianan (*beginning to speak with plaintive intensity*), for it's of many a fine thing your voice would put a poor dark fellow in mind, and the day I'd hear it it's of little else at all I would be thinking.

MOLLY BYRNE: I'll tell your wife if you talk to me the like of that. . . . You've heard, maybe, she's below picking nettles for the widow O'Flinn, who took great pity on her when she seen the two of you fighting, and yourself putting shame on her at the crossing of the roads.

MARTIN DOUL *impatiently*: Is there no living person can speak a score of words to me, or say 'God speed you' itself, without putting me in mind of the old woman or that day either at Grianan?

MOLLY BYRNE *maliciously*: I was thinking it should be a fine thing to put you in mind of the day you called the grand day of your life.

MARTIN DOUL: Grand day, is it? *Plaintively again, throwing aside his work, and leaning towards her.* Or a bad black day when I was roused up and found I was the like of the little children do be listening to the stories of an old woman, and do be dreaming after in the dark night that it's in grand houses of gold they are, with speckled horses to ride, and do be waking again, in a short while, and they destroyed with the cold, and the thatch dripping, maybe, and the starved ass braying in the yard?

MOLLY BYRNE *working indifferently*: You've great romancing this day, Martin Doul. Was it up at the still you were at the fall of night?

MARTIN DOUL *stands up, comes towards her, but stands at far side of well*: It was not, Molly Byrne, but lying down in a little rickety shed. . . . Lying down across a sop of straw, and I thinking I was seeing you walk, and hearing the sound of your step on a dry road, and hearing you again, and you laughing and making great talk in a high room with dry timber lining the roof. For it's a fine sound your voice has that time, and it's better I am, I'm thinking, lying down, the way a blind man does be lying, than to be sitting here in the grey light taking hard words of Timmy the smith.

MOLLY BYRNE *looking at him with interest*: It's queer talk you have if it's a little, old, shabby stump of a man you are itself.

MARTIN DOUL: I'm not so old as you do hear them say.

MOLLY BYRNE: You're old, I'm thinking, to be talking that talk with a girl.

MARTIN DOUL *despondingly*: It's not a lie you're telling maybe, for it's long years I'm after losing from the world, feeling love and talking love, with the old woman, and I fooled the whole while with the lies of Timmy the smith.

MOLLY BYRNE *half invitingly*: It's a fine way you're wanting to pay Timmy the smith. . . . And it's not his *lies* you're making love to this day, Martin Doul.

MARTIN DOUL: It is not, Molly, and the Lord forgive us all. *He passes behind her and comes near her left*. For I've heard tell there are lands beyond in Cahir Iveragh and the Reeks of Cork with warm sun in them, and fine light in the sky. *Bending towards her*. And light's a grand thing for a man ever was blind, or a woman, with a fine neck, and a skin on her the like of you, the way we'd have a right to go off this day till we'd have a fine life passing abroad through them towns of the south, and we telling stories, maybe, or singing songs at the fairs.

MOLLY BYRNE *turning round half amused, and looking him over from head to foot*: Well, isn't it a queer thing when your own wife's after leaving you because you're a pitiful show, you'd talk the like of that to me?

MARTIN DOUL *drawing back a little, hurt, but indignant*: It's a queer thing, maybe, for all things is queer in the world. *In a low voice with peculiar emphasis*. But there's one thing I'm telling you, if she walked off away from me, it wasn't because of seeing me, and I no more than I am, but because I was looking on her with my two eyes, and she getting up, and eating her food, and combing her hair, and lying down for her sleep.

MOLLY BYRNE *interested, off her guard*: Wouldn't any married man you'd have be doing the like of that?

MARTIN DOUL *seizing the moment that he has her attention*: I'm thinking by the mercy of God it's few sees anything but them is blind for a space (*with excitement*). It's few sees the old women rotting for the grave, and it's few sees the like of yourself. *He bends over her*. Though it's shining you are, like a high lamp would drag in the ships out of the sea.

MOLLY BYRNE *shrinking away from him*: Keep off from me, Martin Doul.

MARTIN DOUL *quickly with low, furious intensity*: It's the truth I'm telling you. *He puts his hand on her shoulder and shakes her*. And you'd do right not to marry a man is after looking out a long while on the bad days of the world; for what way would the like of him have fit eyes to look on yourself, when you rise up in the morning and come out of the little door you have above in the lane, the time it'd be a fine thing if a man would be seeing, and losing his sight, the way he'd have your two eyes facing him, and he going the roads, and shining above him, and he looking in the sky, and springing up from the earth, the time he'd lower his head, in place of the muck that seeing men do meet all roads spread on the world.

MOLLY BYRNE *who has listened half mesmerized, starting away*: It's the like of that talk you'd hear from a man would be losing his mind.

MARTIN DOUL *going after her, passing to her right*: It'd be little wonder if a man near the like of you would be losing his mind. Put down your can now, and come along with myself, for I'm seeing you this day, seeing you, maybe, the way no man has seen you in the world. *He takes her by the arm and tries to pull her away softly to the right.* Let you come on now, I'm saying, to the lands of Iveragh and the Reeks of Cork, where you won't set down the width of your two feet and not be crushing fine flowers, and making sweet smells in the air.

MOLLY BYRNE *laying down can, trying to free herself*: Leave me go, Martin Doul! Leave me go, I'm saying!

MARTIN DOUL: Let you not be fooling. Come along now the little path through the trees.

MOLLY BYRNE *crying out towards forge*: Timmy – Timmy the smith.

Timmy comes out of forge, and Martin Doul lets her go. Molly Byrne, excited and breathless, pointing to Martin Doul.

Did ever you hear that them that loses their sight loses their senses along with it, Timmy the smith!

TIMMY *suspicious, but uncertain*: He's no sense, surely, and he'll be having himself driven off this day from where he's good sleeping, and feeding, and wages for his work.

MOLLY BYRNE *as before*: He's a bigger fool than that, Timmy. Look on him now, and tell me if that isn't a grand fellow to think he's only to open his mouth to have a fine woman, the like of me, running along by his heels.

Martin Doul recoils towards centre, with his hand to his eyes; Mary Doul is seen on left coming forward softly.

TIMMY *with blank amazement*: Oh, the blind is wicked people, and it's no lie. But he'll walk off this day and not be troubling us more.

Turns back left and picks up Martin Doul's coat and stick; some things fall out of coat pocket, which he gathers up again.

MARTIN DOUL *turns round, sees Mary Doul, whispers to Molly Byrne with imploring agony*: Let you not put shame on me, Molly, before herself and the smith. Let you not put shame on me and I after saying fine words to you, and dreaming . . . dreams . . . in the night. *He hesitates, and looks round the sky.* Is it a storm of thunder is coming, or the last end of the world? *He staggers towards Mary Doul, tripping slightly over tin can.* The heavens is closing, I'm thinking, with darkness and great trouble passing in the sky. *He reaches Mary Doul, and seizes her left arm with both his hands – with a frantic cry.* Is it the darkness of thunder is coming, Mary Doul? Do you see me clearly with your eyes?

MARY DOUL *snatches her arm away, and hits him with empty sack across the face*: I see you a sight too clearly, and let you keep off from me now.

MOLLY BYRNE *clapping her hands*: That's right, Mary. That's the way to treat the like of him is after standing there at my feet and asking me to go off with him, till I'd grow an old wretched road-woman the like of yourself.

MARY DOUL *defiantly*: When the skin shrinks on your chin, Molly Byrne, there won't be the like of you for a shrunk hag in the four quarters of Ireland. . . . It's a fine pair you'd be, surely!

Martin Doul is standing at back right centre, with his back to the audience.

TIMMY *coming over to Mary Doul*: Is it no shame you have to let on she'd ever be the like of you?

MARY DOUL: It's them that's fat and flabby do be wrinkled young, and that whitish yellowy hair she has does be soon turning the like of a handful of thin grass you'd see rotting, where the wet lies, at the north of a sty. *Turning to go out on right.* Ah, it's a better thing to have a simple, seemly face, the like of my face, for twoscore years, or fifty itself, than to be setting fools mad a short while, and then to be turning a thing would drive off the little children from your feet.

She goes out; Martin Doul has come forward again, mastering himself, but uncertain.

TIMMY: Oh, God protect me, Molly, from the words of the blind. *He throws down Martin Doul's coat and stick.* There's your old rubbish now, Martin Doul, and let you take it up, for it's all you have, and walk off through the world, for if ever I meet you coming again, if it's seeing or blind you are itself, I'll bring out the big hammer and hit you a welt with it will leave you easy till the Judgment Day.

MARTIN DOUL *rousing himself with an effort*: What call have you to talk the like of that with myself?

TIMMY *pointing to Molly Byrne*: It's well you know what call I have. It's well you know a decent girl, I'm thinking to wed, has no right to have her heart scalded with hearing talk – and queer, bad talk, I'm thinking – from a raggy-looking fool the like of you.

MARTIN DOUL *raising his voice*: It's making game of you she is, for what seeing girl would marry with yourself? Look on him, Molly, look on him, I'm saying, for I'm seeing him still, and let you raise your voice, for the time is come, and bid him go up into his forge, and be sitting there by himself, sneezing, and sweating, and he beating pot-hooks till the Judgment Day. *He seizes her arm again.*

MOLLY BYRNE: Keep him off from me, Timmy!

TIMMY *pushing Martin Doul aside*: Would you have me strike you, Martin Doul? Go along now after your wife, who's a fit match for you, and leave Molly with myself.

MARTIN DOUL *despairingly*: Won't you raise your voice, Molly, and lay hell's long curse on his tongue?

MOLLY BYRNE *on Timmy's left*: I'll be telling him it's destroyed I am with the sight of you and the sound of your voice. Go off now after your wife, and if she beats you again, let you go after the tinker girls is above running the hills, or down among the sluts of the town, and you'll learn one day, maybe, the way a man should speak with a well-reared, civil girl the like of me. *She takes Timmy by the arm.* Come up now into the forge till he'll be gone down a bit on the road, for it's near afeard I am of the wild look he has come in his eyes.

She goes into the forge. Timmy stops in the doorway.

TIMMY: Let me not find you here again, Martin Doul. *He bares his arm.* It's well you know Timmy the smith has great strength in his arm, and it's a power of things it has broken a sight harder than the old bone of your skull.

He goes into the forge and pulls the door after him.

MARTIN DOUL *stands a moment with his hand to his eyes*: And that's the last thing I'm to set my sight on in the life of the world – the villainy of a woman and the bloody strength of a man. Oh, God, pity a poor blind fellow, the way I am this day with no strength in me to do hurt to them at all. *He begins groping about for a moment, then stops.* Yet if I've no strength in me I've a voice left for my prayers, and may God blight them this day, and my own soul the same hour with them, the way I'll see them after, Molly Byrne and Timmy the smith, the two of them on a high bed, and they screeching in hell. . . . It'll be a grand thing that time to look on the two of them; and they twisting and roaring out, and twisting and roaring again, one day and the next day, and each day always and ever. It's not blind I'll be that time, and it won't be hell to me, I'm thinking, but the like of heaven itself; and it's fine care I'll be taking the Lord Almighty doesn't know. *He turns to grope out.*

CURTAIN

ACT THREE

The same scene as in first Act, but gap in centre has been filled with briers, or branches of some sort. Mary Doul, blind again, gropes her way in on left, and sits as before. She has a few rushes with her. It is an early spring day.

MARY DOUL *mournfully*: Ah, God help me . . . God help me; the blackness wasn't so black at all the other time as it is this time, and it's destroyed I'll be now, and hard set to get my living working alone, when it's few are passing and the winds are cold. *She begins shredding rushes.* I'm thinking short days will be long days to me from this time, and I sitting here, not seeing a blink or hearing a word, and no thought in my mind but long prayers that Martin Doul'll get his reward in a short while for the villainy of his heart. It's great jokes the people'll be making now, I'm thinking, and they passing me by, pointing their fingers, maybe, and asking what place is himself, the way it's no quiet or decency I'll have from this day till I'm an old woman with long white hair and it twisting from my brow. *She fumbles with her hair, and then seems to hear something. Listens for a moment.* There's a queer slouching step coming on the road. . . . God help me, he's coming surely.

She stays perfectly quiet. Martin Doul gropes in on right, blind also.

MARTIN DOUL *gloomily*: The devil mend Mary Doul for putting lies on me, and letting on she was grand. The devil mend the old Saint for letting me see it was lies. *He sits down near her.* The devil mend Timmy the smith for killing me with hard work, and keeping me with an empty, windy stomach in me, in the day and in the night. Ten thousand devils mend the soul of Molly Byrne – (*Mary Doul nods her head with approval*) – and the bad wicked souls is hidden in all the women of the world. *He rocks himself, with his hand over his face.* It's lonesome I'll be from this day, and if living people is a bad lot, yet Mary Doul, herself, and she a dirty, wrinkled-looking hag, was better maybe to be sitting along with than no one at all. I'll be getting my death now, I'm thinking, sitting alone in the cold air, hearing the night coming, and the blackbirds flying round in the briers crying to themselves, the time you'll hear one cart getting off a long way in the east, and another cart getting off a long way in the west, and a dog barking maybe, and a little wind turning the sticks. *He listens and sighs heavily.* I'll be destroyed sitting alone and losing my senses this time the way I'm after losing my sight, for it'd make any person afeard to be sitting up hearing the sound of his breath – (*he moves his feet on the stones*) – and the noise of his feet, when it's a power of queer things do be stirring, little sticks breaking and the grass moving – (*Mary Doul half sighs, and he turns on her in horror*) – till you'd take your dying oath on sun and moon a thing was breathing on the stones. *He listens towards her for a moment, then starts up nervously and gropes about for his stick.* I'll be going now, I'm thinking, but I'm not sure what place my stick's in, and I'm destroyed with terror and dread. *He touches her face as he is groping about and cries out.* There's a thing with a cold, living face on it sitting up at my side. *He turns to run away, but misses his path and tumbles in against the wall.* My road is lost on me now! Oh, merciful God, set my foot on the path this day, and I'll be saying prayers morning and night, and not straining my ear after young girls, or doing any bad thing till I die –

MARY DOUL *indignantly*: Let you not be telling lies to the Almighty God.

MARTIN DOUL: Mary Doul, is it? *Recovering himself with immense relief.* Is it Mary Doul, I'm saying?

MARY DOUL: There's a sweet tone in your voice I've not heard for a space. You're taking me for Molly Byrne, I'm thinking.

MARTIN DOUL *coming towards her, wiping sweat from his face.* Well, sight's a queer thing for upsetting a man. It's a queer thing to think I'd live to this day to be fearing the like of you; but if it's shaken I am for a short while, I'll soon be coming to myself.

MARY DOUL: You'll be grand then, and it's no lie.

MARTIN DOUL *sitting down shyly some way off*: You've no call to be talking, for I've heard tell you're as blind as myself.

MARY DOUL: If I am I'm bearing in mind I'm married to a little dark stump of a fellow looks the fool of the world, and I'll be bearing in mind from this day the great hullabaloo he's after making from hearing a poor woman breathing quiet in her place.

MARTIN DOUL: And you'll be bearing in mind, I'm thinking, what you seen a while back when you looked down into a well, or a clear pool, maybe, when there was no wind stirring and a good light in the sky.

MARY DOUL: I'm minding that surely, for if I'm not the way the liars were saying below I seen a thing in them pools put joy and blessing in my heart. *She puts her hand to her hair again.*

MARTIN DOUL *laughing ironically*: Well, they were saying below I was losing my senses, but I never went any day the length of that. . . . God help you, Mary Doul, if you're not a wonder for looks, you're the maddest female woman is walking the counties of the east.

MARY DOUL *scornfully*: You were saying all times you'd a great ear for hearing the lies in a word. A great ear, God help you, and you think you're using it now.

MARTIN DOUL: If it's not lies you're telling would you have me think you're not a wrinkled poor woman is looking like three scores, maybe, or two scores and a half!

MARY DOUL: I would not, Martin. *She leans forward earnestly*. For when I seen myself in them pools, I seen my hair would be grey or white, maybe, in a short while, and I seen with it that I'd a face would be a great wonder when it'll have soft white hair falling around it, the way when I'm an old woman there won't be the like of me surely in the seven counties of the east.

MARTIN DOUL *with real admiration*: You're a cute thinking woman, Mary Doul, and it's no lie.

MARY DOUL *triumphantly*: I am, surely, and I'm telling you a beautiful white-haired woman is a grand thing to see, for I'm told when Kitty Bawn was selling poteen below, the young men itself would never tire to be looking in her face.

MARTIN DOUL *taking off his hat and feeling his head, speaking with hesitation*: Did you think to look, Mary Doul, would there be a whiteness the like of that coming upon me?

MARY DOUL *with extreme contempt*: On you, God help you! . . . In a short while you'll have a head on you as bald as an old turnip you'd see rolling round in the muck. You need never talk again of your fine looks, Martin Doul, for the day of that talk's gone for ever.

MARTIN DOUL: That's a hard word to be saying, for I was thinking if I'd a bit of comfort, the like of yourself, it's not far off we'd be from the good days went before, and that'd be a wonder surely. But I'll never rest easy, thinking you're a grey beautiful woman, and myself a pitiful show.

MARY DOUL: I can't help your looks, Martin Doul. It wasn't myself made you with your rat's eyes, and your big ears, and your griseldy chin.

MARTIN DOUL *rubs his chin ruefully, then beams with delight*: There's one thing you've forgot, if you're a cute thinking woman itself.

MARY DOUL: Your slouching feet, is it? Or your hooky neck, or your two knees is black with knocking one on the other?

MARTIN DOUL *with delighted scorn*: There's talking for a cute woman. There's talking, surely!

MARY DOUL *puzzled at joy of his voice*: If you'd anything but lies to say you'd be talking yourself.

MARTIN DOUL *bursting with excitement*: I've this to say, Mary Doul. I'll be letting my beard grow in a short while, a beautiful, long, white, silken, streamy beard, you wouldn't see the like of in the eastern world. . . . Ah, a white beard's a grand thing on an old man, a grand thing for making the quality stop and be stretching out their hands with good silver or gold, and a beard's a thing you'll never have, so you may be holding your tongue.

MARY DOUL *laughing cheerfully*: Well, we're a great pair, surely, and it's great times we'll have yet, maybe, and great talking before we die.

MARTIN DOUL: Great times from this day, with the help of the Almighty God, for a priest itself would believe the lies of an old man would have a fine white beard growing on his chin.

MARY DOUL: There's the sound of one of them twittering yellow birds do be coming in the springtime from beyond the sea, and there'll be a fine warmth now in the sun, and a sweetness in the air, the way it'll be a grand thing to be sitting here quiet and easy, smelling the things growing up, and budding from the earth.

MARTIN DOUL: I'm smelling the furze a while back sprouting on the hill, and if you'd hold your tongue you'd hear the lambs of Grianan, though it's near drowned their crying is with the full river making noises in the glen.

MARY DOUL *listens*: The lambs is bleating, surely, and there's cocks and laying hens making a fine stir a mile off on the face of the hill. *She starts.*

MARTIN DOUL: What's that is sounding in the west?

A faint sound of a bell is heard.

MARY DOUL: It's not the churches, for the wind's blowing from the sea.

MARTIN DOUL *with dismay*: It's the old Saint, I'm thinking, ringing his bell.

MARY DOUL: The Lord protect us from the saints of God!

They listen.

He's coming this road, surely.

MARTIN DOUL *tentatively*: Will we be running off, Mary Doul?

MARY DOUL: What place would we run?

MARTIN DOUL: There's the little path going up through the sloughs. . . . If we reached the bank above, where the elders do be growing, no person would see a sight of us, if it was a hundred yeoman were passing itself; but I'm afeard after the time we were with our sight we'll not find our way to it at all.

MARY DOUL *standing up*: You'd find the way, surely. You're a grand man, the world knows, at finding your way winter or summer, if there was deep snow in it itself, or thick grass and leaves, maybe, growing from the earth.

MARTIN DOUL *taking her hand*: Come a bit this way; it's here it begins. *They grope about gap*. There's a tree pulled into the gap, or a strange thing happened, since I was passing it before.

MARY DOUL: Would we have a right to be crawling in below under the sticks?

MARTIN DOUL: It's hard set I am to know what would be right. And isn't it a poor thing to be blind when you can't run off itself, and you fearing to see?

MARY DOUL *nearly in tears*: It's a poor thing, God help us, and what good'll our grey hairs be itself, if we have our sight, the way we'll see them falling each day, and turning dirty in the rain.

The bells sounds near by.

MARTIN DOUL *in despair*: He's coming now, and we won't get off from him at all.

MARY DOUL: Could we hide in the bit of a brier is growing at the west butt of the church?

MARTIN DOUL: We'll try that, surely. *He listens a moment*. Let you make haste; I hear them trampling in the wood.

They grope over to church.

MARY DOUL: It's the words of the young girls making a great stir in the trees.

The find the bush.

Here's the brier on my left, Martin; I'll go in first, I'm the big one, and I'm easy to see.

MARTIN DOUL *turning his head anxiously*: It's easy heard you are; and will you be holding your tongue?

MARY DOUL *partly behind bush*: Come in now beside of me.

The kneel down, still clearly visible.

Do you think they can see us now, Martin Doul?

MARTIN DOUL: I'm thinking they can't, but I'm hard set to know; for the lot of them young girls, the devil save them, have sharp, terrible eyes, would pick out a poor man, I'm thinking, and he lying below hid in his grave.

MARY DOUL: Let you not be whispering sin, Martin Doul, or maybe it's the finger of God they'd see pointing to ourselves.

MARTIN DOUL: It's yourself is speaking madness, Mary Doul; haven't you heard the Saint say it's the wicked do be blind?

MARY DOUL: If it is you'd have a right to speak a big, terrible word would make the water not cure us at all.

MARTIN DOUL: What way would I find a big, terrible word, and I shook with the fear; and if I did itself, who'd know rightly if it's good words or bad would save us this day from himself?

MARY DOUL: They're coming. I hear their feet on the stones.

The Saint comes in on right, with Timmy and Mary Byrne in holiday clothes, the others as before.

TIMMY: I've heard tell Martin Doul and Mary Doul were seen this day about on the road, holy father, and we were thinking you'd have pity on them and cure them again.

SAINT: I would, maybe, but where are they at all? I'll have little time left when I have the two of you wed in the church.

MAT SIMON *at their seat*: There are the rushes they do have lying round on the stones. It's not far off they'll be, surely.

MOLLY BYRNE *pointing with astonishment*: Look beyond, Timmy.

They all look over and see Martin Doul.

TIMMY: Well, Martin's a lazy fellow to be lying in there at the height of the day. *He goes over shouting.* Let you get up out of that. You were near losing a great chance by your sleepiness this day, Martin Doul. . . . The two of them's in it, God help us all!

MARTIN DOUL *scrambling up with Mary Doul*: What is it you want, Timmy, that you can't leave us in peace?

TIMMY: The Saint's come to marry the two of us, and I'm after speaking a word for yourselves, the way he'll be curing you now; for if you're a foolish man itself, I do be pitying you, for I've a kind heart, when I think of you sitting dark again, and you after seeing a while, and working for your bread.

Martin Doul takes Mary Doul's hand and tries to grope his way off right; he has lost his hat, and they are both covered with dust and grass seeds.

PEOPLE: You're going wrong. It's this way, Martin Doul.

They push him over in front of the Saint, near centre. Martin Doul and Mary Doul stand with piteous hang-dog dejection.

SAINT: Let you not be afeard, for there's great pity with the Lord.

MARTIN DOUL: We aren't afeard, holy father.

SAINT: It's many a time those that are cured with the well of the four beauties of God lose their sight when a time is gone, but those I cure a second time go on seeing till the hour of death. *He takes the cover from his can.* I've a few drops only left of the water, but, with the help of God, it'll be enough for the two of you, and let you kneel down now upon the road.

Martin Doul wheels round with Mary Doul and tries to get away.

You can kneel down here, I'm saying, we'll not trouble this time going to the church.

TIMMY *turning Martin Doul round, angrily*: Are you going mad in your head, Martin Doul? It's here you're to kneel. Did you not hear his reverence, and he speaking to you now?

SAINT: Kneel down, I'm saying, the ground's dry at your feet.

MARTIN DOUL *with distress*: Let you go on your way, holy father. We're not calling you at all.

SAINT: I'm not saying a word of penance, or fasting itself, for I'm thinking the Lord has brought you great teaching in the blinding of your eyes; so you've no call now to be fearing me, let you kneel down till I give you your sight.

MARTIN DOUL: We're not asking our sight, holy father, and let you be walking on and leaving us in our peace at the crossing roads, for it's best we are this way, and we're not asking to see.

SAINT *to the people*: Is his mind gone that he's no wish to be cured this day, and looking out on the wonders of the world?

MARTIN DOUL: It's wonders enough I seen in a short space, holy father, for the life of one man only.

TIMMY: Is it he see wonders?

PATCH: He's making game.

MAT SIMON: He's may be drunk, holy father.

SAINT *puzzled*: I never heard tell of any person wouldn't have great joy to be looking on the earth, and the image of the Lord is thrown upon men.

MARTIN DOUL *raising his voice, by degrees*: That's great sights, holy father. . . . What was it I seen my first day, but your own bleeding feet and they cut with the stones, and my last day, but the villainy of herself you're wedding, God forgive you, Timmy the smith. . . . That was great sights maybe. . . . And wasn't it great sights seeing the roads when the north winds would be driving and the skies would be harsh and you'd see the horses, and the asses, and the dogs itself, maybe, with their heads hanging, and they closing their eyes –

TIMMY: There's talking.

MAT SIMON: He's maybe right, it's lonesome living when the days are dark.

MOLLY BYRNE: He's not right. Let you speak up, holy father, and confound him now.

SAINT *coming close to Martin Doul and putting his hand on his shoulder*: Did you never hear tell of the summer and the fine spring in places where the holy men of Ireland have built up churches to the Lord, that you'd wish to be closed up and seeing no sight of the glittering seas, and the furze is opening above, will soon have the hills shining as if it was fine creels of gold they were, rising to the sky?

PATCH: That's it, holy father.

MAT SIMON: What will you say now, Martin Doul?

MARTIN DOUL *fiercely*: I'll say it's ourselves have finer sight than the lot of you, and we sitting abroad in the sweetness of the warmth of night (*the Saint draws back from him*), hearing a late thrush, maybe, and the swift crying things do be racing in the air, till we do be looking up in our own minds into a grand sky, and seeing lakes, and broadening rivers, and hills are waiting for the spade and plough.

MAT SIMON *roaring laughing*: It's songs he's making now, holy father.

PATCH: It's mad he is.

MOLLY BYRNE: It's not, but lazy, holy father, and not wishing to work; for, awhile since, he was all times longing and screeching for the light of day.

MARTIN DOUL *with vehement bitterness*: If I was, I seen my fill in a short while with the look of my wife, and the look of your own wicked grin, the time you do be making game with a man.

MOLLY BYRNE: There's talking. . . . Let you not mind him more, holy father, but leave him in darkness, if it's that is best fitting the blackness of his heart.

TIMMY: Cure Mary Doul, your reverence, who is a quiet poor woman, never said a hard word but when she'd be vexed with himself, or with the young girls do be making game of her below.

MAT SIMON: That's it. Cure Mary Doul, your reverence.

SAINT: There's little use, I'm thinking, talking to the like of him, but if you've any sense, Mary Doul, let you kneel down at my feet, and I'll bring sight into your eyes.

MARTIN DOUL *more defiantly*: You will not, holy father. . . . Would you have her looking on me, and saying hard words to me till the hour of death?

SAINT *severely*: If she's wanting her sight, I wouldn't have the like of you stop her at all. *To Mary Doul*. Kneel down, I'm saying.

MARY DOUL *confused*: Let us be as we are, holy father, and then we'll be known again, in a short while, as the people is happy and blind, and we'll be having an easy time with no trouble to live, and we getting half-pence on the road.

MOLLY BYRNE: Let you not be raving. Kneel down and get your sight, and let himself be taking half-pence if he likes it best.

TIMMY: If it's choosing a wilful blindness you are, there isn't anyone will give you a ha'p'orth of meal, or be doing the little things you do need to keep you living in the world at all.

MAT SIMON: If you had your sight you could be keeping a watch on him that no other woman came near him in the night or day.

MARY DOUL *partly convinced*: That's true, maybe.

SAINT: Kneel down, for I must be hastening with the marriage, and going my own way before the fall of night.

ALL *together*: Kneel down, Mary, kneel down when you're bid by the Saint.

MARY DOUL *looking uneasily towards Martin Doul*: Maybe it's right they are, and I will if you wish it, holy father.

She kneels down. The Saint takes off his hat and gives it to someone near him. All the men take off their hats. He goes forward a step to take Martin Doul's hand away from Mary Doul.

SAINT *to Martin Doul*: Go aside now. We're not wanting you here.

Martin Doul pushes him away roughly, and stands with his left hand on Mary Doul's shoulder.

MARTIN DOUL: Keep off yourself, holy father, and let you not be taking my rest from me in the darkness of my wife. . . . What call has the likes of you coming where you're not wanted, and making a great mess with the holy water you have, and the length of your prayers? *Defiantly*. Go on, I'm saying, and leave us this place on the road.

SAINT: If it was a seeing man I heard talking the like of that I'd put a black curse on him would weigh down his soul, till it'd be falling to hell, but you're a poor blind sinner, God forgive you, and I don't mind you at all. *He raises his can*. Go aside now till I give the blessing to your wife, and if you won't go of your own will, there are those standing by will make you, surely.

MARTIN DOUL: Well, there's bitter hardness in the pity of your like, and what is it you want coming for to break our happiness and hour of ease. Let you rise up, Mary, and not heed them more. *He pulls Mary Doul.*

SAINT *imperiously*: Let you take that man and drive him down upon the road.

MAT SIMON: Come on, now.

PATCH: Come on from talking badness to the holy saint.

They seize Martin Doul.

MARTIN DOUL *throwing himself down on the ground*: I'll not come, I'm saying, and let you take his holy water to cure the blackness of your souls today.

MARY DOUL: Leave him easy, holy father, when I'd liefer live dark all times beside him, than be getting eyesight and new torments now.

SAINT: You have taken your choice. Drag him off from her, I'm saying.

PEOPLE: That's it. That's it. Come forward till we drop him in the pool beyond.

MARTIN DOUL *screaming*: Make them leave me go, holy father. Make them leave me go, I'm saying, and let you not think badly of my heathen talk, but cure her this day, or do anything you will.

SAINT (*to people*): Let him be. . . . Let him be, if his sense has come to him at all.

MARTIN DOUL *shakes himself loose, feels for Mary Doul, sinking his voice to a plausible whine*: You may cure herself surely, holy father; I wouldn't stop you at all – and it's great joy she'll have looking on your face – but let you cure myself along with her, the way I'll see when it's lies she's telling, and be looking out day and night upon the holy men of God. *He kneels down a little before Mary Doul.*

SAINT *speaking half to the people*: Men who are dark a long while and thinking over queer thoughts in their heads, aren't the like of simple men, who do be working every day, and praying, and living like ourselves; so if he has found a right mind at the last minute itself, I'll cure him, if the Lord will, and not be thinking of the hard, foolish words he's after saying this day to us all.

MARTIN DOUL *listening eagerly*: I'm waiting now, holy father.

SAINT *with can in his hand, close to Martin Doul*: With the power of the water from the grave of the four beauties of God, with the power of this water, I'm saying, that I put upon your eyes – *He raises can. Martin Doul with a sudden movement strikes the can from the Saint's hand and sends it rocketing across stage.*

PEOPLE *with a terrified murmur*: Will you look what he's done. Oh, glory be to God.

MARTIN DOUL *stands up triumphantly, and pulls Mary Doul up*: If I'm a poor dark sinner I've sharp ears, God help me, and it's well I heard the little splash of the water you had there in the can. Go on now holy father, for if you're a fine Saint itself, it's more sense is in a blind man, and more power maybe than you're thinking at all. Let you walk on now with your worn feet, and your welted knees, and your fasting, holy ways have left you with a big head on you and a thin pitiful arm. For if it's a right some of you have to be working and sweating the like of Timmy the smith, and a right some of you have to be fasting and praying and talking holy talk the like of yourself, I'm thinking it's a good right ourselves have to be sitting blind, hearing a soft wind turning round the little leaves of the spring and feeling the sun, and we not tormenting our souls with the sight of the grey days, and the holy men, and the dirty feet is trampling the world. *He gropes towards his stone with Mary Doul.*

MAT SIMON: It'd be an unlucky fearful thing, I'm thinking, to have the like of that man living near us at all in the townland of Grianan. Wouldn't he bring down a curse upon us, holy father, from the heavens of God?

SAINT *tying his girdle*: God has great mercy, but great wrath for them that sin.

THE PEOPLE: Go on now, Martin Doul. Go on from this place. Let you not be bringing great storms or droughts on us maybe from the power of the Lord.

Some of them throw things at him.

MARTIN DOUL *turning round defiantly and picking up a stone*: Keep off now, the yelping lot of you, or it's more than one maybe will get a bloody head on him with the pitch of my stone. Keep off now, and let you not be afeard; for we're going on the two of us to the towns of the south, where the people will have kind voices maybe, and we won't know their bad looks or their villainy at all. *He takes Mary Doul's hand again.* Come along now and we'll be walking to the south, for we've seen too much of every one in this place, and it's small joy we'd have living near them, or hearing the lies they do be telling from the grey of dawn till the night.

MARY DOUL *despondingly*: That's the truth, surely; and we'd have a right to be gone, if it's a long way itself, as I've heard them say, where you do have to be walking with a slough of wet on the one side and a slough of wet on the other, and you going a stony path with the north wind blowing behind.

They go out.

TIMMY: There's a power of deep rivers with floods in them where you do have to be lepping the stones and you going to the south, so I'm thinking the two of them will be drowned together in a short while, surely.

SAINT: They have chosen their lot, and the Lord have mercy on their souls. *He rings his bell.* And let the two of you come up now into the church, Molly Byrne and Timmy the smith, till I make your marriage and put my blessing on you all.

He turns to the church; procession forms, and the curtain comes down as they go slowly into the church.

The Playboy of the Western World

PERSONS IN THE PLAY

CHRISTOPHER MAHON

OLD MAHON, his father, a squatter

MICHAEL JAMES FLAHERTY (called MICHAEL JAMES), a
  publican

MARGARET FLAHERTY (called PEGEEN MIKE), his daughter

WIDOW QUIN, a woman of about thirty

SHAWN KEOGH, her cousin, a young farmer

PHILLY CULLEN and JIMMY FARRELL, small farmers

SARA TANSEY, SUSAN BRADY, and HONOR BLAKE, village
  girls

A BELLMAN

SOME PEASANTS

*The action takes place near a village, on a wild coast of Mayo.
The first Act passes on an evening of autumn, the other two Acts on the
following day*

Preface

In writing 'The Playboy of the Western World', as in my other plays, I have used one or two words only that I have not heard among the country people of Ireland, or spoken in my own nursery before I could read the newspapers. A certain number of the phrases I employ I have heard also from herds and fishermen along the coast from Kerry to Mayo or from beggar-women and ballad-singers nearer Dublin; and I am glad to acknowledge how much I owe to the folk-imagination of these fine people. Any one who has lived in real intimacy with the Irish peasantry will know that the wildest sayings and ideas in this play are tame indeed, compared with the fancies one may hear in any little hillside cabin in Geesala, or Carraroe, or Dingle Bay. All art is a collaboration; and there is little doubt that in the happy ages of literature, striking and beautiful phrases were as ready to the story-teller's or the playwright's hand, as the rich cloaks and dresses of his time. It is probable that when the Elizabethan dramatist took his ink-horn and sat down to his work he used many phrases that he had just heard, as he sat at dinner, from his mother or his children. In Ireland, those of us who know the people have the same privilege. When I was writing 'The Shadow of the Glen', some years ago, I got more aid than any learning could have given me from a chink in the floor of the old Wicklow house where I was staying, that let me hear what was being said by the servant girls in the kitchen. This matter, I think, is of importance, for in countries where the imagination of the people, and the language they use, is rich and living, it is possible for a writer to be rich and copious in his words, and at the same time to give the reality, which is the root of all poetry, in a comprehensive and natural form. In the modern literature of towns, however, richness is found only in sonnets, or prose poems, or in one or two elaborate books that are far away from the profound and common interests of life. One has, on one side, Mallarmé and Huysmans producing this literature; and on the other, Ibsen and Zola dealing with the reality of life in joyless and pallid words. On the stage one must have reality, and one must have joy; and that is why the intellectual modern drama has failed, and people have grown sick of the false joy of the musical comedy, that has been given them in place of the rich joy found only in what is superb and wild in reality. In a good play every speech should be as fully flavoured as a nut or apple, and such speeches cannot be written by any one who works among people who have shut their lips on poetry. In Ireland, for a few years more, we have a popular imagination that is fiery, and magnificent, and tender; so that those of us who wish to write start with a chance that is not given to writers in places where the springtime of the local life has been forgotten, and the harvest is a memory only, and the straw has been turned into bricks.

J.M.S.

21st January 1907

ACT ONE

Country public house or shebeen, very rough and untidy. There is a sort of counter on the right with shelves, holding many bottles and jugs, just seen above it. Empty barrels stand near the counter. At back, a little to left of counter, there is a door into the open air, then, more to the left, there is a settle with shelves above it, with more jugs, and a table beneath a window. At the left there is a large open fire-place, with turf fire, and a small door into inner room. Pegeen, a wild-looking but fine girl, of about twenty, is writing at table. She is dressed in the usual peasant dress.

PEGEEN *slowly as she writes*: Six yards of stuff for to make a yellow gown. A pair of lace boots with lengthy heels on them and brassy eyes. A hat is suited for a wedding-day. A fine-tooth comb. To be sent with three barrels of porter in Jimmy Farrell's creel cart on the evening of the coming Fair to Mister Michael James Flaherty. With the best compliments of this season. Margaret Flaherty.

SHAWN KEOGH *a fat and fair young man comes in as she signs, looks around awkwardly, when he sees she is alone*: Where's himself?

PEGEEN *without looking at him*: He's coming. *She directs letter*. To Mister Sheamus Mulroy, Wine and Spirit Dealer, Castlebar.

SHAWN *uneasily*: I didn't see him on the road.

PEGEEN: How would you see him (*licks stamp and puts it on letter*) and it dark night this half-hour gone by?

SHAWN *turning towards door again*: I stood a while outside wondering would I have a right to pass on or to walk in and see you, Pegeen Mike (*comes to fire*), and I could hear the cows breathing and sighing in the stillness of the air, and not a step moving any place from this gate to the bridge.

PEGEEN *putting letter in envelope*: It's above at the crossroads he is, meeting Philly Cullen and a couple more are going along with him to Kate Cassidy's wake.

SHAWN *looking at her blankly*: And he's going that length in the dark night.

PEGEEN *impatiently*: He is surely, and leaving me lonesome on the scruff of the hill. *She gets up and puts envelope on dresser, then winds clock.* Isn't it long the nights are now, Shawn Keogh, to be leaving a poor girl with her own self counting the hours to the dawn of day?

SHAWN *with awkward humour*: If it is, when we're wedded in a short while you'll have no call to complain, for I've little will to be walking off to wakes or weddings in the darkness of the night.

PEGEEN *with rather scornful good humour*: You're making mighty certain, Shaneen, that I'll wed you now.

SHAWN: Aren't we after making a good bargain, the way we're only waiting these days on Father Reilly's dispensation from the bishops, or the Court of Rome.

PEGEEN *looking at him teasingly, washing up at dresser*: It's a wonder, Shaneen, the Holy Father'd be taking notice of the likes of you; for if I was him I wouldn't bother with this place where you'll meet none but Red Linahan, has a squint in his eye, and Patcheen is lame in his heel, or the mad Mulrannies were driven from California and they lost in their wits. We're a queer lot these times to go troubling the Holy Father on his sacred seat.

SHAWN *scandalized*: If we are, we're as good this place as another, maybe, and as good these times as we were for ever.

PEGEEN *with scorn*: As good is it? Where now will you meet the like of Daneen Sullivan knocked the eye from a peeler; or Marcus Quin, God rest him, got six months for maiming ewes, and he a great warrant to tell stories of holy Ireland till he'd have the old women shedding down tears about their feet. Where will you find the like of them, I'm saying?

SHAWN *timidly*: If you don't, it's a good job, maybe; for (*with peculiar emphasis on the words*) Father Reilly has small conceit to have that kind walking around and talking to the girls.

PEGEEN *impatiently throwing water from basin out of the door*: Stop tormenting me with Father Reilly (*imitating his voice*) when I'm asking only what way I'll pass these twelve hours of dark, and not take my death with the fear. *Looking out of door.*

SHAWN *timidly*: Would I fetch you the Widow Quin, maybe?

PEGEEN: Is it the like of that murderer? You'll not, surely.

SHAWN *going to her, soothingly*: Then I'm thinking himself will stop

along with you when he sees you taking on; for it'll be a long
night-time with great darkness, and I'm after feeling a kind of
fellow above in the furzy ditch, groaning wicked like a
maddening dog, the way it's good cause you have, maybe, to be
fearing now.

PEGEEN *turning on him sharply*: What's that? Is it a man you seen?

SHAWN *retreating*: I couldn't see him at all, but I heard him
groaning out, and breaking his heart. It should have been a
young man from his words speaking.

PEGEEN *going after him*: And you never went near to see was he
hurted or what ailed him at all?

SHAWN: I did not, Pegeen Mike. It was a dark, lonesome place to
be hearing the like of him.

PEGEEN: Well, you're a daring fellow, and if they find his corpse
stretched above in the dews of dawn, what'll you say then to the
peelers, or the Justice of the Peace?

SHAWN *thunderstruck*: I wasn't thinking of that. For the love of
God, Pegeen Mike, don't let on I was speaking of him. Don't
tell your father and the men is coming above; for if they heard
that story they'd have great blabbing this night at the wake.

PEGEEN: I'll maybe tell them, and I'll maybe not.

SHAWN: They are coming at the door. Will you whisht, I'm saying?

PEGEEN: Whisht yourself.

*She goes behind counter. Michael James, fat, jovial publican, comes in
followed by Philly Cullen, who is thin and mistrusting, and Jimmy
Farrell, who is fat and amorous, about forty-five.*

MEN *together*: God bless you! The blessing of God on this place!

PEGEEN: God bless you kindly.

MICHAEL *to men, who go to the counter*: Sit down now, and take
your rest. *Crosses to Shawn at the fire*. And how is it you are
Shawn Keogh? Are you coming over the sands to Kate
Cassidy's wake?

SHAWN: I am not, Michael James. I'm going home the short cut to
my bed.

PEGEEN *speaking across the counter*: He's right, too, and have you
no shame, Michael James, to be quitting off for the whole night,
and leaving myself lonesome in the shop?

MICHAEL *good-humouredly*: Isn't it the same whether I go for the whole night or a part only? and I'm thinking it's a queer daughter you are if you'd have me crossing backward through the Stooks of the Dead Women, with a drop taken.

PEGEEN: If I am a queer daughter, it's a queer father'd be leaving me lonesome these twelve hours of dark, and I piling the turf with the dogs barking, and the calves mooing, and my own teeth rattling with the fear.

JIMMY *flatteringly*: What is there to hurt you, and you a fine, hardy girl would knock the heads of any two men in the place?

PEGEEN *working herself up*: Isn't there the harvest boys with their tongues red for drink, and the ten tinkers is camped in the east glen, and the thousand militia – bad cess to them! – walking idle through the land. There's lots surely to hurt me, and I won't stop alone in it, let himself do what he will.

MICHAEL: If you're that afeard, let Shawn Keogh stop along with you. It's the will of God, I'm thinking, himself should be seeing to you now.

They all turn on Shawn.

SHAWN *in horrified confusion*: I would and welcome, Michael James, but I'm afeard of Father Reilly; and what at all would the Holy Father and the Cardinals of Rome be saying if they heard I did the like of that.

MICHAEL *with contempt*: God help you! Can't you sit in by the hearth with the light lit and herself beyond in the room? You'll do that surely, for I've heard tell there's a queer fellow above, going mad or getting his death, maybe, in the gripe of the ditch, so she'd be safer this night with a person here.

SHAWN *with plaintive despair*: I'm afeard of Father Reilly, I'm saying. Let you not be tempting me, and we near married itself.

PHILLY *with cold contempt*: Lock him in the west room. He'll stay then and have no sin to be telling to the priest.

MICHAEL *to Shawn, getting between him and the door*: Go up now.

SHAWN *at the top of his voice*: Don't stop me, Michael James. Let me out of the door, I'm saying, for the love of the Almighty God. Let me out. *Trying to dodge past him.* Let me out of it, and may God grant you His indulgence in the hour of need.

MICHAEL *loudly*: Stop your noising, and sit down by the hearth. *Gives him a push and goes to counter, laughing.*

SHAWN *turning back, wringing his hands*: Oh, Father Reilly, and the saints of God, where will I hide myself to-day? Oh, St Joseph and St Patrick and St Brigid and St James, have mercy on me now!

Shawn turns round, sees door clear, and makes a rush for it.

MICHAEL *catching him by the coat-tail*: You'd be going, is it?

SHAWN *screaming*: Leave me go, Michael James, leave me go, you old Pagan, leave me go, or I'll get the curse of the priests on you, and of the scarlet-coated bishops of the Courts of Rome.

With a sudden movement he pulls himself out of his coat, and disappears out of the door, leaving his coat in Michael's hands.

MICHAEL *turning round, and holding up coat*: Well, there's the coat of a Christian man. Oh, there's sainted glory this day in the lonesome west; and by the will of God I've got you a decent man, Pegeen, you'll have no call to be spying after if you've a score of young girls, maybe, weeding in your fields.

PEGEEN *taking up the defence of her property*: What right have you to be making game of a poor fellow for minding the priest, when it's your own fault is, not paying a penny pot-boy to stand along with me and give me courage in the doing of my work. *She snaps the coat away from him, and goes behind counter with it.*

MICHAEL *taken aback*: Where would I get a pot-boy? Would you have me send the bell-man screaming in the streets of Castlebar?

SHAWN *opening the door a chink and putting in his hand, in a small voice*: Michael James!

MICHAEL *imitating him*: What ails you?

SHAWN: The queer dying fellow's beyond looking over the ditch. He's come up, I'm thinking, stealing your hens. *Looks over his shoulder.* God help me, he's following me now (*he runs into room*) and if he's heard what I said, he'll be having my life, and I going home lonesome in the darkness of the night.

For a perceptible moment they watch the door with curiosity. Someone coughs outside. Then Christy Mahon, a slight young man, comes in very tired and frightened and dirty.

CHRISTY *in a small voice*: God save all here!

MEN: God save you kindly!

CHRISTY *going to the counter*: I'd trouble you for a glass of porter, woman of the house. *He puts down coin.*

PEGEEN *serving him*: You're one of the tinkers, young fellow, is beyond camped in the glen?

CHRISTY: I am not; but I'm destroyed walking.

MICHAEL *patronizingly*: Let you come up then to the fire. You're looking famished with the cold.

CHRISTY: God reward you. *He takes up his glass and goes a little way across to the left, then stops and looks about him.* Is it often the polis do be coming into this place, master of the house?

MICHAEL: If you'd come in better hours, you'd have seen 'Licensed for the Sale of Beer and Spirits, to be Consumed on the Premises,' written in white letters above the door, and what would the polis want spying on me, and not a decent house within four miles, the way every living Christian is a bona fide, saving one widow alone?

CHRISTY *with relief*: It's a safe house, so.

He goes over to the fire, sighing and moaning. Then he sits down, putting his glass beside him, and begins gnawing a turnip, too miserable to feel the others staring at him with curiosity.

MICHAEL *going after him*: Is it yourself is fearing the polis? You're wanting, maybe?

CHRISTY: There's many wanting.

MICHAEL: Many, surely, with the broken harvest and the ended wars. *He picks up some stockings, etc., that are near the fire, and carries them away furtively.* It should be larceny, I'm thinking?

CHRISTY *dolefully*: I had it in my mind it was a different word and a bigger.

PEGEEN: There's a queer lad. Were you never slapped in school, young fellow, and you don't know the name of your deed?

CHRISTY *bashfully*: I'm slow at learning, a middling scholar only.

MICHAEL: If you're a dunce itself, you'd have a right to know that larceny's robbing and stealing. Is it for the like of that you're wanting?

CHRISTY *with a flash of family pride*: And I the son of a strong farmer (*with a sudden qualm*), God rest his soul, could have bought up the whole of your old house a while since, from the butt of his tail-pocket, and not have missed the weight of it gone.

MICHAEL *impressed*: If it's not stealing, it's maybe something big.

CHRISTY *flattered*: Aye, it's maybe something big.

JIMMY: He's a wicked-looking young fellow. Maybe he followed after a young woman on a lonesome night.

CHRISTY *shocked*: Oh, the saints forbid, mister; I was all times a decent lad.

PHILLY *turning on Jimmy*: You're a silly man, Jimmy Farrell. He said his father was a farmer a while since, and there's himself now in a poor state. Maybe the land was grabbed from him, and he did what any decent man would do.

MICHAEL *to Christy, mysteriously*: Was it bailiffs?

CHRISTY: The divil a one.

MICHAEL: Agents?

CHRISTY: The divil a one.

MICHAEL: Landlords?

CHRISTY *peevishly*: Ah, not at all, I'm saying. You'd see the like of them stories on any little paper of a Munster town. But I'm not calling to my mind any person, gentle, simple, judge or jury, did the like of me.

They all draw nearer with delighted curiosity.

PHILLY: Well, that lad's a puzzle-the-world.

JIMMY: He'd beat Dan Davies' circus, or the holy missioners making sermons on the villainy of man. Try him again, Philly.

PHILLY: Did you strike golden guineas out of solder, young fellow, or shilling coins itself?

CHRISTY: I did not, mister, not sixpence nor a farthing coin.

JIMMY: Did you marry three wives maybe? I'm told there's a sprinkling have done that among the holy Luthers of the preaching north.

CHRISTY *shyly*: I never married with one, let alone with a couple or three.

PHILLY: Maybe he went fighting for the Boers, the like of the man beyond, was judged to be hanged, quartered, and drawn. Were you off east, young fellow, fighting bloody wars for Kruger and the freedom of the Boers?

CHRISTY: I never left my own parish till Tuesday was a week.

PEGEEN *coming from counter*: He's done nothing, so. *To Christy*. If you didn't commit murder or a bad, nasty thing; or false coining, or robbery, or butchery, or the like of them, there isn't anything that would be worth your troubling for to run from now. You did nothing at all.

CHRISTY *his feelings hurt*: That's an unkindly thing to be saying to a poor orphaned traveller, has a prison behind him, and hanging before, and hell's gap gaping below.

PEGEEN *with a sign to the men to be quiet*: You're only saying it. You did nothing at all. A soft lad the like of you wouldn't slit the wind pipe of a screeching sow.

CHRISTY *offended*: You're not speaking the truth.

PEGEEN *in mock rage*: Not speaking the truth, is it? Would you have me knock the head of you with the butt of the broom?

CHRISTY *twisting round on her with a sharp cry of horror*: Don't strike me. I killed my poor father, Tuesday was a week, for doing the like of that.

PEGEEN *with blank amazement*: Is it killed your father?

CHRISTY *subsiding*: With the help of God I did, surely, and that the Holy Immaculate Mother may intercede for his soul.

PHILLY *retreating with Jimmy*: There's a daring fellow.

JIMMY: Oh, glory be to God!

MICHAEL *with great respect*: That was a hanging crime, mister honey. You should have had good reason for doing the like of that.

CHRISTY *in a very reasonable tone*: He was a dirty man, God forgive him, and he getting old and crusty, the way I couldn't put up with him at all.

PEGEEN: And you shot him dead?

CHRISTY *shaking his head*: I never used weapons. I've no licence, and I'm a law-fearing man.

MICHAEL: It was with a hilted knife maybe? I'm told, in the big world, it's bloody knives they use.

CHRISTY *loudly, scandalized*: Do you take me for a slaughter-boy?

PEGEEN: You never hanged him, the way Jimmy Farrell hanged

og from the licence, and had it screeching and wriggling
e hours at the butt of a string, and himself swearing it was
ead dog, and the peelers swearing it had life?

CHRISTY: I did not, then. I just riz the loy and let fall the edge of
it on the ridge of his skull, and he went down at my feet like an
empty sack, and never let a grunt or groan from him at all.

MICHAEL *making a sign to Pegeen to fill Christy's glass*: And what
way weren't you hanged, mister? Did you bury him then?

CHRISTY *considering*: Aye. I buried him then. Wasn't I digging
spuds in the field?

MICHAEL: And the peelers never followed after you the eleven
days that you're out?

CHRISTY *shaking his head*: Never a one of them, and I walking
forward facing hog, dog, or divil on the highway of the road.

PHILLY *nodding wisely*: It's only with a common week-day kind of
a murderer them lads would be trusting their carcass, and that
man should be a great terror when his temper's roused.

MICHAEL: He should then. *To Christy*. And where was it, mister
honey, that you did the deed?

CHRISTY *looking at him with suspicion*: Oh, a distant place, master
of the house, a windy corner of high, distant hills.

PHILLY *nodding with approval*: He's a close man, and he's right,
surely.

PEGEEN: That'd be a lad with the sense of Solomon to have for a
pot-boy, Michael James, if it's the truth you're seeking one at all.

PHILLY: The peelers is fearing him, and if you'd that lad in the
house there isn't one of them would come smelling around if the
dogs itself were lapping poteen from the dung-pit of the yard.

JIMMY: Bravery's a treasure in a lonesome place, and a lad would
kill his father, I'm thinking, would face a foxy divil with a
pitchpike on the flags of hell.

PEGEEN: It's the truth they're saying, and if I'd that lad in the
house, I wouldn't be fearing the loosèd khaki cut-throats, or the
walking dead.

CHRISTY *swelling with surprise and triumph*: Well, glory be to God!

MICHAEL *with deference*: Would you think well to stop here and be
pot-boy, mister honey, if we gave you good wages, and didn't
destroy you with the weight of work?

SHAWN *coming forward uneasily*: That'd be a queer kind to bring into a decent, quiet household with the like of Pegeen Mike.

PEGEEN *very sharply*: Will you whisht? Who's speaking to you?

SHAWN *retreating*: A bloody-handed murderer the like of . . .

PEGEEN *snapping at him*: Whisht, I am saying: we'll take no fooling from your like at all. *To Christy, with a honeyed voice*. And you young fellow, you'd have a right to stop, I'm thinking, for we'd do our all and utmost to content your needs.

CHRISTY *overcome with wonder*: And I'd be safe this place from the searching law?

MICHAEL: You would, surely. If they're not fearing you, itself, the peelers in this place is decent, drouthy poor fellows, wouldn't touch a cur dog and not give warning in the dead of night.

PEGEEN *very kindly and persuasively*: Let you stop a short while anyhow. Aren't you destroyed walking with your feet in bleeding blisters, and your whole skin needing washing like a Wicklow sheep.

CHRISTY *looking round with satisfaction*: It's a nice room, and if it's not humbugging me you are, I'm thinking that I'll surely stay.

JIMMY *jumps up*: Now, by the grace of God, herself will be safe this night, with a man killed his father holding danger from the door, and let you come on, Michael James, or they'll have the best stuff drunk at the wake.

MICHAEL *going to the door with men*: And begging your pardon mister, what name will we call you, for we'd like to know?

CHRISTY: Christopher Mahon.

MICHAEL: Well, God bless you, Christy, and a good rest till we meet again when the sun'll be rising to the noon of day.

CHRISTY: God bless you all.

MEN: God bless you.

They go out, except Shawn, who lingers at the door.

SHAWN *to Pegeen*: Are you wanting me to stop along with you and keep you from harm?

PEGEEN *gruffly*: Didn't you say you were fearing Father Reilly?

SHAWN: There'd be no harm staying now, I'm thinking, and himself in it too.

PEGEEN: You wouldn't stay when there was need for you, and let you step off nimble this time when there's none.

SHAWN: Didn't I say it was Father Reilly . . .

PEGEEN: Go on, then, to Father Reilly (*in a jeering tone*), and let him put you in the holy brotherhoods, and leave that lad to me.

SHAWN: If I meet the Widow Quin . . .

PEGEEN: Go on, I'm saying, and don't be waking this place with your noise. *She hustles him out and bolts door.* That lad would wear the spirits from the saints of peace. *Bustles about, then takes off her apron and pins it up in the window as a blind, Christy watching her timidly. Then she comes to him and speaks with bland good humour.* Let you stretch out now by the fire, young fellow. You should be destroyed travelling.

CHRISTY *shyly again, drawing off his boots*: I'm tired surely, walking wild eleven days, and waking fearful in the night. *He holds up one of his feet, feeling his blisters, and looking at them with compassion.*

PEGEEN *standing beside him, watching him with delight*: You should have had great people in your family, I'm thinking, with the little, small feet you have, and you with a kind of a quality name, the like of what you'd find on the great powers and potentates of France and Spain.

CHRISTY *with pride*: We were great, surely, with wide and windy acres of rich Munster land.

PEGEEN: Wasn't I telling you, and you a fine, handsome young fellow with a noble brow?

CHRISTY *with a flush of delighted surprise*: Is it me?

PEGEEN: Aye. Did you never hear that from the young girls where you come from in the west or south?

CHRISTY *with venom*: I did not, then. Oh, they're bloody liars in the naked parish where I grew a man.

PEGEEN: If they are itself, you've heard it these days, I'm thinking, and you walking the world telling out your story to young girls or old.

CHRISTY: I've told my story no place till this night, Pegeen Mike, and it's foolish I was here, maybe, to be talking free; but you're decent people, I'm thinking, and yourself a kindly woman, the way I wasn't fearing you at all.

PEGEEN *filling a sack with straw*: You've said the like of that, maybe, in every cot and cabin where you've met a young girl on your way.

CHRISTY *going over to her, gradually raising his voice*: I've said it nowhere till this night, I'm telling you; for I've seen none the like of you the eleven long days I am walking the world, looking over a low ditch or a high ditch on my north or south, into stony, scattered fields, or scribes of bog, where you'd see young, limber girls, and fine, prancing women making laughter with the men.

PEGEEN: If you weren't destroyed travelling, you'd have as much talk and streeleen, I'm thinking, as Owen Roe O'Sullivan or the poets of the Dingle Bay; and I've heard all times it's the poets are your like – fine, fiery fellows with great rages when their temper's roused.

CHRISTY *drawing a little nearer to her*: You've a power of rings, God bless you, and would there be any offence if I was asking are you single now?

PEGEEN: What would I want wedding so young?

CHRISTY *with relief*: We're alike, so.

PEGEEN *she puts sack on settle and beats it up*: I never killed my father. I'd be afeard to do that, except I was the like of yourself with blind rages tearing me within, for I'm thinking you should have had great tussling when the end was come.

CHRISTY *expanding with delight at the first confidential talk he has ever had with a woman*: We had not then. It was a hard woman was come over the hill; and if he was always a crusty kind, when he'd a hard woman setting him on, not the divil himself or his four fathers could put up with him at all.

PEGEEN *with curiosity*: And isn't it a great wonder that one wasn't fearing you?

CHRISTY *very confidentially*: Up to the day I killed my father, there wasn't a person in Ireland knew the kind I was, and I there drinking, waking, eating, sleeping, a quiet, simple poor fellow with no man giving me heed.

PEGEEN *getting a quilt out of cupboard and putting it on the sack*: It was the girls were giving you heed, maybe, and I'm thinking it's most conceit you'd have to be gaming with their like.

CHRISTY *shaking his head, with simplicity*: Not the girls itself, and I won't tell you a lie. There wasn't any one heeding me in that place saving only the dumb beasts of the field. *He sits down at fire.*

PEGEEN *with disappointment*: And I thinking you should have been living the like of a king of Norway or the eastern world. *She comes and sits beside him after placing bread and mug of milk on the table.*

CHRISTY *laughing piteously*: The like of a king, is it? And I after toiling, moiling, digging, dodging from the dawn till dusk; with never a sight of joy or sport saving only when I'd be abroad in the dark night poaching rabbits on hills, for I was a divil to poach, God forgive me (*very naïvely*), and I near got six months for going with a dung fork and stabbing a fish.

PEGEEN: And it's that you'd call sport, is it, to be abroad in the darkness with yourself alone?

CHRISTY: I did, God help me, and there I'd be as happy as the sunshine of St Martin's Day, watching the light passing the north or the patches of fog, till I'd hear a rabbit starting to screech and I'd go running in the furze. Then, when I'd my full share, I'd come walking down where you'd see the ducks and geese stretched sleeping on the highway of the road, and before I'd pass the dunghill, I'd hear himself snoring out – a loud, lonesome snore he'd be making all times, the while he was sleeping; and he a man'd be raging all times, the while he was waking, like a gaudy officer you'd hear cursing and damning and swearing oaths.

PEGEEN: Providence and Mercy, spare us all!

CHRISTY: It's that you'd say surely if you seen him and he after drinking for weeks, rising up in the red dawn, or before it maybe, and going out into the yard as naked as an ash-tree in the moon of May, and shying clods against the visage of the stars till he'd put the fear of death into the banbhs and the screeching sows.

PEGEEN: I'd be well-nigh afeard of that lad myself, I'm thinking. And there was no one in it but the two of you alone?

CHRISTY: The divil a one, though he'd sons and daughters walking all great states and territories of the world, and not a one of them, to this day, but would say their seven curses on him, and they rousing up to let a cough or sneeze, maybe, in the deadness of the night.

PEGEEN *nodding her head*: Well, you should have been a queer lot. I never cursed my father the like of that, though I'm twenty and more years of age.

CHRISTY: Then you'd have cursed mine, I'm telling you, and he a man never gave peace to any, saving when he'd get two months or three, or be locked in the asylums for battering peelers or assaulting men (*with depression*), the way it was a bitter life he led me till I did up a Tuesday and halve his skull.

PEGEEN *putting her hand on his shoulder*: Well, you'll have peace in this place, Christy Mahon, and none to trouble you, and it's near time a fine lad like you should have your good share of the earth.

CHRISTY: It's time surely, and I a seemly fellow with great strength in me and bravery of . . .

Someone knocks.

Clinging to Pegeen. Oh, glory! it's late for knocking, and this last while I'm in terror of the peelers, and the walking dead.

Knocking again.

PEGEEN: Who's there?
VOICE: Me.
PEGEEN: Who's me?
VOICE: The Widow Quin.
PEGEEN *jumping up and giving him the bread and milk*: Go on now with your supper, and let on to be sleepy, for if she found you were such a warrant to talk, she'd be stringing gabble till the dawn of day.

He takes bread and sits shyly with his back to the door.

Opening door, with temper. What ails you, or what is it you're wanting at this hour of the night?

WIDOW QUIN *coming in a step and peering at Christy*: I'm after meeting Shawn Keogh and Father Reilly below, who told me of your curiosity man, and they fearing by this time he was maybe roaring, romping on your hands with drink.

PEGEEN *pointing to Christy*: Look now is he roaring, and he stretched out drowsy with his supper and his mug of milk. Walk down and tell that to Father Reilly and to Shaneen Keogh.

WIDOW QUIN *coming forward*: I'll not see them again, for I've their word to lead that lad forward for to lodge with me.

PEGEEN *in blank amazement*: This night is it?

WIDOW QUIN *going over*: This night. 'It isn't fitting,' says the priesteen, 'to have his likeness lodging with an orphaned girl.' *To Christy.* God save you, mister!

CHRISTY *shyly*: God save you kindly!

WIDOW QUIN *looking at him with half amused curiosity*: Well, aren't you a little smiling fellow? It should have been great and bitter torments did rouse your spirits to a deed of blood.

CHRISTY *doubtfully*: It should, maybe.

WIDOW QUIN: It's more than 'maybe' I'm saying, and it'd soften my heart to see you sitting so simple with your cup and cake, and you fitter to be saying your catechism than slaying your da.

PEGEEN *at counter, washing glasses*: There's talking when any'd see he's fit to be holding his head high with the wonders of the world. Walk on from this, for I'll not have him tormented, and he destroyed travelling since Tuesday was a week.

WIDOW QUIN *peaceably*: We'll be walking surely when his supper's done, and you'll find we're great company, young fellow, when it's of the like of you and me you'd hear the penny poets singing in an August Fair.

CHRISTY *innocently*: Did you kill your father?

PEGEEN *contemptuously*: She did not. She hit himself with a worn pick, and the rusted poison did corrode his blood the way he never overed it, and died after. That was a sneaky kind of murder did win small glory with the boys itself. *She crosses to Christy's left.*

WIDOW QUIN *with good humour*: If it didn't, maybe all knows a widow woman has buried her children and destroyed her man is a wiser comrade for a young lad than a girl, the like of you, who'd go helter-skeltering after any man would let you a wink upon the road.

PEGEEN *breaking out into wild rage*: And you'll say that, Widow Quin, and you gasping with the rage you had racing the hill beyond to look on his face.

WIDOW QUIN *laughing derisively*: Me, is it? Well, Father Reilly has cuteness to divide you now. *She pulls Christy up.* There's great temptation in a man did slay his da, and we'd best be going, young fellow; so rise up and come with me.

PEGEEN *seizing his arm*: He'll not stir. He's pot-boy in this place, and I'll not have him stolen off and kidnapped while himself's abroad.

WIDOW QUIN: It'd be a crazy pot-boy'd lodge him in the shebeen where he works by day, so you'd have a right to come on, young fellow, till you see my little houseen, a perch off on the rising hill.

PEGEEN: Wait till morning, Christy Mahon. Wait till you lay eyes on her leaky thatch is growing more pasture for her buck goat than her square of fields, and she without a tramp itself to keep in order her place at all.

WIDOW QUIN: When you see me contriving in my little gardens, Christy Mahon, you'll swear the Lord God formed me to be living lone, and that there isn't my match in Mayo for thatching, or mowing, or shearing a sheep.

PEGEEN *with noisy scorn*: It's true the Lord God formed you to contrive indeed. Doesn't the world know you reared a black ram at your own breast, so that the Lord Bishop of Connaught felt the elements of a Christian, and he eating it after in a kidney stew? Doesn't the world know you've been shaving the foxy skipper from France for a threepenny-bit and a sop of grass tobacco would wring the liver from a mountain goat you'd meet leaping the hills?

WIDOW QUIN *with amusement*: Do you hear her now, young fellow? Do you hear the way she'll be rating at your own self when a week is by?

PEGEEN *to Christy*: Don't heed her. Tell her to go on into the pigsty and not plague us here.

WIDOW QUIN: I'm going; but he'll come with me.

PEGEEN *shaking him*: Are you dumb, young fellow?

CHRISTY *timidly to Widow Quin*: God increase you; but I'm pot-boy in this place, and it's here I liefer stay.

PEGEEN *triumphantly*: Now you have heard him, and go on from this.

WIDOW QUIN *looking round the room*: It's lonesome this hour crossing the hill, and if he won't come along with me, I'd have a right maybe to stop this night with yourselves. Let me stretch out on the settle, Pegeen Mike; and himself can lie by the hearth.

PEGEEN *short and fiercely*: Faith, I won't. Quit off or I will send you now.

WIDOW QUIN *gathering her shawl up*: Well, it's a terror to be aged a score. *To Christy*. God bless you now, young fellow, and let you be wary, or there's right torment will await you here if you go romancing with her like, and she waiting only, as they bade me say, on a sheepskin parchment to be wed with Shawn Keogh of Killakeen.

CHRISTY *going to Pegeen as she bolts door*: What's that she's after saying?

PEGEEN: Lies and blather, you've no call to mind. Well, isn't Shawn Keogh an impudent fellow to send up spying on me? Wait till I lay hands on him. Let him wait, I'm saying.

CHRISTY: And you're not wedding him at all?

PEGEEN: I wouldn't wed him if a bishop came walking for to join us here.

CHRISTY: That God in glory may be thanked for that.

PEGEEN: There's your bed now. I've put a quilt upon you I'm after quilting a while since with my own two hands, and you'd best stretch out now for your sleep, and may God give you a good rest till I call you in the morning when the cocks will crow.

CHRISTY *as she goes to inner room*: May God and Mary and St Patrick bless you and reward you for your kindly talk.

She shuts the door behind her. He settles his bed slowly, feeling the quilt with immense satisfaction.

Well, it's a clean bed and soft with it, and it's great luck and company I've won me in the end of time – two fine women fighting for the likes of me – till I'm thinking this night wasn't I a foolish fellow not to kill my father in the years gone by.

CURTAIN

ACT TWO

Scene as before. Brilliant morning light. Christy, looking bright and cheerful, is cleaning a girl's boots.

CHRISTY *to himself, counting jugs on dresser:* Half a hundred beyond. Ten there. A score that's above. Eighty jugs. Six cuts and a broken one. Two plates. A power of glasses. Bottles, a school-master'd be hard set to count, and enough in them, I'm thinking, to drunken all the wealth and wisdom of the county Clare. *He puts down the boot carefully.* There's her boots now, nice and decent for her evening use, and isn't it grand brushes she has? *He puts them down and goes by degrees to the looking-glass.* Well, this'd be a fine place to be my whole life talking out with swearing Christians, in place of my old dogs and cat; and I stalking around, smoking my pipe and drinking my fill, and never a day's work but drawing a cork an odd time, or wiping a glass, or rinsing out a shiny tumbler for a decent man. *He takes the looking-glass from the wall and puts it on the back of a chair; then sits down in front of it and begins washing his face.* Didn't I know rightly, I was handsome, though it was the divil's own mirror we had beyond, would twist a squint across an angel's brow; and I'll be growing fine from this day, the way I'll have a soft lovely skin on me and won't be the like of the clumsy young fellows do be ploughing all times in the earth and dung. *He starts.* Is she coming again? *He looks out.* Stranger girls. God help me, where'll I hide myself away and my long neck naked to the world? *He looks out.* I'd best go to the room maybe till I'm dressed again.

He gathers up his coat and the looking-glass, and runs into the inner room. The door is pushed open, and Susan Brady looks in, and knocks on door.

SUSAN: There's nobody in it. *Knocks again.*
NELLY *pushing her in and following her, with Honor Blake and Sara Tansey:* It'd be early for them both to be out walking the hill.
SUSAN: I'm thinking Shawn Keogh was making game of us, and there's no such man in it at all.

HONOR *pointing to straw and quilt*: Look at that. He's been sleeping there in the night. Well, it'll be a hard case if he's gone off now the way we'll never set our eyes on a man killed his father, and we after rising early and destroying ourselves running fast on the hill.

NELLY: Are you thinking them's his boots?

SARA *taking them up*: If they are, there should be his father's track on them. Did you never read in the papers the way murdered men do bleed and drip?

SUSAN: Is that blood there, Sara Tansey?

SARA *smelling it*: That's bog water, I'm thinking; but it's his own they are, surely, for I never seen the like of them for whitey mud, and red mud, and turf on them, and the fine sands of the sea. That man's been walking, I'm telling you. *She goes down right, putting on one of his boots.*

SUSAN *going to window*: Maybe he's stolen off to Belmullet with the boots of Michael James, and you'd have a right so to follow after him, Sara Tansey, and you the one yoked the ass-cart and drove ten miles to set your eyes on the man bit the yellow lady's nostril on the northern shore. *She looks out.*

SARA *running to window, with one boot on*: Don't be talking, and we fooled to-day. *Putting on the other boot.* There's a pair do fit me well and I'll be keeping them for walking to the priest, when you'd be ashamed this place, going up winter and summer with nothing worth while to confess at all.

HONOR *who has been listening at door*: Whisht! there's someone inside the room. *She pushes door a chink open.* It's a man.

Sara kicks off boots and puts them where they were. They all stand in a line looking through chink.

SARA: I'll call him. Mister! Mister! *He puts in his head.* Is Pegeen within?

CHRISTY *coming in as meek as a mouse, with the looking-glass held behind his back*: She's above on the cnuceen, seeking the nanny goats, the way she'd have a sup of goat's milk for to colour my tea.

SARA: And asking your pardon, is it you's the man killed his father?

CHRISTY *sidling towards the nail where the glass was hanging*: I am, God help me!

SARA *taking eggs she has brought*: Then my thousand welcomes to you, and I've run up with a brace of duck's eggs for your food to-day. Pegeen's ducks is no use, but these are the real rich sort. Hold out your hand and you'll see it's no lie I'm telling you.

CHRISTY *coming forward shyly, and holding out his left hand*: They're a great and weighty size.

SUSAN: And I run up with a pat of butter, for it'd be a poor thing to have you eating your spuds dry, and you after running a great way since you did destroy your da.

CHRISTY: Thank you kindly.

HONOR: And I brought you a little cut of a cake, for you should have a thin stomach on you, and you that length walking the world.

NELLY: And I brought you a little laying pullet – boiled and all she is – was crushed at the fall of night by the curate's car. Feel the fat of the breast, mister.

CHRISTY: It's bursting, surely. *He feels it with the back of his hand in which he holds the presents.*

SARA: Will you pinch it? Is your right hand too sacred for to use at all? *She slips round behind him.* It's a glass he has. Well, I never seen to this day a man with a looking-glass held to his back. Them that kills their fathers is a vain lot surely.

Girls giggle.

CHRISTY *smiling innocently and piling presents on glass*: I'm very thankful to you all to-day. . . .

WIDOW QUIN *coming in quickly, at door*: Sara Tansey, Susan Brady, Honor Blake! What in glory has you here at this hour of day?

GIRLS *giggling*: That's the man killed his father.

WIDOW QUIN *coming to them*: I know well it's the man; and I'm after putting him down in the sports below for racing, leaping, pitching, and the Lord knows what.

SARA *exuberantly*: That's right, Widow Quin. I'll bet my dowry that he'll lick the world.

WIDOW QUIN: If you will, you'd have a right to have him fresh and nourished in place of nursing a feat. *Taking presents.* Are you fasting or fed, young fellow?

CHRISTY: Fasting, if you please.

WIDOW QUIN *loudly*: Well, you're the lot. Stir up now and give him his breakfast. *To Christy.* Come here to me (*she puts him on bench beside her while the girls make tea and get his breakfast*), and let you tell us your story before Pegeen will come, in place of grinning your ears off like the moon of May.

CHRISTY *beginning to be pleased*: It's a long story; you'd be destroyed listening.

WIDOW QUIN: Don't be letting on to be shy, a fine, gamy, treacherous lad the like of you. Was it in your house beyond you cracked his skull?

CHRISTY *shy but flattered*: It was not. We were digging spuds in his cold, sloping, stony, divil's patch of a field.

WIDOW QUIN: And you went asking money of him, or making talk of getting a wife would drive him from his farm?

CHRISTY: I did not, then; but there I was, digging and digging, and 'You squinting idiot,' says he, 'let you walk down now and tell the priest you'll wed the Widow Casey in a score of days.'

WIDOW QUIN: And what kind was she?

CHRISTY *with horror*: A walking terror from beyond the hills, and she two score and five years, and two hundred-weights and five pounds in the weighing scales, with a limping leg on her, and a blinded eye, and she a woman of noted misbehaviour with the old and young.

GIRLS *clustering round him, serving him*: Glory be.

WIDOW QUIN: And what did he want driving you to wed with her? *She takes a bit of the chicken.*

CHRISTY *eating with growing satisfaction*: He was letting on I was wanting a protector from the harshness of the world, and he without a thought the whole while but how he'd have her hut to live in and her gold to drink.

WIDOW QUIN: There's maybe worse than a dry hearth and a widow woman and your glass at night. So you hit him then?

CHRISTY *getting almost excited*: I did not. 'I won't wed her,' says I, 'when all know she did suckle me for six weeks when I came into the world, and she a hag this day with a tongue on her has the crows and seabirds scattered, the way they wouldn't cast a shadow on her garden with the dread of her curse.'

WIDOW QUIN *teasingly*: That one should be right company.

SARA *eagerly*: Don't mind her. Did you kill him then?

CHRISTY: 'She's too good for the like of you,' says he, 'and go on now or I'll flatten you out like a crawling beast has passed under a dray.' 'You will not if I can help it,' says I. 'Go on,' says he, 'or I'll have the divil making garters of your limbs to-night.' 'You will not if I can help it,' says I. *He sits up brandishing his mug.*

SARA: You were right surely.

CHRISTY *impressively*: With that the sun came out between the cloud and the hill, and it shining green in my face. 'God have mercy on your soul,' says he, lifting a scythe. 'Or on your own,' says I, raising the loy.

SUSAN: That's a grand story.

HONOR: He tells it lovely.

CHRISTY *flattered and confident, waving bone*: He gave a drive with the scythe, and I gave a lep to the east. Then I turned around with my back to the north, and I hit a blow on the ridge of his skull, laid him stretched out, and he split to the knob of his gullet. *He raises the chicken bone to his Adam's apple.*

GIRLS *together*: Well, you're a marvel! Oh, God bless you! You're the lad, surely!

SUSAN: I'm thinking the Lord God sent him this road to make a second husband to the Widow Quin, and she with a great yearning to be wedded, though all dread her here. Lift him on her knee, Sara Tansey.

WIDOW QUIN: Don't tease him.

SARA *going over to dresser and counter very quickly and getting two glasses and porter*: You're heroes, surely, and let you drink a supeen with your arms linked like the outlandish lovers in the sailor's song. *She links their arms and gives them the glasses.* There now. Drink a health to the wonders of the western world, the pirates, preachers, poteen-makers, with the jobbing jockies; parching peelers, and the juries fill their stomachs selling judgments of the English law. *Brandishing the bottle.*

WIDOW QUIN: That's a right toast, Sara Tansey. Now, Christy.

They drink with their arms linked, he drinking with his left hand, she with her right. As they are drinking, Pegeen Mike comes in with a milk-can and stands aghast. They all spring away from Christy. He goes down left. Widow Quin remains seated.

PEGEEN *angrily to Sara*: What is it you're wanting?

SARA *twisting her apron*: An ounce of tobacco.

PEGEEN: Have you tuppence?

SARA: I've forgotten my purse.

PEGEEN: Then you'd best be getting it and not be fooling us here. *To the Widow Quin, with more elaborate scorn*. And what is it you're wanting, Widow Quin?

WIDOW QUIN *insolently*: A penn-orth of starch.

PEGEEN *breaking out*: And you without a white shift or a shirt in your whole family since the drying of the flood. I've no starch for the like of you, and let you walk on now to Killamuck.

WIDOW QUIN *turning to Christy, as she goes out with the girls*: Well, you're mighty huffy this day, Pegeen Mike, and you, young fellow, let you not forget the sports and racing when the noon is by.

They go out.

PEGEEN *imperiously*: Fling out that rubbish and put them cups away.

Christy tidies away in great haste.

Shove in the bench by the wall.

He does so.

And hang that glass on the nail. What disturbed it at all?

CHRISTY *very meekly*: I was making myself decent only, and this a fine country for young lovely girls.

PEGEEN *sharply*: Whisht your talking of girls. *Goes to counter on right*.

CHRISTY: Wouldn't any wish to be decent in a place . . .

PEGEEN: Whisht, I'm saying.

CHRISTY *looks at her face for a moment with great misgivings, then as a last effort takes up a loy, and goes towards her, with feigned assurance*: It was with a loy the like of that I killed my father.

PEGEEN *still sharply*: You've told me that story six times since the dawn of day.

CHRISTY *reproachfully*: It's a queer thing you wouldn't care to be hearing it and them girls after walking four miles to be listening to me now.

PEGEEN *turning round astonished*: Four miles?

CHRISTY *apologetically*: Didn't himself say there were only bona fides living in the place?

PEGEEN: It's bona fides by the road they are, but that lot came over the river lepping the stones. It's not three perches when you go like that, and I was down this morning looking on the papers the post-boy does have in his bag. *With meaning and emphasis*. For there was great news this day, Christopher Mahon. *She goes into room on left.*

CHRISTY *suspiciously*: Is it news of my murder?

PEGEEN *inside*: Murder, indeed.

CHRISTY *loudly*: A murdered da?

PEGEEN *coming in again and crossing right*: There was not, but a story filled half a page of the hanging of a man. Ah, that should be a fearful end, young fellow, and it worst of all for a man destroyed his da; for the like of him would get small mercies, and when it's dead he is they'd put him in a narrow grave, with cheap sacking wrapping him round, and pour down quicklime on his head, the way you'd see a woman pouring any frish-frash from a cup.

CHRISTY *very miserably*: Oh, God help me. Are you thinking I'm safe? You were saying at the fall of night I was shut of jeopardy and I here with yourselves.

PEGEEN *severely*: You'll be shut of jeopardy no place if you go talking with a pack of wild girls the like of them do be walking abroad with the peelers, talking whispers at the fall of night.

CHRISTY *with terror*: And you're thinking they'd tell?

PEGEEN *with mock sympathy*: Who know, God help you?

CHRISTY *loudly*: What joy would they have to bring hanging to the likes of me?

PEGEEN: It's queer joys they have, and who knows the thing they'd do, if it'd make the green stones cry itself to think of you swaying and swiggling at the butt of a rope, and you with a fine,

neck, God bless you! the way you'd be a half an hour, in
anguish, getting your death.

CHRISTY *getting his boots and putting them on*: If there's that terror
of them, it'd be best, maybe, I went on wandering like Esau or
Cain and Abel on the sides of Neifin or the Erris plain.

PEGEEN *beginning to play with him*: It would, maybe, for I've heard
the circuit judges this place is a heartless crew.

CHRISTY *bitterly*: It's more than judges this place is a heartless crew.
Looking up at her. And isn't it a poor thing to be starting again,
and I a lonesome fellow will be looking out on women and girls
the way the needy fallen spirits do be looking on the Lord.

PEGEEN: What call have you to be that lonesome when there's
poor girls walking Mayo in their thousands now?

CHRISTY *grimly*: It's well you know what call I have. It's well you
know it's a lonesome thing to be passing small towns with the
lights shining sideways when the night is down, or going in
strange places with a dog noising before you and a dog noising
behind, or drawn to the cities where you'd hear a voice kissing
and talking deep love in every shadow of the ditch, and you
passing on with an empty, hungry stomach failing from your
heart.

PEGEEN: I'm thinking you're an odd man, Christy Mahon. The
oddest walking fellow I ever set my eyes on to this hour to-day.

CHRISTY: What would any be but odd men and they living
lonesome in the world?

PEGEEN: I'm not odd, and I'm my whole life with my father only.

CHRISTY *with infinite admiration*: How would a lovely, handsome
woman the like of you be lonesome when all men should be
thronging around to hear the sweetness of your voice, and the
little infant children should be pestering your steps, I'm
thinking, and you walking the roads.

PEGEEN: I'm hard set to know what way a coaxing fellow the like
of yourself should be lonesome either.

CHRISTY: Coaxing?

PEGEEN: Would you have me think a man never talked with the
girls would have the words you've spoken to-day? It's only
letting on you are to be lonesome, they way you'd get around
me now.

CHRISTY: I wish to God I was letting on; but I was lonesome all times, and born lonesome, I'm thinking, as the moon of dawn. *Going to door.*

PEGEEN *puzzled by his talk*: Well, it's a story I'm not understanding at all why you'd be worse than another, Christy Mahon, and you a fine lad with the great savagery to destroy your da.

CHRISTY: It's little I'm understanding myself, saving only that my heart's scalded this day, and I going off stretching out the earth between us, the way I'll not be waking near you another dawn of the year till the two of us do arise to hope or judgment with the saints of God, and now I'd best be going with my wattle in my hand, for hanging is a poor thing (*turning to go*), and it's little welcome only is left me in this house to-day.

PEGEEN *sharply*: Christy.

He turns round.

Come here to me.

He goes towards her.

Lay down that switch and throw some sods on the fire. You're pot-boy in this place, and I'll not have you mitch off from us now.

CHRISTY: You were saying I'd be hanged if I stay.

PEGEEN *quite kindly at last*: I'm after going down and reading the fearful crimes of Ireland for two weeks or three, and there wasn't a word of your murder. *Getting up and going over to the counter.* They've likely not found the body. You're safe so with ourselves.

CHRISTY *astonished, slowly*: It's making game of me you were (*following her with fearful joy*), and I can stay so, working at your side, and I not lonesome from this mortal day.

PEGEEN: What's to hinder you staying, except the widow woman or the young girls would inveigle you off?

CHRISTY *with rapture*: And I'll have your words from this day filling my ears, and that look is come upon you meeting my two eyes, and I watching you loafing around in the warm sun, or rinsing your ankles when the night is come.

PEGEEN *kindly, but a little embarrassed*: I'm thinking you'll be a loyal young lad to have working around, and if you vexed me a while since with your leaguing with the girls, I wouldn't give a thraneen for a lad hadn't a mighty spirit in him and a gamy heart.

Shawn Keogh runs in carrying a cleeve on his back, followed by the Widow Quin.

SHAWN *to Pegeen*: I was passing below, and I seen your mountainy sheep eating cabbages in Jimmy's field. Run up or they'll be bursting surely.

PEGEEN: Oh, God mend them!

She puts a shawl over her head and runs out.

CHRISTY *looking from one to the other. Still in high spirits*: I'd best go to her aid maybe. I'm handy with ewes.

WIDOW QUIN *closing the door*: She can do that much, and there is Shaneen has long speeches for to tell you now. *She sits down with an amused smile.*

SHAWN *taking something from his pocket and offering it to Christy*: Do you see that, mister?

CHRISTY *looking at it*: The half of a ticket to the Western States!

SHAWN *trembling with anxiety*: I'll give it to you and my new hat (*pulling it out of hamper*); and my breeches with the double seat (*pulling it out*); and my new coat is woven from the blackest shearings for three miles around (*giving him the coat*); I'll give you the whole of them, and my blessing, and the blessing of Father Reilly itself, maybe, if you'll quit from this and leave us in the peace we had till last night at the fall of dark.

CHRISTY *with a new arrogance*: And for what is it you're wanting to get shut of me?

SHAWN *looking to the Widow for help*: I'm a poor scholar with middling faculties to coin a lie, so I'll tell you the truth, Christy Mahon. I'm wedding with Pegeen beyond, and I don't think well of having a clever fearless man the like of you dwelling in her house.

CHRISTY *almost pugnaciously*: And you'd be using bribery for to banish me?

SHAWN *in an imploring voice*: Let you not take it badly, mister honey; isn't beyond the best place for you, where you'll have golden chains and shiny coats and you riding upon hunters with the ladies of the land. *He makes an eager sign to the Widow Quin to come to help him.*

WIDOW QUIN *coming over*: It's true for him, and you'd best quit off and not have that poor girl setting her mind on you, for there's Shaneen thinks she wouldn't suit you, though all is saying that she'll wed you now.

Christy beams with delight.

SHAWN *in terrified earnest*: She wouldn't suit you, and she with the divil's own temper the way you'd be strangling one another in a score of days. *He makes the movement of strangling with his hands.* It's the like of me only that she's fit for; a quiet simple fellow wouldn't raise a hand upon her if she scratched itself.

WIDOW QUIN *putting Shawn's hat on Christy*: Fit them clothes on you anyhow, young fellow, and he'd maybe loan them to you for the sports. *Pushing him towards inner door.* Fit them on and you can give your answer when you have them tried.

CHRISTY *beaming, delighted with the clothes*: I will then. I'd like herself to see me in them tweeds and hat.

He goes into room and shuts the door.

SHAWN *in great anxiety*: He'd like herself to see them. He'll not leave us, Widow Quin. He's a score of divils in him the way it's well-nigh certain he will wed Pegeen.

WIDOW QUIN *jeeringly*: It's true all girls are fond of courage and do hate the like of you.

SHAWN *walking about in desperation*: Oh, Widow Quin, what'll I be doing now? I'd inform again him, but he'd burst from Kilmainham and he'd be sure and certain to destroy me. If I wasn't so God-fearing, I'd near have courage to come behind him and run a pike into his side. Oh, it's a hard case to be an orphan and not to have your father that you're used to, and you'd easy kill and make yourself a hero in the sight of all. *Coming up to her.* Oh, Widow Quin, will you find me some contrivance when I've promised you a ewe?

WIDOW QUIN: A ewe's a small thing, but what would you give me if I did wed him and did save you so?

SHAWN *with astonishment*: You?

WIDOW QUIN: Aye. Would you give me the red cow you have and the mountainy ram, and the right of way across your rye path, and a load of dung at Michaelmas, and turbary upon the western hill?

SHAWN *radiant with hope*: I would, surely, and I'd give you the wedding-ring I have, and the loan of a new suit, the way you'd have him decent on the wedding-day. I'd give you two kids for your dinner, and a gallon of poteen, and I'd call the piper on the long car to your wedding from Crossmolina or from Ballina. I'd give you . . .

WIDOW QUIN: That'll do, so, and let you whisht, for he's coming now again.

Christy comes in very natty in the new clothes. Widow Quin goes to him admiringly.

If you seen yourself now, I'm thinking you'd be too proud to speak to at all, and it'd be a pity surely to have your like sailing from Mayo to the western world.

CHRISTY *as proud as a peacock*: I'm not going. If this is a poor place itself, I'll make myself contented to be lodging here.

Widow Quin makes a sign to Shawn to leave them.

SHAWN: Well, I'm going measuring the racecourse while the tide is low, so I'll leave you the garments and my blessing for the sports to-day. God bless you!

He wriggles out.

WIDOW QUIN *admiring Christy*: Well, you're mighty spruce, young fellow. Sit down now while you're quiet till you talk with me.

CHRISTY *swaggering*: I'm going abroad on the hillside for to seek Pegeen.

WIDOW QUIN: You'll have time and plenty for to seek Pegeen, and you heard me saying at the fall of night the two of us should be great company.

CHRISTY: From this out I'll have no want of company when all sorts is bringing me their food and clothing (*he swaggers to the door, tightening his belt*), the way they'd set their eyes upon a gallant orphan cleft his father with one blow to the breeches

belt. *He opens door, then staggers back.* Saints of Glory! Holy
angels from the throne of light!

WIDOW QUIN *going over*: What ails you?

CHRISTY: It's the walking spirit of my murdered da!

WIDOW QUIN *looking out*: Is it that tramper?

CHRISTY *wildly*: Where'll I hide my poor body from that ghost of
hell?

*The door is pushed open, and old Mahon appears on threshold. Christy
darts in behind door.*

WIDOW QUIN *in great amazement*: God save you, my poor man.

MAHON *gruffly*: Did you see a young lad passing this way in the
early morning or the fall of night?

WIDOW QUIN: You're a queer kind to walk in not saluting at all.

MAHON: Did you see the young lad?

WIDOW QUIN *stiffly*: What kind was he?

MAHON: An ugly young streeler with a murderous gob on him,
and a little switch in his hand. I met a tramper seen him coming
this way at the fall of night.

WIDOW QUIN: There's harvest hundreds do be passing these days
for the Sligo boat. For what is it you're wanting him, my poor
man?

MAHON: I want to destroy him for breaking the head on me with
the clout of a loy. *He takes off a big hat, and shows his head in a
mass of bandages and plaster, with some pride.* It was he did that,
and amn't I a great wonder to think I've traced him ten days
with that rent in my crown?

WIDOW QUIN *taking his head in both hands and examining it with
extreme delight*: That was a great blow. And who hit you? A
robber maybe?

MAHON: It was my own son hit me, and he the divil a robber, or
anything else, but a dirty, stuttering lout.

WIDOW QUIN *letting go his skull and wiping her hands in her apron*:
You'd best be wary of a mortified scalp, I think they call it,
lepping around with that wound in the splendour of the sun. It
was a bad blow, surely, and you should have vexed him fearful
to make him strike that gash in his da.

MAHON: Is it me?

WIDOW QUIN *amusing herself*: Aye. And isn't it a great shame when the old and hardened do torment the young?

MAHON *raging*: Torment him is it? And I after holding out with the patience of a martyred saint till there's nothing but destruction on me, and I'm driven out in my old age with none to aid me.

WIDOW QUIN *greatly amused*: It's a sacred wonder the way that wickedness will spoil a man.

MAHON: My wickedness, is it? Amn't I after saying it is himself has me destroyed, and he a lier on walls, a talker of folly, a man you'd see stretched the half of the day in the brown ferns with his belly to the sun.

WIDOW QUIN: Not working at all?

MAHON: The divil a work, or if he did itself, you'd see him raising up a haystack like the stalk of a rush, or driving our last cow till he broke her leg at the hip, and when he wasn't at that he'd be fooling over little birds he had – finches and felts – or making mugs at his own self in the bit of a glass we had hung on the wall.

WIDOW QUIN *looking at Christy*: What way was he so foolish? It was running wild after the girls maybe?

MAHON *with a shout of derision*: Running wild, is it? If he seen a red petticoat coming swinging over the hill, he'd be off to hide in the sticks, and you'd see him shooting out his sheep's eyes between the little twigs and the leaves, and his two ears rising like a hare looking out through a gap. Girls, indeed!

WIDOW QUIN: It was drink maybe?

MAHON: And he a poor fellow would get drunk on the smell of a pint. He'd a queer rotten stomach, I'm telling you, and when I gave him three pulls from my pipe a while since, he was taken with contortions till I had to send him in the ass-cart to the females' nurse.

WIDOW QUIN *clasping her hands*: Well, I never, till this day, heard tell of a man the like of that!

MAHON: I'd take a mighty oath you didn't, surely, and wasn't he the laughing joke of every female woman where four baronies meet, the way the girls would stop their weeding if they seen him coming the road to let a roar at him, and call him the loony of Mahon's?

WIDOW QUIN: I'd give the world and all to see the like of him. What kind was he?

MAHON: A small, low, fellow.

WIDOW QUIN: And dark?

MAHON: Dark and dirty.

WIDOW QUIN *considering*: I'm thinking I seen him.

MAHON *eagerly*: An ugly young blackguard.

WIDOW QUIN: A hideous, fearful villain, and the spit of you.

MAHON: What way is he fled?

WIDOW QUIN: Gone over the hills to catch a coasting steamer to the north or south.

MAHON: Could I pull up on him now?

WIDOW QUIN: If you'll cross the sands below where the tide is out, you'll be in it as soon as himself, for he had to go round ten miles by the top of the bay. *She points to the door.* Strike down by the head beyond and then follow on the roadway to the north and east.

Mahon goes abruptly.

Shouting after him. Let you give him a good vengeance when you come up with him, but don't put yourself in the power of the law, for it'd be a poor thing to see a judge in his black cap reading out his sentence on a civil warrior the like of you. *She swings the door to and looks at Christy, who is cowering in terror, for a moment, then she bursts into a laugh.* Well, you're the walking Playboy of the Western World, and that's the poor man you had divided to his breeches belt.

CHRISTY *looking out; then, to her*: What'll Pegeen say when she hears that story? What'll she be saying to me now?

WIDOW QUIN: She'll knock the head of you, I'm thinking, and drive you from the door. God help her to be taking you for a wonder, and you a little schemer making up a story you destroyed your da.

CHRISTY *turning to the door, nearly speechless with rage, half to himself*: To be letting on he was dead, and coming back to his life, and following after me like an old weasel tracing a rat, and coming in here laying desolation between my own self and the fine women of Ireland, and he a kind of carcass that you'd fling upon the sea. . . .

WIDOW QUIN *more soberly*: There's talking for a man's one only son.

CHRISTY *breaking out*: His one son, is it? May I meet him with one tooth and it aching, and one eye to be seeing seven and seventy divils in the twists of the road, and one old timber leg on him to limp into the scalding grave. *Looking out.* There he is now crossing the strands, and that the Lord God would send a high wave to wash him from the world.

WIDOW QUIN *scandalized*: Have you no shame? *Putting her hand on his shoulder and turning him round.* What ails you? Near crying, is it?

CHRISTY *in despair and grief*: Amn't I after seeing the love-light of the star of knowledge shining from her brow, and hearing words would put you thinking on the holy Brigid speaking to the infant saints, and now she'll be turning again, and speaking hard words to me, like an old woman with a spavindy ass she'd have, urging on a hill.

WIDOW QUIN: There's poetry talk for a girl you'd see itching and scratching, and she with a stale stink of poteen on her from selling in the shop.

CHRISTY *impatiently*: It's her like is fitted to be handling merchandise in the heavens above, and what'll I be doing now, I ask you, and I a kind of wonder was jilted by the heavens when a day was by.

There is a distant noise of girls' voices. Widow Quin looks from window and comes to him, hurriedly.

WIDOW QUIN: You'll be doing like myself, I'm thinking, when I did destroy my man, for I'm above many's the day, odd times in great spirits, abroad in the sunshine, darning a stocking or stitching a shift; and odd times again looking out on the schooners, hookers, trawlers is sailing the sea, and I thinking on the gallant hairy fellows are drifting beyond, and myself long years living alone.

CHRISTY *interested*: You're like me, so.

WIDOW QUIN: I am your like, and it's for that I'm taking a fancy to you, and I with my little houseen above where there'd be myself to tend you, and none to ask were you a murderer or what at all.

CHRISTY: And what would I be doing if I left Pegeen?

WIDOW QUIN: I've nice jobs you could be doing – gathering shells to make a whitewash for our hut within, building up a little goose-house, or stretching a new skin on an old curragh I have, and if my hut is far from all sides, it's there you'll meet the wisest old men, I tell you, at the corner of my wheel, and it's there yourself and me will have great times whispering and hugging. . . .

VOICES *outside, calling far away*: Christy! Christy Mahon! Christy!

CHRISTY: Is it Pegeen Mike?

WIDOW QUIN: It's the young girls, I'm thinking, coming to bring you to the sports below, and what is it you'll have me to tell them now?

CHRISTY: Aid me for to win Pegeen. It's herself only that I'm seeking now.

Widow Quin gets up and goes to window.

Aid me for to win her, and I'll be asking God to stretch a hand to you in the hour of death, and lead you short cuts through the Meadows of Ease, and up the floor of heaven to the Footstool of the Virgin's Son.

WIDOW QUIN: There's praying!

VOICES *nearer*: Christy! Christy Mahon!

CHRISTY *with agitation*: They're coming. Will you swear to aid and save me, for the love of Christ?

WIDOW QUIN *looks at him for a moment*: If I aid you, will you swear to give me a right of way I want, and a mountainy ram, and a load of dung at Michaelmas, the time that you'll be master here?

CHRISTY: I will, by the elements and stars of night.

WIDOW QUIN: Then we'll not say a word of the old fellow, the way Pegeen won't know your story till the end of time.

CHRISTY: And if he chances to return again?

WIDOW QUIN: We'll swear he's a maniac and not your da. I could take an oath I seen him raving on the sands to-day.

Girls run in.

SUSAN: Come on to the sports below. Pegeen says you're to come.

SARA TANSEY: The lepping's beginning, and we've a jockey's suit to fit upon you for the mule race on the sands below.

HONOR: Come on, will you?

CHRISTY: I will then if Pegeen's beyond.

SARA: She's in the boreen making game of Shaneen Keogh.

CHRISTY: Then I'll be going to her now.

He runs out, followed by the girls.

WIDOW QUIN: Well, if the worst comes in the end of all, it'll be great game to see there's none to pity him but a widow woman, the like of me, has buried her children and destroyed her man.

She goes out.

CURTAIN

ACT THREE

Scene as before. Later in the day. Jimmy comes in, slightly drunk.

JIMMY *calls*: Pegeen! *Crosses to inner door.* Pegeen Mike! *Comes back again into the room.* Pegeen!

Philly comes in in the same state.

To Philly. Did you see herself?

PHILLY: I did not; but I sent Shawn Keogh with the ass-cart for to bear him home. *Trying cupboards, which are locked.* Well, isn't he a nasty man to get into such staggers at a morning wake; and isn't herself the divil's daughter for locking, and she so fussy after that young gaffer, you might take your death with drouth and none to heed you?

JIMMY: It's little wonder she'd be fussy, and he after bringing bankrupt ruin on the roulette man, and the tick-o'-the-loop man, and breaking the noise of the cockshot-man, and winning all in the sports below, racing, lepping, dancing, and the Lord knows what! He's right luck, I'm telling you.

PHILLY: If he has, he'll be rightly hobbled yet, and he not able to say ten words without making a brag of the way he killed his father, and the great blow he hit with the loy.

JIMMY: A man can't hang by his own informing, and his father should be rotten by now.

Old Mahon passes window slowly.

PHILLY: Supposing a man's digging spuds in that field with a long spade, and supposing he flings up the two halves of that skull, what'll be said then in the papers and the courts of law?

JIMMY: They'd say it was an old Dane, maybe, was drowned in the flood.

Old Mahon comes in and sits down near door listening.

Did you never hear tell of the skulls they have in the city of Dublin, ranged out like blue jugs in a cabin of Connaught?

PHILLY: And you believe that?

JIMMY *pugnaciously*: Didn't a lad see them and he after coming from harvesting in the Liverpool boat? 'They have them there,' says he, 'making a show of the great people there was one time walking the world. White skulls and black skulls and yellow skulls, and some with full teeth, and some haven't only but one.'

PHILLY: It was no lie, maybe, for when I was a young lad there was a graveyard beyond the house with the remnants of a man who had thighs as long as your arm. He was a horrid man, I'm telling you, and there was many a fine Sunday I'd put him together for fun, and he with shiny bones, you wouldn't meet the like of these days in the cities of the world.

MAHON *getting up*: You wouldn't, is it? Lay your eyes on that skull, and tell me where and when there was another the like of it, is splintered only from the blow of a loy.

PHILLY: Glory be to God! And who hit you at all?

MAHON *triumphantly*: It was my own son hit me. Would you believe that?

JIMMY: Well, there's wonders hidden in the heart of man!

PHILLY *suspiciously*: And what way was it done?

MAHON *wandering about the room*: I'm after walking hundreds and long scores of miles, winning clean beds and the fill of my belly four times in the day, and I doing nothing but telling stories of that naked truth. *He comes to them a little aggressively*. Give me a supeen and I'll tell you now.

Widow Quin comes in and stands aghast behind him. He is facing Jimmy and Philly, who are on the left.

JIMMY: Ask herself beyond. She's the stuff hidden in her shawl.

WIDOW QUIN *coming to Mahon quickly*: You here, is it? You didn't go far at all?

MAHON: I seen the coasting steamer passing, and I got a drouth upon me and a cramping leg, so I said: 'The divil go along with him,' and turned again. *Looking under her shawl*. And let you give me a supeen, for I'm destroyed travelling since Tuesday was last week.

WIDOW QUIN *getting a glass, in a cajoling tone*: Sit down then by the fire and take your ease for a space. You've a right to be destroyed indeed, with your walking, and fighting, and facing the sun. *Giving him poteen from a stone jar she has brought in*. There now is a drink for you, and may it be to your happiness and length of life.

MAHON *taking glass greedily, and sitting down by fire*: God increase you!

WIDOW QUIN *taking men to the right stealthily*: Do you know what? That man's raving from his wound to-day, for I met him a while since telling a rambling tale of a tinker had him destroyed. Then he heard of Christy's deed, and he up and says it was his son had cracked his skull. Oh, isn't madness a fright, for he'll go killing someone yet, and he thinking it's the man has struck him so?

JIMMY *entirely convinced*: It's a fright surely. I knew a party was kicked in the head by a red mare, and he went killing horses a great while, till he eat the insides of a clock and died after.

PHILLY *with suspicion*: Did he see Christy?

WIDOW QUIN: He didn't. *With a warning gesture*. Let you not be putting him in mind of him, or you'll be likely summoned if there's murder done. *Looking round at Mahon*. Whisht! He's listening. Wait now till you hear me taking him easy and unravelling all. *She goes to Mahon*. And what way are you feeling, mister? Are you in contentment now?

MAHON *slightly emotional from his drink*: I'm poorly only, for it's a hard story the way I'm left to-day, when it was I did tend him from his hour of birth, and he a dunce never reached his second book, the way he'd come from school, many's the day, with his legs lamed under him, and he blackened with his beatings like a tinker's ass. It's a hard story, I'm saying, the way some do have their next and nighest raising up a hand of murder on them, and some is lonesome getting their death with lamentation in the dead of night.

WIDOW QUIN *not knowing what to say*: To hear you talking so quiet, who'd know you were the same fellow we seen pass to-day?

MAHON: I'm the same surely. The wrack and ruin of threescore years; and it's a terror to live that length, I tell you, and to have your sons going to the dogs against you, and you wore out scolding them, and skelping them, and Gods knows what.

PHILLY *to Jimmy*: He's not raving. *To Widow Quin*. Will you ask him what kind was his son?

WIDOW QUIN *to Mahon, with a peculiar look*: Was your son that hit you a lad of one year and a score maybe, a great hand at racing and lepping and licking the world?

MAHON *turning on her with a roar of rage*: Didn't you hear me say he was the fool of men, the way from this out he'll know the orphan's lot, with old and young making game of him, and they swearing, raging, kicking at him like a mangy cur.

A great burst of cheering outside, some way off.

> *Putting his hands to his ears.* What in the name of God do they want roaring below?

WIDOW QUIN *with the shade of a smile*: They're cheering a young lad, the champion Playboy of the Western World.

More cheering.

MAHON *going to window*: It'd split my heart to hear them, and I with pulses in my brain-pan for a week gone by. Is it racing they are?

JIMMY *looking from door*: It is, then. They are mounting him for the mule race will be run upon the sands. That's the playboy on the winkered mule.

MAHON *puzzled*: That lad, is it? If you said it was a fool he was, I'd have laid a mighty oath he was the likeness of my wandering son. *Uneasily, putting his hand to his head.* Faith, I'm thinking I'll go walking for to view the race.

WIDOW QUIN *stopping him, sharply*: You will not. You'd best take the road to Belmullet, and not be dilly-dallying in this place where there isn't a spot you could sleep.

PHILLY *coming forward*: Don't mind her. Mount there on the bench and you'll have a view of the whole. They're hurrying before the tide will rise, and it'd be near over if you went down the pathway through the crags below.

MAHON *mounts on bench, Widow Quin beside him*: That's a right view again the edge of the sea. They're coming now from the point. He's leading. Who is he at all?

WIDOW QUIN: He's the champion of the world, I tell you, and there isn't a ha'p'orth isn't falling lucky to his hands to-day.

PHILLY *looking out, interested in the race*: Look at that. They're pressing him now.

JIMMY: He'll win it yet.

PHILLY: Take your time, Jimmy Farrell. It's too soon to say.

WIDOW QUIN *shouting*: Watch him taking the gate. There's riding!

JIMMY *cheering*: More power to the young lad!

MAHON: He's passing the third.

JIMMY: He'll lick them yet.

WIDOW QUIN: He'd lick them if he was running races with a score itself.

MAHON: Look at the mule he has, kicking the stars.

WIDOW QUIN: There was a lep! *Catching hold of Mahon in her excitement.* He's fallen? He's mounted again! Faith, he's passing them all!

JIMMY: Look at him skelping her!

PHILLY: And the mountain girls hooshing him on!

JIMMY: It's the last turn! The post's cleared for them now!

MAHON: Look at the narrow place. He'll be into the bogs! *With a yell.* Good rider! He's through it again.

JIMMY: He's neck and neck!

MAHON: Good boy to him! Flames, but he's in!

Great cheering, in which all join.

> *With hesitation.* What's that? They're raising him up. They're coming this way. *With a roar of rage and astonishment.* It's Christy, by the stars of God! I'd know his way of spitting and he astride the moon.

He jumps down and makes a run for the door, but Widow Quin catches him and pulls him back.

WIDOW QUIN: Stay quiet, will you? That's not your son. *To Jimmy.* Stop him, or you'll get a month for the abetting of manslaughter and be fined as well.

JIMMY: I'll hold him.

MAHON *struggling*: Let me out! Let me out, the lot of you, till I have my vengence on his head to-day.

WIDOW QUIN *shaking him, vehemently*: That's not your son. That's a man is going to make marriage with the daughter of this house, a place with fine trade, a licence, and with poteen too.

MAHON *amazed*: That man marrying a decent and a moneyed girl! Is it mad yous are? Is it in a crazy-house for females that I'm landed now?

WIDOW QUIN: It's mad yourself is with the blow upon your head. That lad is the wonder of the western world.

MAHON: I seen it's my son.

WIDOW QUIN: You seen that you're mad. *Cheering outside.* Do you hear them cheering him in the zigzags of the road? Aren't you after saying that your son's a fool, and how would they be cheering a true idiot born?

MAHON *getting distressed*: It's maybe out of reason that that man's himself. *Cheering again.* There's none surely will go cheering him. Oh, I'm raving with a madness that would fright the world! *He sits down with his hand to his head.* There was one time I seen ten scarlet divils letting on they'd cork my spirit in a gallon can; and one time I seen rats as big as badgers sucking the lifeblood from the butt of my lug; but I never till this day confused that dribbling idiot with a likely man. I'm destroyed surely.

WIDOW QUIN: And who'd wonder when it's your brain-pan that is gaping now?

MAHON: Then the blight of the sacred drouth upon myself and him, for I never went mad to this day, and I not three weeks with the Limerick girls drinking myself silly and parlatic from the dusk to dawn. *To Widow Quin, suddenly.* Is my visage astray?

WIDOW QUIN: It is, then. You're a sniggering maniac, a child could see.

MAHON *getting up more cheerfully*: Then I'd best be going to the union beyond, and there'll be a welcome before me, I tell you (*with great pride*), and I a terrible and fearful case, the way that there I was one time, screeching in a straitened waistcoat, with seven doctors writing out my sayings in a printed book. Would you believe that?

WIDOW QUIN: If you're a wonder itself, you'd best be hasty, for them lads caught a maniac one time and pelted the poor creature till he ran out, raving and foaming, and was drowned in the sea.

MAHON *with philosophy*: It's true mankind is the divil when your head's astray. Let me out now and I'll slip down the boreen, and not see them so.

WIDOW QUIN *showing him out*: That's it. Run to the right, and not a one will see.

He runs off.

PHILLY *wisely*: You're at some gaming, Widow Quin; but I'll walk after him and give him his dinner and a time to rest, and I'll see then if he's raving or as sane as you.

WIDOW QUIN *annoyed*: If you go near that lad, let you be wary of your head, I'm saying. Didn't you hear him telling he was crazed at times?

PHILLY: I heard him telling a power; and I'm thinking we'll have right sport before night will fall.

He goes out.

JIMMY: Well, Philly's a conceited and foolish man. How could that madman have his senses and his brain-pan slit? I'll go after them and see him turn on Philly now.

He goes; Widow Quin hides poteen behind counter. Then hubbub outside.

VOICES: There you are! Good jumper! Grand lepper! Darlint boy! He's the racer! Bear him on, will you!

Christy comes in, in jockey's dress, with Pegeen Mike, Sara, and other girls and men.

PEGEEN *to crowd*: Go on now, and don't destroy him, and he drenching with sweat. Go along, I'm saying, and have your tug-of-warring till he's dried his skin.

CROWD: Here's his prizes! A bagpipes! A fiddle was played by a poet in the years gone by! A flat and three-thorned blackthorn would lick the scholars out of Dublin town!

CHRISTY *taking prizes from the men*: Thank you kindly, the lot of you. But you'd say it was little only I did this day if you'd seen me a while since striking my one single blow.

TOWN CRIER *outside ringing a bell*: Take notice, last event of this day! Tug-of-warring on the green below! Come on, the lot of you! Great achievements for all Mayo men!

PEGEEN: Go on and leave him for to rest and dry. Go on, I tell you, for he'll do no more.

She hustles crowd out; Widow Quin following them.

MEN *going*: Come on, then. Good luck for the while!

PEGEEN *radiantly, wiping his face with her shawl*: Well, you're the lad, and you'll have great times from this out when you could win that wealth of prizes, and you sweating in the heat of noon!

CHRISTY *looking at her with delight*: I'll have great times if I win the crowning prize I'm seeking now, and that your promise that you'll wed me in a fortnight, when our banns is called.

PEGEEN *backing away from him*: You've right daring to go ask me that, when all knows you'll be starting to some girl in your own townland, when your father's rotten in four months, or five.

CHRISTY *indignantly*: Starting from you, is it? *He follows her.* I will not, then, and when the airs is warming, in four months or five, it's then yourself and me should be pacing Neifin in the dews of night, the times sweet smells do be rising, and you'd see a little, shiny, new moon, maybe sinking on the hills.

PEGEEN *looking at him playfully*: And it's that kind of a poacher's love you'd make, Christy Mahon, on the sides of Neifin, when the night is down?

CHRISTY: It's little you'll think if my love's a poacher's, or an earl's itself, when you'll feel my two hands stretched around you, and I squeezing kisses on your puckered lips, till I'd feel a kind of pity for the Lord God is all ages sitting lonesome in His golden chair.

PEGEEN: That'll be right fun, Christy Mahon, and any girl would walk her heart out before she'd meet a young man was your like for eloquence, or talk at all.

CHRISTY *encouraged*: Let you wait, to hear me talking, till we're astray in Erris, when Good Friday's by, drinking a sup from a well, and making mighty kisses with our wetted mouths, or gaming in a gap of sunshine, with yourself stretched back unto your necklace, in the flowers of the earth.

PEGEEN *in a low voice, moved by his tone*: I'd be nice so, is it?

CHRISTY *with rapture*: If the mitred bishops seen you that time, they'd be the like of the holy prophets, I'm thinking, do be straining the bars of Paradise to lay eyes on the Lady Helen of Troy, and she abroad, pacing back and forward, with a nosegay in her golden shawl.

PEGEEN *with real tenderness*: And what is it I have, Christy Mahon, to make me fitting entertainment for the like of you, that has such poet's talking, and such bravery of heart.

CHRISTY *in a low voice*: Isn't there the light of seven heavens in your heart alone, the way you'll be an angel's lamp to me from this out, and I abroad in the darkness, spearing salmons in the Owen or the Carrowmore?

PEGEEN: If I was your wife I'd be along with you those nights, Christy Mahon, the way you'd see I was a great hand at coaxing bailiffs, or coining funny nicknames for the stars of night.

CHRISTY: You, is it? Taking your death in the hailstones, or in the fogs of dawn.

PEGEEN: Yourself and me would shelter easy in a narrow bush (*with a qualm of dread*); but we're only talking, maybe, for this would be a poor, thatched place to hold a fine lad is the like of you.

CHRISTY *putting his arm round her*: If I wasn't a good Christian, it's on my naked knees I'd be saying my prayers and paters to every jackstraw you have roofing your head, and every stony pebble is paving the laneway to your door.

PEGEEN *radiantly*: If that's the truth I'll be burning candles from this out to the miracles of God that have brought you from the south to-day, and I with my gowns bought ready, the way that I can wed you, and not wait at all.

CHRISTY: It's miracles, and that's the truth. Me there toiling a long while, and walking a long while, not knowing at all I was drawing all times nearer to this holy day.

PEGEEN: And myself, a girl, was tempted often to go sailing the seas till I'd marry a Jew-man, with ten kegs of gold, and I not knowing at all there was the like of you drawing nearer, like the stars of God.

CHRISTY: And to think I'm long years hearing women talking that talk, to all bloody fools, and this the first time I've heard the like of your voice talking sweetly for my own delight.

PEGEEN: And to think it's me is talking sweetly, Christy Mahon, and I the fright of seven townlands for my biting tongue. Well, the heart's a wonder; and, I'm thinking, there won't be our like in Mayo, for gallant lovers, from this hour to-day. (*Drunken singing is heard outside.*) There's my father coming from the wake, and when he's had his sleep we'll tell him, for he's peaceful then.

They separate.

MICHAEL *singing outside:*

> The jailer and the turnkey
> They quickly ran us down,
> And brought us back as prisoners
> Once more to Cavan town.

He comes in supported by Shawn.

> There we lay bewailing
> All in a prison bound. . . .

He see Christy. Goes and shakes him drunkenly by the hand, while Pegeen and Shawn talk on the left.

To Christy. The blessing of God and the holy angels on your head, young fellow. I hear tell you're after winning all in the sports below; and wasn't it a shame I didn't bear you along with me to Kate Cassidy's wake, a fine, stout lad, the like of you, for you'd never see the match of it for flows of drink, the way when we sunk her bones at noonday in her narrow grave, there were five men, aye, and six men, stretched out retching speechless on the holy stones.

CHRISTY *uneasily, watching Pegeen*: Is that the truth?

MICHAEL: It is, then; and aren't you a louty schemer to go burying your poor father unbeknownst when you'd a right to throw him on the crupper of a Kerry mule and drive him westwards, like holy Joseph in the days gone by, the way we could have given him a decent burial, and not have him rotting beyond, and not a Christian drinking a smart drop to the glory of his soul?

CHRISTY *gruffly*: It's well enough he's lying, for the likes of him.

MICHAEL *slapping him on the back*: Well, aren't you a hardened slayer? It'll be a poor thing for the household man where you go sniffing for a female wife; and (*pointing to Shawn*) look beyond at that shy and decent Christian I have chosen for my daughter's hand, and I after getting the gilded dispensation this day for to wed them now.

CHRISTY: And you'll be wedding them this day, is it?

MICHAEL *drawing himself up*: Aye. Are you thinking, if I'm drunk itself, I'd leave my daughter living single with a little frisky rascal is the like of you?

PEGEEN *breaking away from Shawn*: Is it the truth the dispensation's come?

MICHAEL *triumphantly*: Father Reilly's after reading it in gallous Latin, and 'It's come in the nick of time,' says he; 'so I'll wed them in a hurry, dreading that young gaffer who'd capsize the stars.'

PEGEEN *fiercely*: He's missed his nick of time, for it's that lad, Christy Mahon, that I'm wedding now.

MICHAEL *loudly, with horror*: You'd be making him a son to me, and he wet and crusted with his father's blood?

PEGEEN: Aye. Wouldn't it be a bitter thing for a girl to go marrying the like of Shaneen, and he a middling kind of a scarecrow, with no savagery or fine words in him at all?

MICHAEL *gasping and sinking on a chair*: Oh, aren't you a heathen daughter to go shaking the fat of my heart, and I swamped and drownded with the weight of drink? Would you have them turning on me the way that I'd be roaring to the dawn of day with the wind upon my heart? Have you not a word to aid me, Shaneen? Are you not jealous at all?

SHAWN *in great misery*: I'd be afeard to be jealous of a man did slay his da.

PEGEEN: Well, it'd be a poor thing to go marrying your like. I'm seeing there's a world of peril for an orphan girl, and isn't it a great blessing I didn't wed you before himself came walking from the west or south?

SHAWN: It's a queer story you'd go picking a dirty tramp up from the highways of the world.

PEGEEN *playfully*: And you think you're a likely beau to go straying along with, the shiny Sundays of the opening year, when it's sooner on a bullock's liver you'd put a poor girl thinking than on the lily or the rose?

SHAWN: And have you no mind of my weight of passion, and the holy dispensation, and the drift of heifers I'm giving, and the golden ring?

PEGEEN: I'm thinking you're too fine for the like of me, Shawn Keogh of Killakeen, and let you go off till you'd find a radiant lady with droves of bullocks on the plains of Meath, and herself bedizened in the diamond jewelleries of Pharaoh's ma. That'd be your match, Shaneen. So God save you now! *She retreats behind Christy.*

SHAWN: Won't you hear me telling you . . .?

CHRISTY *with ferocity*: Take yourself from this, young fellow, or I'll maybe add a murder to my deeds to-day.

MICHAEL *springing up with a shriek*: Murder is it? Is it mad yous are? Would you go making murder in this place, and it piled with poteen for our drink to-night? Go on to the foreshore if it's fighting you want, where the rising tide will wash all traces from the memory of man. *Pushing Shawn towards Christy.*

SHAWN *shaking himself free, and getting behind Michael*: I'll not fight him, Michael James, I'd liefer live a bachelor, simmering in passions to the end of time, than face a lepping savage the like of him has descended from the Lord knows where. Strike him

yourself, Michael James, or you'll lose my drift of heifers and
my blue bull from Sneem.

MICHAEL: Is it me fight him, when it's father-slaying he's bred to
now? *Pushing Shawn.* Go on, you fool, and fight him now.

SHAWN *coming forward a little*: Will I strike him with my hand?

MICHAEL: Take the loy is on your western side.

SHAWN: I'd be afeard of the gallows if I struck with that.

CHRISTY *taking up the loy*: Then I'll make you face the gallows or
quit off from this.

Shawn flies out of the door.

Well, fine weather be after him (*going to Michael, coaxingly*),
and I'm thinking you wouldn't wish to have that quaking
blackguard in your house at all. Let you give us your blessing
and hear her swear her faith to me, for I'm mounted on the
spring-tide of the stars of luck, the way it'll be good for any to
have me in the house.

PEGEEN *at the other side of Michael*: Bless us now, for I swear to
God I'll wed him, and I'll not renege.

MICHAEL *standing up in the centre, holding on to both of them*: It's the
will of God, I'm thinking, that all should win an easy or a cruel
end, and it's the will of God that all should rear up lengthy
families for the nurture of the earth. What's a single man, I ask
you, eating a bit in one house and drinking a sup in another,
and he with no place of his own, like an old braying jackass
strayed upon the rocks? *To Christy.* It's many would be in dread
to bring your like into their house for to end them, maybe, with
a sudden end; but I'm a decent man of Ireland, and I liefer face
the grave untimely and I seeing a score of grandsons growing
up little gallant swearers by the name of God, than go peopling
my bedside with puny weeds the like of what you'd breed, I'm
thinking, out of Shaneen Keogh. *He joins their hands.* A daring
fellow is the jewel of the world, and a man did split his father's
middle with a single clout should have the bravery of ten, so
may God and Mary and St Patrick bless you, and increase you
from this mortal day.

CHRISTY *and* PEGEEN: Amen, O Lord!

Hubbub outside. Old Mahon rushes in, followed by all the crowd, and

Widow Quin. He makes a rush at Christy, knocks him down, and begins to beat him.

PEGEEN *dragging back his arm*: Stop that, will you? Who are you at all?

MAHON: His father, God forgive me!

PEGEEN *drawing back*: Is it rose from the dead?

MAHON: Do you think I look so easy quenched with the tap of a loy? *Beats Christy again.*

PEGEEN *glaring at Christy*: And it's lies you told, letting on you had him slitted, and you nothing at all.

CHRISTY *catching Mahon's stick*: He's not my father. He's a raving maniac would scare the world. *Pointing to Widow Quin.* Herself knows it is true.

CROWD: You're fooling, Pegeen! The Widow Quin seen him this day, and you likely knew! You're a liar!

CHRISTY *dumbfounded*: It's himself was a liar, lying stretched out with an open head on him, letting on he was dead.

MAHON: Weren't you off racing the hills before I got my breath with the start I had seeing you turn on me at all?

PEGEEN: And to think of the coaxing glory we had given him, and he after doing nothing but hitting a soft blow and chasing northward in a sweat of fear. Quit off from this.

CHRISTY *piteously*: You've seen my doings this day, and let you save me from the old man; for why would you be in such a scorch of haste to spur me to destruction now?

PEGEEN: It's there your treachery is spurring me, till I'm hard set to think you're the one I'm after lacing in my heart-strings half an hour gone by. *To Mahon.* Take him on from this, for I think bad the world should see me raging for a Munster liar, and the fool of men.

MAHON: Rise up now to retribution, and come on with me.

CROWD *jeeringly*: There's the playboy! There's the lad thought he'd rule the roost in Mayo! Slate him now, mister.

CHRISTY *getting up in shy terror*: What is it drives you to torment me here, when I'd asked the thunders of the might of God to blast me if I ever did hurt to any saving only that one single blow.

MAHON *loudly*: If you didn't, you're a poor good-for-nothing, and isn't it by the like of you the sins of the whole world are committed?

CHRISTY *raising his hands*: In the name of the Almighty God . . .

MAHON: Leave troubling the Lord God. Would you have Him sending down droughts, and fevers, and the old hen and the cholera morbus?

CHRISTY *to Widow Quin*: Will you come between us and protect me now?

WIDOW QUIN: I've tried a lot, God help me, and my share is done.

CHRISTY *looking round in desperation*: And I must go back into my torment is it, or run off like a vagabond straying through the unions with the dust of August making mudstains in the gullet of my throat; or the winds of March blowing on me till I'd take an oath I felt them making whistles of my ribs within?

SARA: Ask Pegeen to aid you. Her like does often change.

CHRISTY: I will not, then, for there's torment in the splendour of her like, and she a girl any moon of midnight would take pride to meet, facing southwards on the heaths of Keel. But what did I want crawling forward to scorch my understanding at her flaming brow?

PEGEEN *to Mahon, vehemently, fearing she will break into tears*: Take him on from this or I'll set the young lads to destroy him here.

MAHON *going to him, shaking his stick*: Come on now if you wouldn't have the company to see you skelped.

PEGEEN *half laughing, through her tears*: That's it, now the world will see him pandied, and he an ugly liar was playing off the hero, and the fright of men.

CHRISTY *to Mahon, very sharply*: Let me go!

CROWD: That's it. Now, Christy. If them two set fighting, it will lick the world.

MAHON *making a grab at Christy*: Come here to me.

CHRISTY *more threateningly*: Leave me go, I'm saying.

MAHON: I will, maybe, when your legs is limping, and your back is blue.

CROWD: Keep it up, the two of you. I'll back the old one. Now the playboy.

CHRISTY *in low and intense voice*: Shut your yelling, for if you're after making a mighty man of me this day by the power of a lie, you're setting me now to think if it's a poor thing to be lonesome it's worse, maybe, go mixing with the fools of earth.

Mahon makes a movement towards him.

Almost shouting. Keep off . . . lest I do show a blow unto the lot of you would set the guardian angels winking in the clouds above. *He swings round with a sudden rapid movement and picks up a loy.*

CROWD *half frightened, half amused*: He's going mad! Mind yourselves! Run from the idiot!

CHRISTY: If I am an idiot, I'm after hearing my voice this day saying words would raise the top-knot on a poet in a merchant's town. I've won your racing, and your lepping, and . . .

MAHON: Shut your gullet and come on with me.

CHRISTY: I'm going, but I'll stretch you first.

He runs at old Mahon with the loy, chases him out of the door, followed by crowd and Widow Quin. There is a great noise outside, then a yell, and dead silence for a moment. Christy comes in, half dazed, and goes to fire.

WIDOW QUIN *coming in hurriedly, and going to him*: They're turning again you. Come on, or you'll be hanged, indeed.

CHRISTY: I'm thinking, from this out, Pegeen'll be giving me praises, the same as in the hours gone by.

WIDOW QUIN *impatiently*: Come by the back door. I'd think bad to have you stifled on the gallows tree.

CHRISTY *indignantly*: I will not, then. What good'd be my lifetime if I left Pegeen?

WIDOW QUIN: Come on, and you'll be no worse than you were last night; and you with a double murder this time to be telling to the girls.

CHRISTY: I'll not leave Pegeen Mike.

WIDOW QUIN *impatiently*: Isn't there the match of her in every parish public, from Binghamstown unto the plain of Meath? Come on, I tell you, and I'll find you finer sweethearts at each waning moon.

CHRISTY: It's Pegeen I'm seeking only, and what'd I care if you brought me a drift of chosen females, standing in their shifts itself, maybe, from this place to the eastern world?

SARA *runs in, pulling off one of her petticoats*: They're going to hang him. *Holding out petticoat and shawl.* Fit these upon him, and let him run off to the east.

WIDOW QUIN: He's raving now; but we'll fit them on him, and I'll take him in the ferry to the Achill boat.

CHRISTY *struggling feebly*: Leave me go, will you? when I'm thinking of my luck to-day, for she will wed me surely, and I a proven hero in the end of all.

They try to fasten petticoat round him.

WIDOW QUIN: Take his left hand and we'll pull him now. Come on, young fellow.

CHRISTY *suddenly starting up*: You'll be taking me from her? You're jealous, is it, of her wedding me? Go on from this. *He snatches up a stool, and threatens them with it.*

WIDOW QUIN *going*: It's in the madhouse they should put him, not in jail, at all. We'll go by the back door to call the doctor, and we'll save him so.

She goes out, with Sara, through inner room. Men crowd in the doorway. Christy sits down again by the fire.

MICHAEL *in a terrified whisper*: Is the old lad killed surely?

PHILLY: I'm after feeling the last gasps quitting his heart.

They peer in at Christy.

MICHAEL *with a rope*: Look at the way he is. Twist a hangman's knot on it, and slip it over his head, while he's not minding at all.

PHILLY: Let you take it, Shaneen. You're the soberest of all that's here.

SHAWN: Is it me to go near him, and he the wickedest and worst with me? Let you take it, Pegeen Mike.

PEGEEN: Come on, so.

She goes forward with the others, and they drop the double hitch over his head.

CHRISTY: What ails you?

SHAWN *triumphantly, as they pull the rope tight on his arms*: Come on to the peelers, till they stretch you now.

CHRISTY: Me!

MICHAEL: If we took pity on you the Lord God would, maybe, bring us ruin from the law to-day, so you'd best come easy, for hanging is an easy and a speedy end.

CHRISTY: I'll not stir. *To Pegeen.* And what is it you'll say to me, and I after doing it this time in the face of all?

PEGEEN: I'll say, a strange man is a marvel, with his mighty talk; but what's a squabble in your back yard, and the blow of a loy, have taught me that there's a great gap between a gallous story and a dirty deed. *To men.* Take him on from this, or the lot of us will be likely put on trial for his deed to-day.

CHRISTY *with horror in his voice*: And it's yourself will send me off, to have a horny-fingered hangman hitching slip-knots at the butt of my ear.

MEN *pulling rope*: Come on, will you?

He is pulled down on the floor.

CHRISTY *twisting his legs round the table*: Cut the rope, Pegeen, and I'll quit the lot of you, and live from this out, like the madman of Keel, eating muck and green weeds on the faces of the cliffs.

PEGEEN: And leave us to hang, is it, for a saucy liar, the like of you? *To men.* Take him on, out from this.

SHAWN: Pull a twist on his neck, and squeeze him so.

PHILLY: Twist yourself. Sure he cannot hurt you, if you keep your distance from his teeth alone.

SHAWN: I'm afeard of him. *To Pegeen.* Lift a lighted sod, will you, and scorch his leg.

PEGEEN *blowing the fire with a bellows*: Leave go now, young fellow, or I'll scorch your shins.

CHRISTY: You're blowing for to torture me. *His voice rising and growing stronger.* That's your kind, is it? Then let the lot of you be wary, for, if I've to face the gallows, I'll have a gay march down, I tell you, and shed the blood of some of you before I die.

SHAWN *in terror*: Keep a good hold, Philly. Be wary, for the love of God. For I'm thinking he would liefest wreak his pains on me.

CHRISTY *almost gaily*: If I do lay my hands on you, it's the way you'll be at the fall of night, hanging as a scarecrow for the fowls of hell. Ah, you'll have a gallous jaunt, I'm saying, coaching out through limbo with my father's ghost.

SHAWN *to Pegeen*: Make haste, will you? Oh, isn't he a holy terror, and isn't it true for Father Reilly, that all drink's a curse that has the lot of you so shaky and uncertain now?

CHRISTY: If I can wring a neck among you, I'll have a royal judgment looking on the trembling jury in the courts of law. And won't there by crying out in Mayo the day I'm stretched upon the rope, with ladies in their silks and satins snivelling in their lacy kerchiefs, and they rhyming songs and ballads on the terror of my fate? *He squirms round on the floor and bites Shawn's leg.*

SHAWN *shrieking*: My leg's bit on me. He's the like of a mad dog, I'm thinking, the way that I will surely die.

CHRISTY *delighted with himself*: You will, then, the way you can shake out hell's flags of welcome for my coming in two weeks or three, for I'm thinking Satan hasn't many have killed their da in Kerry, and in Mayo too.

Old Mahon comes in behind on all fours and looks on unnoticed.

MEN *to Pegeen*: Bring the sod, will you?
PEGEEN *coming over*: God help him so. *Burns his leg.*
CHRISTY *kicking and screaming*: Oh, glory be to God!
JIMMY *seeing old Mahon*: Will you look what's come in?

The all drop Christy and run left.

CHRISTY *scrambling on his knees face to face with old Mahon*: Are you coming to be killed a third time, or what ails you now?
MAHON: For what is it they have you tied?
CHRISTY: They're taking me to the peelers to have me hanged for slaying you.
MICHAEL *apologetically*: It is the will of God that all should guard their little cabins from the treachery of law, and what would my daughter be doing if I was ruined or was hanged itself?
MAHON *grimly, loosening Christy*: It's little I care if you put a bag

228

on her back, and went picking cockles till the hour of death; but my son and myself will be going our own way, and we'll have great times from this out telling stories of the villainy of Mayo, and the fools is here. *To Christy, who is freed.* Come on now.

CHRISTY: Go with you, is it? I will then, like a gallant captain with his heathen slave. Go on now and I'll see you from this day stewing my oatmeal and washing my spuds, for I'm master of all fights from now. *Pushing Mahon.* Go on, I'm saying.

MAHON: Is it me?

CHRISTY: Not a word out of you. Go on from this.

MAHON *walking out and looking back at Christy over his shoulder*: Glory be to God! *With a broad smile.* I am crazy again.

Goes.

CHRISTY: Ten thousand blessings upon all that's here, for you've turned me a likely gaffer in the end of all, the way I'll go romancing through a romping lifetime from this hour to the dawning of the Judgment Day.

He goes out.

MICHAEL: By the will of God, we'll have peace now for our drinks. Will you draw the porter, Pegeen?

SHAWN *going up to her*: It's a miracle Father Reilly can wed us in the end of all, and we'll have none to trouble us when his vicious bite is healed.

PEGEEN *hitting him a box on the ear*: Quit my sight. *Putting her shawl over her head and breaking out into wild lamentations.* Oh, my grief, I've lost him surely. I've lost the only Playboy of the Western World.

CURTAIN

Deirdre of the Sorrows

———

LAVARCHAM, Deirdre's nurse

OLD WOMAN, Lavarcham's servant

OWEN, Conchubor's attendant and spy

CONCHUBOR, High King of Ulster

FERGUS, Conchubor's friend

DEIRDRE

NAISI, Deirdre's lover

AINNLE, Naisi's brother

ARDAN, Naisi's brother

TWO SOLDIERS

*Scene: Act I, Lavarcham's house in Slieve Fuadh. Act II, Alban.
Early morning in the beginning of winter. Outside the tent of Deirdre
and Naisi. Act III, tent below Emain Macha*

ACT ONE

Lavarcham's house on Slieve Fuadh. There is a door to inner room on the left, and a door to open air on the right. Window at back and a frame with a half-finished piece of tapestry. There are also a large press and heavy oak chest near the back wall. The place is neat and clean but bare. Lavarcham, woman of fifty, is working at tapestry frame. Old Woman comes in from left.

OLD WOMAN: She hasn't come yet, is it, and it falling to the night?

LAVARCHAM: She has not. . . . *Concealing her anxiety.* It's dark with the clouds are coming from the west and south, but it isn't later than the common.

OLD WOMAN: It's later surely, and I hear tell the Sons of Usna, Naisi and his brothers, are above chasing hares for two days or three, and the same awhile since when the moon was full.

LAVARCHAM *more anxiously*: The gods send they don't set eyes on her – (*with a sign of helplessness*) yet if they do itself, it wasn't my wish brought them or could send them away.

OLD WOMAN *reprovingly*: If it wasn't you'd do well to keep a check on her, and she turning a woman that was meant to be a queen.

LAVARCHAM: Who'd check her like was made to have her pleasure only, the way if there were no warnings told about her you'd see troubles coming when an old king is taking her, and she without a thought but for her beauty and to be straying the hills.

OLD WOMAN: The gods help the lot of us. . . . Shouldn't she be well pleased getting the like of Conchubor, and he middling settled in his years itself? I don't know what he wanted putting her this wild place to be breaking her in, or putting myself to be roasting her supper and she with no patience for her food at all. *She looks out.*

LAVARCHAM: Is she coming from the glen?

OLD WOMAN: She is not. But whisht – there's two men leaving the furze – (*crying out*) it's Conchubor and Fergus along with him. Conchubor'll be in a blue stew this night and herself abroad.

LAVARCHAM *settling room hastily*: Are they close by?

OLD WOMAN: Crossing the stream, and there's herself on the

hillside with a load of twigs. Will I run out and put her in order before they'll set eyes on her at all?

LAVARCHAM: You will not. Would you have him see you, and he a man would be jealous of a hawk would fly between her and the rising sun. *She looks out.* Go up to the hearth and be as busy as if you hadn't seen them at all.

OLD WOMAN *sitting down to polish vessel*: There'll be trouble this night, for he should be in his tempers from the way he's stepping out, and he swinging his hands.

LAVARCHAM *wearied with the whole matter*: It'd be best of all, maybe, if he got in tempers with herself, and made an end quickly, for I'm in a poor way between the pair of them. *Going back to tapestry frame.* There they are now at the door.

Conchubor and Fergus come in.

CONCHUBOR *and* FERGUS: The gods save you.

LAVARCHAM *getting up and curtsying*: The gods save and keep you kindly, and stand between you and all harm for ever.

CONCHUBOR *looking round*: Where is Deirdre?

LAVARCHAM *trying to speak with indifference*: Abroad upon Slieve Fuadh. She does be all times straying around picking flowers or nuts, or sticks itself; but so long as she's gathering new life I've a right not to heed her, I'm thinking, and she taking her will.

Fergus talks to Old Woman.

CONCHUBOR *stiffly*: A night with thunder coming is no night to be abroad.

LAVARCHAM *more uneasily*: She's used to every track and pathway, and the lightning itself wouldn't let down its flame to singe the beauty of her like.

FERGUS *cheerfully*: She's right, Conchubor, and let you sit down and take your ease (*he takes a wallet from under his cloak*), and I'll count out what we've brought, and put it in the presses within.

He goes into the inner room with the Old Woman.

CONCHUBOR *sitting down and looking about*: Where are the mats and hangings and the silver skillets I sent up for Deirdre?

LAVARCHAM: The mats and hangings are in this press, Conchubor. She wouldn't wish to be soiling them, she said, running out and in with mud and grasses on her feet, and it raining since the night of Samhain. The silver skillets and the golden cups we have beyond locked in the chest.

CONCHUBOR: Bring them out and use them from this day.

LAVARCHAM: We'll do it, Conchubor.

CONCHUBOR *getting up and going to frame*: Is this hers?

LAVARCHAM *pleased to speak of it*: It is, Conchubor. All say there isn't her match at fancying figures and throwing purple upon crimson, and she edging them all times with her greens and gold.

CONCHUBOR *a little uneasily*: Is she keeping wise and busy since I passed before, and growing ready for her life in Emain?

LAVARCHAM *drily*: That is a question will give small pleasure to yourself or me. *Making up her mind to speak out.* If it's the truth I'll tell you, she's growing too wise to marry a big king and she a score only. Let you not be taking it bad, Conchubor, but you'll get little good seeing her this night, for with all my talking it's wilfuller she's growing these two months or three.

CONCHUBOR *severely, but relieved things are no worse*: Isn't it a poor thing you're doing so little to school her to meet what is to come?

LAVARCHAM: I'm after serving you two score of years, and I'll tell you this night, Conchubor, she's little call to mind an old woman when she has the birds to school her, and the pools in the rivers where she goes bathing in the sun. I'll tell you if you seen her that time, with her white skin, and her red lips, and the blue water and the ferns about her, you'd know, maybe, and you greedy itself, it wasn't for your like she was born at all.

CONCHUBOR: It's little I heed for what she was born; she'll be my comrade, surely. *He examines her workbox.*

LAVARCHAM *sinking into sadness again*: I'm in dread so they were right, saying she'd bring destruction on the world, for it's a poor thing when you see a settled man putting the love he has for a young child, and the love he has for a full woman, on a girl the like of her; and it's a poor thing, Conchubor, to see a High King, the way you are this day, prying after her needles and numbering her lines of thread.

CONCHUBOR *getting up*: Let you not be talking too far and you old itself. *Walks across room and back.* Does she know the troubles are foretold?

LAVARCHAM *in the tone of the earlier talk*: I'm after telling her one time and another, but I'd do as well speaking to a lamb of ten weeks and it racing the hills. . . . It's not the dread of death or troubles that would tame her like.

CONCHUBOR *he looks out*: She's coming now, and let you walk in and keep Fergus till I speak with her a while.

LAVARCHAM *going left*: If I'm after vexing you itself, it'd be best you weren't taking her hasty or scolding her at all.

CONCHUBOR *very stiffly*: I've no call to. I'm well pleased she's light and airy.

LAVARCHAM *offended at his tone*: Well pleased is it? *With a snort of irony*. It's a queer thing the way the likes of me do be telling the truth, and the wise are lying all times.

She goes into room on left. Conchubor arranges himself before a mirror for a moment, then goes a little to the left and waits. Deirdre comes in poorly dressed, with a little bag and a bundle of twigs in her arms. She is astonished for a moment when she sees Conchubor; then she makes a curtsy to him, and goes to the hearth without any embarrassment.

CONCHUBOR: The gods save you, Deirdre. I have come up bringing you rings and jewels from Emain Macha.

DEIRDRE: The gods save you.

CONCHUBOR: What have you brought from the hills?

DEIRDRE *quite self-possessed*: A bag of nuts, and twigs for our fires at the dawn of day.

CONCHUBOR *showing annoyance in spite of himself*: And it's that way you're picking up the manners will fit you to be Queen of Ulster?

DEIRDRE *made a little defiant by his tone*: I have no wish to be a queen.

CONCHUBOR *almost sneeringly*: You'd wish to be dressing in your duns and grey, and you herding your geese or driving your calves to their shed – like the common lot scattered in the glens.

DEIRDRE *very defiant*: I would not, Conchubor. *She goes to tapestry and begins to work.* A girl born the way I'm born is more likely to wish for a mate who'd be her likeness. . . . A man with his hair like the raven, maybe, and his skin like the snow and his lips like blood spilt on it.

CONCHUBOR *sees his mistake, and after a moment takes a flattering tone, looking at her work*: Whatever you wish, there's no queen but would be well pleased to have your skill at choosing colours and making pictures on the cloth. *Looking closely*. What is it you're figuring?

DEIRDRE *deliberately*: Three young men and they chasing in the green gap of a wood.

CONCHUBOR *now almost pleading*: It's soon you'll have dogs with silver chains to be chasing in the woods of Emain, for I have white hounds rearing up for you, and grey horses, that I've chosen from the finest in Ulster and Britain and Gaul.

DEIRDRE *unmoved as before*: I've heard tell, in Ulster and Britain and Gaul, Naisi and his brothers have no match and they chasing in the woods.

CONCHUBOR *very gravely*: Isn't it a strange thing you'd be talking of Naisi and his brothers, or figuring them either, when you know the things that are foretold about themselves and you? Yet you've little knowledge, and I'd do wrong taking it bad when it'll be my share from this out to keep you in the way you'll have little call to trouble for knowledge, or its want either.

DEIRDRE: Yourself should be wise, surely.

CONCHUBOR: The like of me has a store of knowledge that's a weight and terror. It's for that we do choose out the like of yourself that are young and glad only. . . . I'm thinking you are gay and lively each day in the year?

DEIRDRE: I don't know if that's true, Conchubor. There are lonesome days and bad nights in this place like another.

CONCHUBOR: You should have as few sad days, I'm thinking, as I have glad and good ones.

DEIRDRE: What is it has you that way ever coming this place, when you'd hear the old woman saying a good child's as happy as a king?

CONCHUBOR: How would I be happy seeing age coming on me each year, when the dry leaves are blowing back and forward at the gate of Emain? And yet this last while I'm saying out, when I see the furze breaking and the daws sitting two and two on ash-trees by the duns of Emain, Deirdre's a year nearer her full age when she'll be my mate and comrade, and then I'm glad surely.

DEIRDRE *almost to herself*: I will not be your mate in Emain.

CONCHUBOR *not heeding her*: It's there you'll be proud and happy and you'll learn that, if young men are great hunters, yet it's with the like of myself you'll find a knowledge of what is priceless in your own like. What we all need is a place is safe and splendid, and it's that you'll get in Emain in two days or three.

DEIRDRE *aghast*: Two days!

CONCHUBOR: I have the rooms ready, and in a little while you'll be brought down there, to be my queen and queen of the five parts of Ireland.

DEIRDRE *standing up frightened and pleading*: I'd liefer stay this place, Conchubor. . . . Leave me this place, where I'm well used to the tracks and pathways and the people of the glens. . . . It's for this life I'm born, surely.

CONCHUBOR: You'll be happier and greater with myself in Emain. It is I will be your comrade and will stand between you and the great troubles are foretold.

DEIRDRE: I will not be your queen in Emain when it's my pleasure to be having freedom on the edges of the hills.

CONCHUBOR: It's my wish to have you quickly; I'm sick and weary thinking of the day you'll be brought down to me, and seeing you walking into my big, empty halls. I've made all sure to have you, and yet all said there's a fear in the back of my mind I'd miss you and have great troubles in the end. It's for that, Deirdre, I'm praying that you'll come quickly; and you may take the word of a man has no lies, you'll not find, with any other, the like of what I'm bringing you in wildness and confusion in my own mind.

DEIRDRE: I cannot go, Conchubor.

CONCHUBOR *taking a triumphant tone*: It is my pleasure to have you, and I a man is waiting a long while on the throne of Ulster. Wouldn't you liefer be my comrade, growing up the like of Emer and Maeve, than to be in this place and you a child always?

DEIRDRE: You don't know me and you'd have little joy taking me, Conchubor. . . . I'm a long while watching the days getting a great speed passing me by. I'm too long taking my will, and it's that way I'll be living always.

CONCHUBOR *drily*: Call Fergus to come with me. This is your last night upon Slieve Fuadh.

DEIRDRE *now pleading*: Leave me a short space longer, Conchubor. Isn't it a poor thing I should be hastened away, when all these troubles are foretold? Leave me a year, Conchubor; it isn't much I'm asking.

CONCHUBOR: It's much to have me twoscore and two weeks waiting for your voice in Emain, and you in this place growing lonesome and shy. I'm a ripe man and in great love, and yet, Deirdre, I'm the King of Ulster. *He gets up.* I'll call Fergus, and we'll make Emain ready in the morning. *He goes towards door on left.*

DEIRDRE *clinging to him*: Do not call him, Conchubor. . . . Promise me a year of quiet. . . . It's one year I'm asking only.

CONCHUBOR: You'd be asking a year next year, and the years that follow. *Calling.* Fergus! Fergus! *To Deirdre.* Young girls are slow always; it is their lovers that must say the word. *Calling.* Fergus!

Deirdre springs away from him as Fergus comes in with Lavarcham and the Old Woman.

(*To Fergus.*) There is a storm coming, and we'd best be going to our people when the night is young.

FERGUS *cheerfully*: The gods shield you, Deirdre. *To Conchubor.* We're late already, and it's no work the High King to be slipping on stepping-stones and hilly pathways when the floods are rising with the rain. *He helps Conchubor into his cloak.*

CONCHUBOR *glad that he has made his decision – to Lavarcham*: Keep your rules a few days longer, and you'll be brought down to Emain, you and Deirdre with you.

LAVARCHAM *obediently*: Your rules are kept always.

CONCHUBOR: The gods shield you.

He goes out with Fergus. Old Woman bolts door.

LAVARCHAM *looking at Deirdre, who has covered her face*: Wasn't I
saying you'd do it? You've brought your marriage a sight nearer
not heeding those are wiser than yourself.

DEIRDRE *with agitation*: It wasn't I did it. Will you take me from
this place, Lavarcham, and keep me safe in the hills?

LAVARCHAM: He'd have us tracked in the half of a day, and then
you'd be his queen in spite of you, and I and mine would be
destroyed for ever.

DEIRDRE *terrified with the reality that is before her*: Are there none
can go against Conchubor?

LAVARCHAM: Maeve of Connaught only, and those that are her
like.

DEIRDRE: Would Fergus go against him?

LAVARCHAM: He would, maybe, and his temper roused.

DEIRDRE *in a lower voice with sudden excitement*: Would Naisi and
his brothers?

LAVARCHAM *impatiently*: Let you not be dwelling on Naisi and
his brothers. . . . In the end of all there is none can go against
Conchubor, and it's folly that we're talking, and if any went
against Conchubor it's sorrows he'd earn and the shortening of
his day of life.

*She turns away, and Deirdre stands up stiff with excitement and goes
and looks out of the window.*

DEIRDRE: Are the stepping-stones flooding, Lavarcham? Will the
night be stormy in the hills?

LAVARCHAM *looking at her curiously*: The stepping-stones are
flooding, surely, and the night will be the worst, I'm thinking,
we've seen these years gone by.

DEIRDRE *tearing open the press and pulling out clothes and tapestries*:
Lay these mats and hangings by the windows, and at the tables
for our feet, and take out the skillets of silver, and the golden
cups we have, and our two flasks of wine.

LAVARCHAM: What ails you?

DEIRDRE *gathering up a dress*: Lay them out quickly, Lavarcham,
we've no call dawdling this night. Lay them out quickly; I'm
going into the room to put on the rich dresses and jewels have
been sent from Emain.

LAVARCHAM: Putting on dresses at this hour, and it dark and drenching with the weight of rain! Are you away in your head!

DEIRDRE *gathering her things together with an outburst of excitement*: I will dress like Emer in Dundealgan, or Maeve in her house in Connaught. If Conchubor'll make me a queen, I'll have the right of a queen who is a master, taking her own choice and making a stir to the edges of the seas. . . . Lay out your mats and hangings where I can stand this night and look about me. Lay out the skins of the rams of Connaught and of the goats of the west. I will not be a child or plaything; I'll put on my robes that are the richest, for I will not be brought down to Emain as Cuchulain brings his horse to the yoke or Conall Cearneach puts his shield upon his arm; and maybe from this day I will turn the men of Ireland like a wind blowing on the heath.

She goes into room. Lavarcham and Old Woman look at each other, then the Old Woman goes over, looks in at Deirdre through chink of the door, and then closes it carefully.

OLD WOMAN *in a frightened whisper*: She's thrown off the rags she had about her, and there she is in her skin; she's putting her hair in shiny twists. Is she raving, Lavarcham, or has she a good right turning to a queen like Maeve?

LARVARCHAM *putting up hanging very anxiously*: It's more than raving's in her mind, or I'm the more astray; and yet she's as good a right as another, maybe, having her pleasure, though she'd spoil the world.

OLD WOMAN *helping her*: Be quick before she'll come back. . . . Who'd have thought we'd run before her, and she so quiet till to-night. Will the High King get the better of her, Lavarcham? If I was Conchubor, I wouldn't marry with her like at all.

LAVARCHAM: Hang that by the window. That should please her, surely. When all's said, it's her like will be the master till the end of time.

OLD WOMAN *at the window*: There's a mountain of blackness in the sky, and the greatest rain falling has been these long years on the earth. The gods help Conchubor. He'll be a sorry man this night, reaching his dun, and he with all his spirits, thinking to himself he'll be putting his arms around her in two days or three.

LAVARCHAM: It's more than Conchubor'll be sick and sorry, I'm thinking, before this story is told to the end.

Loud knocking on door at the right.

Startled. Who is that?

NAISI *outside*: Naisi, and his brothers.

LAVARCHAM: We are lonely women. What is it you're wanting in the blackness of the night?

NAISI: We met a young girl in the woods who told us we might shelter this place if the rivers rose on the pathways and the floods gathered from the butt of the hills.

Old Woman clasps her hands in horror.

LAVARCHAM *with great alarm*: You cannot come in. . . . There is no one let in here, and no young girl with us.

NAISI: Let us in from the great storm. Let us in and we will go further when the cloud will rise.

LAVARCHAM: Go round east to the shed and you'll have shelter. You cannot come in.

NAISI *knocking loudly*: Open the door or we will burst it.

The door is shaken.

OLD WOMAN *in a timid whisper*: Let them in, and keep Deirdre in her room tonight.

AINNLE *and* ARDAN *outside*: Open! Open!

LAVARCHAM *to Old Woman*: Go in and keep her.

OLD WOMAN: I couldn't keep her. I've no hold on her. Go in yourself and I will free the door.

LAVARCHAM: I must stay and turn them out. *She pulls her hair and cloak over her face.* Go in and keep her.

OLD WOMAN: The gods help us.

She runs into the inner room.

VOICES: Open!

LAVARCHAM *opening the door*: Come in then and ill-luck if you'll have it so.

Naisi and Ainnle and Ardan come in and look round with astonishment.

NAISI: It's a rich man has this place, and no herd at all.

LAVARCHAM *sitting down with her head half covered*: It is not, and you'd best be going quickly.

NAISI *hilariously, shaking rain from his clothes*: When we've had the pick of luck finding princely comfort in the darkness of the night! Some rich man of Ulster should come here and he chasing in the woods. May we drink? *He takes up flask.* Whose wine is this that we may drink his health?

LAVARCHAM: It's no one's that you've call to know.

NAISI: Your own health then and length of life.

Pouring out wine for the three. They drink.

LAVARCHAM *very crossly*: You're great boys taking a welcome where it isn't given, and asking questions where you've no call to. . . . If you'd a quiet place settled up to be playing yourself, maybe, with a gentle queen, what'd you think of young men prying around and carrying tales? When I was a bit of a girl the big men of Ulster had better manners, and they the like of your three selves, in the top folly of youth. That'll be a story to tell out in Tara that Naisi is a tippler and stealer, and Ainnle the drawer of a stranger's cork.

NAISI *quite cheerfully, sitting down beside her*: At your age you should know there are nights when a king like Conchubor would spit upon his arm ring, and queens will stick their tongues out at the rising moon. We're that way this night, and it's not wine we're asking only. Where is the young girl told us we might shelter here?

LAVARCHAM: Asking me you'd be? . . . We're decent people, and I wouldn't put you tracking a young girl, not if you gave me the good clasp you have hanging on your coat.

NAISI *giving it to her*: Where is she?

LAVARCHAM *in confidential whisper, putting her hand on his arm*: Let you walk back into the hills and turn up by the second cnuceen where there are three together. You'll see a path running on the rocks and then you'll hear the dogs barking in the houses, and their noise will guide you till you come to a bit of cabin at the foot of an ash-tree. It's there there is a young and flighty girl that I'm thinking is the one you've seen.

NAISI *hilariously*: Here's health, then, to herself and you!

ARDAN: Here's to the years when you were young as she!

AINNLE *in a frightened whisper*: Naisi!

Naisi looks up and Ainnle beckons to him. He goes over and Ainnle points to something on the golden mug he holds in his hand.

NAISI *looking at it in astonishment*: This is the High King's . . . I see his mark on the rim. Does Conchubor come lodging here?

LAVARCHAM *jumping up with extreme annoyance*: Who says it's Conchubor's? How dare young fools the like of you (*speaking with vehement insolence*) come prying around, running the world into troubles for some slip of a girl? What brings you this place straying from Emain? *Very bitterly*. Though you think, maybe, young men can do their fill of foolery and there is none to blame them.

NAISI *very soberly*: Is the rain easing?

ARDAN: The clouds are breaking. . . . I can see Orion in the gap of the glen.

NAISI *still cheerfully*: Open the door and we'll go forward to the little cabin between the ash-tree and the rocks. Lift the bolt and pull it.

Deirdre comes in on left royally dressed and very beautiful. She stands for a moment, and then as the door opens she calls softly.

DEIRDRE: Naisi! Do not leave me, Naisi. I am Deirdre of the Sorrows.

NAISI *transfixed with amazement*: And it is you who go around in the woods making the thrushes bear a grudge against the heavens for the sweetness of your voice singing.

DEIRDRE: It is with me you've spoken, surely. *To Lavarcham and Old Woman*. Take Ainnle and Ardan, these two princes, into the little hut where we eat, and serve them with what is best and sweetest. I have many things for Naisi only.

LAVARCHAM *overawed by her tone*: I will do it, and I ask their pardon. I have fooled them here.

DEIRDRE *to Ainnle and Ardan*: Do not take it badly that I am asking you to walk into our hut for a little. You will have a supper that is cooked by the cook of Conchubor, and Lavarcham will tell you stories of Maeve and Nessa and Rogh.

AINNLE: We'll ask Lavarcham to tell us stories of yourself, and with that we'll be well pleased to be doing your wish.

The all go out except Deirdre and Naisi.

DEIRDRE *sitting in the high chair in the centre*: Come to this stool, Naisi. *Pointing to the stool.* If it's low itself the High King would sooner be on it this night than on the throne of Emain Macha.

NAISI *sitting down*: You are Fedlimid's daughter that Conchubor has walled up from all the men of Ulster.

DEIRDRE: Do many know what is foretold, that Deirdre will be the ruin of the Sons of Usna, and have a little grave by herself, and a story will be told for ever?

NAISI: It's a long while men have been talking of Deirdre, the child who had all gifts, and the beauty that has no equal; there are many know it, and there are kings would give a great price to be in my place this night and you grown to a queen.

DEIRDRE: It isn't many I'd call, Naisi. . . . I was in the woods at the full moon and I heard a voice singing. Then I gathered up my skirts, and I ran on a little path I have to the verge of a rock, and I saw you pass by underneath, in your crimson cloak, singing a song, and you standing out beyond your brothers are called the Flower of Ireland.

NAISI: It's for that you called us in the dusk?

DEIRDRE *in a low voice*: Since that, Naisi, I have been one time the like of a ewe looking for a lamb that had been taken away from her, and one time seeing new gold on the stars, and a new face on the moon, and all times dreading Emain.

NAISI *pulling himself together and beginning to draw back a little*: Yet it should be a lonesome thing to be in this place and you born for great company.

DEIRDRE *softly*: This night I have the best company in the whole world.

NAISI *still a little formally*: It is I who have the best company, for when you're queen in Emain you will have none to be your match or fellow.

DEIRDRE: I will not be queen in Emain.

NAISI: Conchubor has made an oath you will, surely.

DEIRDRE: It's for that maybe I'm called Deirdre, the girl of many

sorrows . . . for it's a sweet life you and I could have, Naisi
. . . . It should be a sweet thing to have what is best and richest,
if it's for a short space only.

NAISI *very distressed*: And we've a short space only to be
triumphant and brave.

DEIRDRE: You must not go, Naisi, and leave me to the High King,
a man is ageing in his dun, with his crowds round him, and his
silver and gold. *More quickly*. I will not live to be shut up in
Emain, and wouldn't we do well paying, Naisi, with silence and
a near death? *She stands up and walks away from him*. I'm a long
while in the woods with my own self, and I'm in little dread of
death, and it earned with riches would make the sun red with
envy, and he going up the heavens; and the moon pale and
lonesome, and she wasting away. *She comes to him and puts her
hands on his shoulders*. Isn't it a small thing is foretold about the
ruin of ourselves, Naisi, when all men have age coming and
great ruin in the end?

NAISI: Yet it's a poor thing it's I should bring you to a tale of blood
and broken bodies, and the filth of the grave. . . . Wouldn't we
do well to wait, Deirdre, and I each twilight meeting you on the
sides of the hills?

DEIRDRE *despondently*: His messengers are coming.

NAISI: Messengers are coming?

DEIRDRE: To-morrow morning or the next, surely.

NAISI: Then we'll go away. It isn't I will give your like to
Conchubor, not if the grave was dug to be my lodging when a
week was by. *He looks out*. The stars are out, Deirdre, and let
you come with me quickly, for it is the stars will be our lamps
many nights and we abroad in Alban, and taking our journeys
among the little islands in the sea. There has never been the like
of the joy we'll have, Deirdre, you and I, having our fill of love
at the evening and the morning till the sun is high.

DEIRDRE: And yet I'm in dread leaving this place, where I have
lived always. Won't I be lonesome and I thinking on the little
hills beyond, and the apple-trees do be budding in the
springtime by the post of the door? *A little shaken by what has
passed*. Won't I be in great dread to bring you to destruction,
Naisi, and you so happy and young?

NAISI: Are you thinking I'd go on living after this night, Deirdre, and you with Conchubor in Emain? Are you thinking I'd go out after hares when I've had your lips in my sight?

Lavarcham comes in as they cling to each other.

LAVARCHAM: Are you raving, Deirdre? Are you choosing this night to destroy the world?

DEIRDRE *very deliberately*: It's Conchubor has chosen this night calling me to Emain. *To Naisi*. Bring in Ainnle and Ardan, and take me from this place, where I'm in dread from this out of the footsteps of a hare passing.

He goes.

> *Clinging to Lavarcham.* Do not take it bad I'm going, Lavarcham. It's you have been a good friend and given me great freedom and joy, and I living on Slieve Fuadh; and maybe you'll be well pleased one day saying you have nursed Deirdre.

LAVARCHAM *moved*: It isn't I'll be well pleased and I far away from you. Isn't a hard thing you're doing, but who can help it? Birds go mating in the spring of the year, and ewes at the leaves falling, but a young girl must have her lover in all the course of the sun and moon.

DEIRDRE: Will you go to Emain in the morning?

LAVARCHAM: I will not. I'll go to Brandon in the south; and in the course of a piece, maybe, I'll be sailing back and forward on the seas to be looking on your face and the little ways you have that none can equal.

Naisi comes back with Ainnle and Ardan and Old Woman.

DEIRDRE *taking Naisi's hand*: My two brothers, I am going with Naisi to Alban and the north to face the troubles are foretold. Will you take word to Conchubor in Emain?

AINNLE: We will go with you.

ARDAN: We will be your servants and your huntsmen, Deirdre.

DEIRDRE: It isn't one brother only of you three is brave and courteous. Will you wed us, Lavarcham? You have the words and customs.

LAVARCHAM: I will not, then. What would I want meddling in the ruin you will earn?

NAISI: Let Ainnle wed us. . . . He has been with wise men and he
knows their ways.

AINNLE *joining their hands*: By the sun and moon and the whole
earth, I wed Deirdre to Naisi. *He steps back and holds up his
hands.* May the air bless you, and water and the wind, the sea,
and all the hours of the sun and moon.

CURTAIN

ACT TWO

*Alban. Early morning in the beginning of winter. A wood outside the tent
of Deirdre and Naisi. Lavarcham comes in muffled in a cloak.*

LAVARCHAM *calling*: Deirdre. . . . Deirdre. . . .

DEIRDRE *coming from tent*: My welcome, Lavarcham. . . . Whose
curragh is rowing from Ulster? I saw the oars through the tops
of the trees, and I thought it was you were coming towards us.

LAVARCHAM: I came in the shower was before dawn.

DEIRDRE: And who is coming?

LAVARCHAM *mournfully*: Let you not be startled or taking it bad,
Deirdre. It's Fergus bringing messages of peace from Conchubor
to take Naisi and his brothers back to Emain. *Sitting down.*

DEIRDRE *lightly*: Naisi and his brothers are well pleased with this
place; and what would take them back to Conchubor in Ulster?

LAVARCHAM: Their like would go any place where they'd see
death standing. *With more agitation.* I'm in dread Conchubor
wants to have yourself and to kill Naisi, and that that'll be the
ruin of the Sons of Usna. I'm silly, maybe, to be dreading the
like, but those have a great love for yourself have a right to be
in dread always.

DEIRDRE *more anxiously*: Emain should be no safe place for myself
and Naisi. And isn't it a hard thing they'll leave us no peace,
Lavarcham, and we so quiet in the woods?

LAVARCHAM *impressively*: It's a hard thing, surely; but let you
take my word and swear Naisi, by the earth, and the sun over
it, and the four quarters of the moon, he'll not go back to
Emain – for good faith or bad faith – the time Conchubor's

keeping the high throne of Ireland. . . . It's that would save you, surely.

DEIRDRE *without hope*: There's little power in oaths to stop what's coming, and little power in what I'd do, Lavarcham, to change the story of Conchubor and Naisi and the things old men foretold.

LAVARCHAM *aggressively*: Was there little power in what you did the night you dressed in your finery and ran Naisi off along with you, in spite of Conchubor and the big nobles did dread the blackness of your luck? It was power enough you had that night to bring distress and anguish; and now I'm pointing you a way to save Naisi, you'll not stir stick or straw to aid me.

DEIRDRE *a little haughtily*: Let you not raise your voice against me, Lavarcham, if you have will itself to guard Naisi.

LAVARCHAM *breaking out in anger*: Naisi is it? I wouldn't care if the crows were stripping his thigh-bones at the dawn of day. It's to stop your own despair and wailing, and you waking up in a cold bed, without the man you have your heart on, I am raging now. *Starting up with temper*. Yet there is more men than Naisi in it; and maybe I was a big fool thinking his dangers, and this day, would fill you up with dread.

DEIRDRE *sharply*: Let you end; such talking is a fool's only, when it's well you know if a thing harmed Naisi it isn't I would live after him. *With distress*. It's well you know it's this day I'm dreading seven years, and I fine nights watching the heifers walking to the haggard with long shadows on the grass; (*with emotion*) or the time I've been stretched in the sunshine, when I've heard Ainnle and Ardan stepping lightly, and they saying: 'Was there ever the like of Deirdre for a happy and sleepy queen?'

LAVARCHAM *not fully pacified*: And yet you'll go, and welcome is it, if Naisi chooses?

DEIRDRE: I've dread going or staying, Lavarcham. It's lonesome this place, having happiness like ours, till I'm asking each day will this day match yesterday, and will tomorrow take a good place beside the same day in the year that's gone, and wondering all times is it a game worth playing, living on until you're dried and old, and our joy is gone for ever.

LAVARCHAM: If it's that ails you, I tell you there's little hurt getting old, though young girls and poets do be storming at the shapes of age. *Passionately.* There's little hurt getting old, saving when you're looking back, the way I'm looking this day and seeing the young you have a love for breaking up their hearts with folly. *Going to Deirdre.* Take my word and stop Naisi, and the day'll come you'll have more joy having the senses of an old woman and you with your little grandsons shrieking round you, than I'd have this night putting on the red mouth and the white arms you have, to go walking lonesome by-ways with a gamy king.

DEIRDRE: It's little joy of a young woman, or an old woman, I'll have from this day, surely. But what use is in our talking when there's Naisi on the foreshore, and Fergus with him?

LAVARCHAM *despairingly*: I'm late so with my warnings, for Fergus'd talk the moon over to take a new path in the sky. *With reproach.* You'll not stop him this day, and isn't it a strange story you were a plague and torment, since you were that height, to those did hang their lifetimes on your voice. *Overcome with trouble; gathering her cloak about her.* Don't think bad of my crying. I'm not the like of many and I'd see a score of naked corpses and not heed them at all, but I'm destroyed seeing yourself in your hour of joy when the end is coming surely.

Owen comes in quickly, rather ragged, bows to Deirdre.

OWEN *to Lavarcham*: Fergus's men are calling you. You were seen on the path, and he and Naisi want you for their talk below.

LAVARCHAM *looking at him with dislike*: Yourself's an ill-lucky thing to meet a morning is the like of this. Yet if you are a spy itself I'll go and give my word that's wanting surely.

Goes out.

OWEN *to Deirdre*: So I've found you alone, and I after waiting three weeks getting ague and asthma in the chill of the bogs, till I saw Naisi caught with Fergus.

DEIRDRE: I've heard news of Fergus; what brought you from Ulster?

OWEN *who has been searching, finds a loaf and sits down eating greedily, and cutting it with a large knife*: The full moon, I'm thinking, and it squeezing the crack in my skull. Was there ever a man crossed nine waves after a fool's wife and he not away in his head?

DEIRDRE *absently*: It should be a long time since you left Emain, where there's civility in speech with queens.

OWEN: It's a long while, surely. It's three weeks I am losing my manners beside the Saxon bull-frogs at the head of the bog. Three weeks is a long space, and yet you're seven years spancelled with Naisi and the pair.

DEIRDRE *beginning to fold up her silks and jewels*: Three weeks of your days might be long, surely, yet seven years are a short space for the like of Naisi and myself.

OWEN *derisively*: If they're a short space there aren't many the like of you. Wasn't there a queen in Tara had to walk out every morning till she'd meet a stranger and see the flame of courtship leaping up within his eye? Tell me now (*leaning towards her*), are you well pleased that length with the same man snorting next you at the dawn of day?

DEIRDRE *very quietly*: Am I well pleased seven years seeing the same sun throwing light across the branches at the dawn of day? It's a heart-break to the wise that it's for a short space we have the same things only. *With contempt.* Yet the earth itself is a silly place, maybe, when a man's a fool and talker.

OWEN *sharply*: Well, go, take your choice. Stay here and rot with Naisi or go to Conchubor in Emain. Conchubor's a wrinkled fool with a swelling belly on him, and eyes falling downward from his shining crown; Naisi should be stale and weary. Yet there are many roads, Deirdre, and I tell you I'd liefer be bleaching in a bog-hole than living on without a touch of kindness from your eyes and voice. It's a poor thing to be so lonesome you'd squeeze kisses on a cur dog's nose.

DEIRDRE: Are there no women like yourself could be your friends in Emain?

OWEN *vehemently*: There are none like you, Deirdre. It's for that I'm asking are you going back this night with Fergus?

DEIRDRE: I will go where Naisi chooses.

OWEN *with a burst of rage*: It's Naisi, Naisi, is it? Then I tell you,

you'll have great sport one day seeing Naisi getting a harshness
in his two sheep's eyes, and he looking on yourself. Would you
credit it, my father used to be in the broom and heather kissing
Lavarcham, with a little bird chirping out above their heads,
and now she'd scare a raven from a carcass on a hill. *With a sad
cry that brings dignity into his voice.* Queens get old, Deirdre,
with their white and long arms going from them, and their
backs hooping. I tell you it's a poor thing to see a queen's nose
reaching down to scrape her chin.

DEIRDRE *looking out, a little uneasy*: Naisi and Fergus are coming
on the path.

OWEN: I'll go so, for if I had you seven years I'd be jealous of the
midges and the dust is in the air. *Muffles himself in his cloak; with
a sort of warning in his voice.* I'll give you a riddle, Deirdre: Why
isn't my father as ugly and old as Conchubor? You've no
answer? . . . It's because Naisi killed him. *With curious
expression.* Think of that and you awake at night, hearing Naisi
snoring, or the night you hear strange stories of the things I'm
doing in Alban or in Ulster either.

He goes out, and in a moment Naisi and Fergus come in on the other side.

NAISI *gaily*: Fergus has brought messages of peace from
Conchubor.

DEIRDRE *greeting Fergus*: He is welcome. Let you rest, Fergus, you
should be hot and thirsty after mounting the rocks.

FERGUS: It's a sunny nook you've found in Alban; yet any man
would be well pleased mounting higher rocks to fetch yourself
and Naisi back to Emain.

DEIRDRE *with keenness*: They've answered? They would go?

FERGUS *benignly*: They have not, but when I was a young man
we'd have given a lifetime to be in Ireland a score of weeks; and
to this day the old men have nothing so heavy as knowing it's
in a short while they'll lose the high skies are over Ireland, and
the lonesome mornings with birds crying on the bogs. Let you
come this day, for there's no place but Ireland where the Gael
can have peace always.

NAISI *gruffly*: It's true, surely. Yet we're better this place while
Conchubor's in Emain Macha.

FERGUS *giving him parchments*: There are your sureties and
Conchubor's seal. *To Deirdre*. I am your surety with
Conchubor. You'll not be young always, and it's time you were
making yourselves ready for the years will come, building up a
homely dun beside the seas of Ireland, and getting in your
children from the princes' wives. It's little joy wandering till age
is on you and your youth is gone away, so you'd best come this
night, for you'd have great pleasure putting out your foot and
saying: 'I am in Ireland, surely.'

DEIRDRE: It isn't pleasure I'd have while Conchubor is king in
Emain.

FERGUS *almost annoyed*: Would you doubt the seals of Conall
Cearneach and the kings of Meath? *He gets parchments from his
cloak and gives them to Naisi. More gently*. It's easy being fearful
and you alone in the wood, yet it would be a poor thing if a
timid woman (*taunting her a little*) could turn away the Sons of
Usna from the life of kings. Let you be thinking on the years to
come, Deirdre, and the way you'd have a right to see Naisi a
high and white-haired justice beside some king of Emain.
Wouldn't it be a poor story if a queen the like of you should
have no thought but to be scraping up her hours dallying in the
sunshine with the sons of kings?

DEIRDRE *turning away a little haughtily*: I leave the choice to Naisi.
Turning back towards Fergus. Yet you'd do well, Fergus, to go
on your way, for the sake of your own years, so you'll not be
saying till your hour of death, maybe, it was yourself brought
Naisi and his brothers to a grave was scooped by treachery.

Goes into tent.

FERGUS: It is a poor thing to see a queen so lonesome and afraid.
He watches till he is sure Deirdre cannot hear him. Listen now to
what I'm saying. You'd do well to come back to men and
women are your match and comrades, and not be lingering
until the day that you'll grow weary, and hurt Deirdre showing
her the hardness will grow up within your eyes. . . . You're here
years and plenty to know it's truth I'm saying.

*Deirdre comes out of tent with a horn of wine, she catches the beginning
of Naisi's speech and stops with stony wonder.*

NAISI *very thoughtfully*: I'll not tell you a lie. There have been days a while past when I've been throwing a line for salmon or watching for the run of hares, that I've dread upon me a day'd come I'd weary of her voice (*very slowly*), and Deirdre'd see I'd wearied.

FERGUS *sympathetic but triumphant*: I knew it, Naisi. . . . And take my word, Deirdre's seen your dread and she'll have no peace from this out in the woods.

NAISI *with confidence*: She's not seen it. . . . Deirdre's no thought of getting old or wearied; it's that puts wonder in her ways, and she with spirits would keep bravery and laughter in a town with plague.

Deirdre drops the horn of wine and crouches down where she is.

FERGUS: That humour'll leave her. But we've no call going too far, with one word borrowing another. Will you come this night to Emain Macha?

NAISI: I'll not go, Fergus. I've had dreams of getting old and weary, and losing my delight in Deirdre; but my dreams were dreams only. What are Conchubor's seals and all your talk of Emain and the fools of Meath beside one evening in Glen Masain? We'll stay this place till our lives and time are worn out. It's that word you may take in your curragh to Conchubor in Emain.

FERGUS *gathering up his parchments*: And you won't go, surely?

NAISI: I will not. . . . I've had dread, I tell you, dread winter and summer, and the autumn and the springtime, even when there's a bird in every bush making his own stir till the fall of night; but this talk's brought me ease, and I see we're as happy as the leaves on the young trees, and we'll be so ever and always, though we'd live the age of the eagle and the salmon and the crow of Britain.

FERGUS *with anger*: Where are your brothers? My message is for them also.

NAISI: You'll see them above chasing otters by the stream.

FERGUS *bitterly*: It isn't much I was mistaken, thinking you were hunters only.

He goes, Naisi turns towards tent and sees Deirdre crouching down with her cloak round her face. Deirdre comes out.

NAISI: You've heard my words to Fergus?

She does not answer. A pause. He puts his arm around her.

Leave troubling, and we'll go this night to Glen da Ruadh, where the salmon will be running with the tide. *Crosses and sits down.*

DEIRDRE *in a very low voice*: With the tide in a little while we will be journeying again, or it is our own blood maybe will be running away. *She turns and clings to him.* The dawn and evening are a little while, the winter and the summer pass quickly, and what way would you and I, Naisi, have joy for ever?

NAISI: We'll have the joy is highest till our age is come, for it isn't Fergus's talk of great deeds could take us back to Emain.

DEIRDRE: It isn't to great deeds you're going but to near troubles, and the shortening of your days the time that they are bright and sunny; and isn't it a poor thing that I, Deirdre, could not hold you away?

NAISI: I've said we'd stay in Alban always.

DEIRDRE: There's no place to stay always. . . . It's a long time we've had, pressing the lips together, going up and down, resting in our arms, Naisi, waking with the smell of June in the tops of the grasses, and listening to the birds in the branches that are highest. . . . It's a long time we've had, but the end has come, surely.

NAISI: Would you have us go to Emain, though if any ask the reason we do not know it, and we journeying as the thrushes come from the north, or young birds fly out on a dark sea?

DEIRDRE: There's reason all times for an end that's come. And I'm well pleased, Naisi, we're going forward in the winter the time the sun has a low place, and the moon has her mastery in a dark sky, for it's you and I are well lodged our last day, where there is a light behind the clear trees, and the berries on the thorns are a red wall.

NAISI: If our time in this place is ended, come away without Ainnle and Ardan to the woods of the east, for it's right to be away from all people when two lovers have their love only. Come away and we'll be safe always.

DEIRDRE *broken-hearted*: There's no safe place, Naisi, on the ridge of the world. . . . And it's in the quiet woods I've seen them digging our grave, throwing out the clay on leaves are bright and withered.

NAISI *still more eagerly*: Come away, Deirdre, and it's little we'll think of safety or the grave beyond it, and we resting in a little corner between the daytime and the long night.

DEIRDRE *clearly and gravely*: It's this hour we're between the daytime and a night where there is sleep for ever, and isn't it a better thing to be following on to a near death, than to be binding the head down, and dragging with the feet, and seeing one day a blight showing upon love where it is sweet and tender?

NAISI *his voice broken with distraction*: If a near death is coming what will be my trouble losing the earth and the stars over it, and you, Deirdre, are their flame and bright crown? Come away into the safety of the woods.

DEIRDRE *shaking her head slowly*: There are as many ways to wither love as there are stars in a night of Samhain; but there is no way to keep life, or love with it, a short space only. . . . It's for that there's nothing lonesome like a love is watching out the time most lovers do be sleeping. . . . It's for that we're setting out for Emain Macha when the tide turns on the sand.

NAISI *giving in*: You're right, maybe. It should be a poor thing to see great lovers and they sleepy and old.

DEIRDRE *with a more tender intensity*: We're seven years without roughness or growing weary; seven years so sweet and shining, the gods would be hard set to give us seven days the like of them. It's for that we're going to Emain, where there'll be a rest for ever, or a place for forgetting, in great crowds and they making a stir.

NAISI *very softly*: We'll go surely, in place of keeping a watch on a love had no match and it wasting away.

They cling to each other for a moment, then Naisi looks up.

There are Fergus and Lavarcham and my two brothers.

Deirdre goes. Naisi sits with his head bowed. Owen runs in stealthily, comes behind Naisi, and seizes him round the arms. Naisi shakes him off and whips out his sword.

OWEN *screaming with derisive laughter and showing his empty hands*: Ah, Naisi, wasn't it well I didn't kill you that time? There was a fright you got! I've been watching Fergus above – don't be frightened – and I've come down to see him getting the cold shoulder, and going off alone.

Fergus and others come in. They are all subdued like men at a queen's wake.

NAISI *putting up his sword*: There he is. *Goes to Fergus.* We are going back when the tide turns, I and Deirdre with yourself.

ALL: Going back!

AINNLE: And you'll end your life with Deirdre, though she has no match for keeping spirits in a little company is far away by itself?

ARDAN: It's seven years myself and Ainnle have been servants and bachelors for yourself and Deirdre. Why will you take her back to Conchubor?

NAISI: I have done what Deirdre wishes and has chosen.

FERGUS: You've made a choice wise men will be glad of in the five ends of Ireland.

OWEN: Wise men is it, and they going back to Conchubor? I could stop them only Naisi put in his sword among my father's ribs, and when a man's done that he'll not credit your oath. Going to Conchubor! I could tell of plots and tricks, and spies were well paid for their play. *He throws up a bag of gold.* Are you paid, Fergus?

He scatters gold pieces over Fergus.

FERGUS: He is raving. . . . Seize him.

OWEN *flying between them*: You won't. Let the lot of you be off to Emain, but I'll be off before you. . . . Dead men, dead men! Men who'll die for Deirdre's beauty; I'll be before you in the grave!

Runs out with his knife in his hand. They all run after him except Lavarcham, who looks out and then clasps her hands. Deirdre comes out to her in a dark cloak.

DEIRDRE: What has happened?

LAVARCHAM: It's Owen's gone raging mad, and he's after

splitting his gullet beyond at the butt of the stone. There was ill luck this day in his eye. And he knew a power if he'd said it all.

Naisi comes back quickly, followed by the others.

AINNLE *coming in very excited*: That man knew plots of Conchubor's. We'll not go to Emain, where Conchubor may love her and have hatred for yourself.

FERGUS: Would you mind a fool and raver?

AINNLE: It's many times there's more sense in madmen than the wise. We will not obey Conchubor.

NAISI: I and Deirdre have chosen; we will go back with Fergus.

ARDAN: We will not go back. We will burn your curraghs by the sea.

FERGUS: My sons and I will guard them.

AINNLE: We will blow the horn of Usna and our friends will come to aid us.

NAISI: It is my friends will come.

AINNLE: Your friends will bind your hands, and you out of your wits.

Deirdre comes forward quickly and comes between Ainnle and Naisi.

DEIRDRE *in a low voice*: For seven years the Sons of Usna have not raised their voices in a quarrel.

AINNLE: We will not take you to Emain.

ARDAN: It is Conchubor has broken our peace.

AINNLE *to Deirdre*: Stop Naisi going. What way would we live if Conchubor should take you from us?

DEIRDRE: There is no one could take me from you. I have chosen to go back with Fergus. Will you quarrel with me, Ainnle, though I have been your queen these seven years in Alban?

AINNLE *subsiding suddenly*: Naisi has no call to take you.

ARDAN: Why are you going?

DEIRDRE *to both of them and the others*: It is my wish. . . . It may be I will not have Naisi growing an old man in Alban with an old woman at his side, and young girls pointing out and saying: 'That is Deirdre and Naisi had great beauty in their youth.' It may be we do well putting a sharp end to the day is brave and glorious, as our fathers put a sharp end to the days of the kings of Ireland; or that I'm wishing to set my foot on Slieve Fuadh, where I was running one time and leaping the streams (*to Lavarcham*), and that I'd be well pleased to see our little apple-trees, Lavarcham, behind our cabin on the hill; or that I've learned, Fergus, it's a lonesome thing to be away from Ireland always.

AINNLE *giving in*: There is no place but will be lonesome to us from this out, and we thinking on our seven years in Alban.

DEIRDRE *to Naisi*: It's in this place we'd be lonesome in the end. . . . Take down Fergus to the sea. He has been a guest had a hard welcome and he bringing messages of peace.

FERGUS: We will make your curragh ready and it fitted for the voyage of a king.

He goes with Naisi.

DEIRDRE: Take your spears, Ainnle and Ardan, and go down before me, and take your horse-boys to be carrying my cloaks are on the threshold.

AINNLE *obeying*: It's with a poor heart we'll carry your things this day we have carried merrily so often, and we hungry and cold.

They gather up things and go out.

DEIRDRE *to Lavarcham*: Go you, too, Lavarcham. You are old, and I will follow quickly.

LAVARCHAM: I'm old, surely, and the hopes I had my pride in are broken and torn.

She goes out with a look of awe at Deirdre.

DEIRDRE *clasping her hands*: Woods of Cuan, woods of Cuan, dear country of the east! It's seven years we've had a life was joy only, and this day we're going west, this day we're facing death, maybe, and death should be a poor, untidy thing, though it's a queen that dies.

She goes out slowly.

CURTAIN

ACT THREE

Tent below Emain, with shabby skins and benches. There is an opening at each side and at back, the latter closed. Old Woman comes in with food and fruits and arranges them on table. Conchubor comes in on right.

CONCHUBOR *sharply*: Has no one come with news for me?

OLD WOMAN: I've seen no one at all, Conchubor.

CONCHUBOR *watches her working for a moment, then makes sure opening at back is closed*: Go up then to Emain, you're not wanting here.

A noise heard left.

Who is that?

OLD WOMAN *going left*: It's Lavarcham coming again. She's a great wonder for jogging back and forward through the world, and I made certain she'd be off to meet them; but she's coming alone, Conchubor, my dear child Deirdre isn't with her at all.

CONCHUBOR: Go up so and leave us.

OLD WOMAN *pleadingly*: I'd be well pleased to set my eyes on Deirdre if she's coming this night, as we're told.

CONCHUBOR *impatiently*: It's not long till you'll see her. But I've matters with Lavarcham, and let you go now, I'm saying.

He shows her out right, Lavarcham comes in on the left.

LAVARCHAM *looking round her with suspicion*: This is a queer place to find you, and it's a queer place to be lodging Naisi and his brothers, and Deirdre with them, and the lot of us tired out with the long way we have been walking.

CONCHUBOR: You've come along with them the whole journey?

LAVARCHAM: I have, then, though I've no call now to be wandering that length to a wedding or a burial, or the two together. *She sits down wearily.* It's a poor thing the way me and you is getting old, Conchubor, and I'm thinking you yourself have no call to be loitering this place getting your death, maybe, in the cold of night.

CONCHUBOR: I'm waiting only to know is Fergus stopped in the north.

LAVARCHAM *more sharply*: He's stopped, surely, and that's a trick
has me thinking you have it in mind to bring trouble this night
on Emain and Ireland and the big world's east beyond them.
She goes to him. And yet you'd do well to be going to your dun,
and not putting shame on her meeting the High King, and she
seamed and sweaty and in great disorder from the dust of many
roads. *Laughing derisively*. Ah, Conchubor, my lad, beauty goes
quickly in the woods, and you'd let a great gasp, I tell you, if
you set your eyes this night on Deirdre.

CONCHUBOR *fiercely*: It's little I care if she's white and worn, for
it's I did rear her from a child. I should have a good right to
meet and see her always.

LAVARCHAM: A good right is it? Haven't the blind a good right to
be seeing, and the lame to be dancing, and the dummies
singing tunes? It's that right you have to be looking for gaiety
on Deirdre's lips. *Coaxingly*. Come on to your dun, I'm saying,
and leave her quiet for one night itself.

CONCHUBOR *with sudden anger*: I'll not go, when it's long enough
I am above in my dun stretching east and west without a
comrade, and I more needy, maybe, than the thieves of Meath.
. . . You think I'm old and wise, but I tell you the wise know the
old must die, and they'll leave no chance for a thing slipping
from them they've set their blood to win.

LAVARCHAM *nodding her head*: If you're old and wise, it's I'm the
same, Conchubor, and I'm telling you you'll not have her
though you're ready to destroy mankind and skin the gods to
win her. There's things a king can't have, Conchubor, and if
you go rampaging this night you'll be apt to win nothing but
death for many, and a sloppy face of trouble on your own self
before the day will come.

CONCHUBOR: It's too much talk you have. *Goes right*. Where is
Owen? Did you see him no place and you coming the road?

LAVARCHAM: I seen him surely. He went spying on Naisi, and
now the worms is spying on his own inside.

CONCHUBOR *exultingly*: Naisi killed him?

LAVARCHAM: He did not then. It was Owen destroyed himself
running mad because of Deirdre. Fools and kings and scholars
are all one in a story with her like, and Owen thought he'd be a

great man, being the first corpse in the game you'll play this
night in Emain.

CONCHUBOR: It's yourself should be the first corpse, but my
other messengers are coming, men from the clans that hated
Usna.

LAVARCHAM *drawing back hopelessly*: Then the gods have pity on
us all!

Men with weapons come in.

CONCHUBOR *to soldiers*: Are Ainnle and Ardan separate from Naisi?

MEN: They are, Conchubor. We've got them off, saying they were
needed to make ready Deirdre's house.

CONCHUBOR: And Naisi and Deirdre are coming?

SOLDIER: Naisi's coming, surely, and a woman with him is
putting out the glory of the moon is rising and the sun is going
down.

CONCHUBOR *looking at Lavarcham*: That's your story that she's
seamed and ugly?

SOLDIER: I have more news. *Pointing to Lavarcham.* When that
woman heard you were bringing Naisi this place, she sent a
horse-boy to call Fergus from the north.

CONCHUBOR *to Lavarcham*: It's for that you've been playing your
tricks, but what you've won is a nearer death for Naisi. *To
soldiers.* Go up and call my fighters, and take that woman up to
Emain.

LAVARCHAM: I'd liefer stay this place. I've done my best, but if a
bad end is coming, surely it would be a good thing maybe I was
here to tend her.

CONCHUBOR *fiercely*: Take her to Emain; it's too many tricks
she's tried this day already.

A soldier goes to her.

LAVARCHAM: Don't touch me. *She puts her cloak round her and
catches Conchubor's arm.* I thought to stay your hand with my
stories till Fergus would come to be beside them, the way I'd
save yourself, Conchubor, and Naisi and Emain Macha; but I'll
walk up now into your halls, and I'll say (*with a gesture*) it's here
nettles will be growing and beyond thistles and docks. I'll go

into your high chambers, where you've been figuring yourself stretching out your neck for the kisses of a queen of women; and I'll say its here there'll be deer stirring and goats scratching, and sheep waking and coughing when there is a great wind from the north. *Shaking herself loose.*

Conchubor makes a sign to soldiers.

I'm going, surely. In a short space I'll be sitting up with many listening to the flames crackling, and the beams breaking, and I looking on the great blaze will be the end of Emain.

She goes out.

CONCHUBOR *looking out*: I see two people in the trees; it should be Naisi and Deirdre. *To soldier.* Let you tell them they'll lodge here to-night.

Conchubor goes out right. Naisi and Deirdre come in on left, very weary.

NAISI *to soldiers*: Is it this place he's made ready for myself and Deirdre?

SOLDIER: The Red Branch House is being aired and swept and you'll be called there when a space is by; till then you'll find fruits and drink on this table, and so the gods be with you.

Goes out right.

NAISI *looking round*: It's a strange place he's put us camping and we come back as his friends.

DEIRDRE: He's likely making up a welcome for us, having curtains shaken out and rich rooms put in order; and it's right he'd have great state to meet us, and you his sister's son.

NAISI *gloomily*: It's little we want with state or rich rooms or curtains, when we're used to the ferns only and cold streams and they making a stir.

DEIRDRE *roaming around room*: We want what is our right in Emain (*looking at hangings*), and though he's riches in store for us it's a shabby, ragged place he's put us waiting, with frayed rugs and skins are eaten by the moths.

NAISI *a little impatiently*: There are few would worry over skins and moths on this first night that we've come back to Emain.

DEIRDRE *brightly*: You should be well pleased it's for that I'd worry all times, when it's I have kept your tent these seven years as tidy as a bee-hive or a linnet's nest. If Conchubor'd a queen like me in Emain he'd not have stretched these rags to meet us. *She pulls hanging, and it opens.* There's new earth on the ground and a trench dug. . . . It's a grave, Naisi, that is wide and deep.

NAISI *goes over and pulls back curtain showing grave*: And that'll be our home in Emain. . . . He's dug it wisely at the butt of a hill, with fallen trees to hide it. He'll want to have us killed and buried before Fergus comes.

DEIRDRE: Take me away. . . . Take me to hide in the rocks, for the night is coming quickly.

NAISI *pulling himself together*: I will not leave my brothers.

DEIRDRE *vehemently*: It's of us two he's jealous. Come away to the places where we're used to have our company. . . . Wouldn't it be a good thing to lie hid in the high ferns together? *She pulls him left.* I hear strange words in the trees.

NAISI: It should be the strange fighters of Conchubor. I saw them passing as we come.

DEIRDRE *pulling him towards the right*: Come to this side. Listen, Naisi!

NAISI: There are more of them. . . . We are shut in, and I have not Ainnle and Ardan to stand near me. Isn't it a hard thing that we three who have conquered many may not die together?

DEIRDRE *sinking down*: And isn't it a hard thing that you and I are this place by our opened grave; though none have lived had happiness like ours those days in Alban that went by so quick.

NAISI: It's a hard thing, surely, we've lost those days for ever; and yet it's a good thing, maybe, that all goes quick, for when I'm in that grave it's soon a day'll come you'll be too wearied to be crying out, and that day'll bring you ease.

DEIRDRE: I'll not be here to know if that is true.

NAISI: It's our three selves he'll kill to-night, and then in two months or three you'll see him walking down for courtship with yourself.

DEIRDRE: I'll not be here.

NAISI *hard*: You'd best keep him off, maybe, and then, when the time comes, make your way to some place west in Donegal, and it's there you'll get used to stretching out lonesome at the fall of night, and waking lonesome for the day.

DEIRDRE: Let you not be saying things are worse than death.

NAISI *a little recklessly*: I've one word left. If a day comes in the west that the larks are cocking their crests on the edge of the clouds, and the cuckoos making a stir, and there's a man you'd fancy, let you not be thinking that day I'd be well pleased you'd go on keening always.

DEIRDRE *turning to look at him*: And if it was I that died, Naisi, would you take another woman to fill up my place?

NAISI *very mournfully*: It's little I know, saving only that it's a hard and bitter thing leaving the earth, and a worse and harder thing leaving yourself alone and desolate to be making lamentation on its face always.

DEIRDRE: I'll die when you do, Naisi. I'd not have come from Alban but I knew I'd be along with you in Emain, and you living or dead. . . . Yet this night it's strange and distant talk you're making only.

NAISI: There's nothing, surely, the like of a new grave of open earth for putting a great space between two friends that love.

DEIRDRE: If there isn't it's that grave when it's closed will make us one for ever, and we two lovers have had great space without weariness or growing old or any sadness of the mind.

CONCHUBOR *coming in on right*: I'd bid you welcome, Naisi.

NAISI *standing up*: You're welcome, Conchubor, I'm well pleased you've come.

CONCHUBOR *blandly*: Let you not think bad of this place where I've put you till other rooms are readied.

NAISI *breaking out*: We know the room you've readied. We know what stirred you to send your seals and Fergus into Alban and stop him in the north (*opening curtain and pointing to the grave*), and dig that grave before us. Now I ask what brought you here?

CONCHUBOR: I've come to look on Deirdre.

NAISI: Look on her. You're a knacky fancier, and it's well you chose the one you'd lure from Alban. Look on her, I tell you, and when you've looked I've got ten fingers will squeeze your mottled goose neck, though you're king itself.

DEIRDRE *coming between them*: Hush, Naisi! Maybe Conchubor'll make peace. . . . Do not mind him, Conchubor; he has cause to rage.

CONCHUBOR: It's little I heed his raging, when a call would bring my fighters from the trees. . . . But what do you say, Deirdre?

DEIRDRE: I'll say so near that grave we seem three lonesome people, and by a new-made grave there's no man will keep brooding on a woman's lips, or on the man he hates. It's not long till your own grave will be dug in Emain, and you'd go down to it more easy if you'd let call Ainnle and Ardan, the way we'd have a supper all together, and fill that grave, and you'll be well pleased from this out, having four new friends the like of us in Emain.

CONCHUBOR *looking at her for a moment*: That's the first friendly word I've heard you speaking, Deirdre. A game the like of yours should be the proper thing for softening the heart and putting sweetness in the tongue; and yet this night when I hear you I've small blame left for Naisi that he stole you off from Ulster.

DEIRDRE *to Naisi*: Now, Naisi, answer gently, and we'll be friends to-night.

NAISI *doggedly*: I have no call but to be friendly. I'll answer what you will.

DEIRDRE *taking Naisi's hand*: Then you'll call Conchubor your friend and king, the man who reared me up upon Slieve Fuadh.

As Conchubor is going to clasp Naisi's hand cries are heard behind.

CONCHUBOR: What noise is that?

AINNLE *behind*: Naisi. . . . Naisi. . . . Come to us; we are betrayed and broken.

NAISI: It's Ainnle crying out in a battle.

CONCHUBOR: I was near won this night, but death's between us now.

He goes out.

DEIRDRE *clinging to Naisi*: There is no battle. . . . Do not leave me, Naisi.

NAISI: I must go to them.

DEIRDRE *beseechingly*: Do not leave me, Naisi. Let us creep up in

265

the darkness behind the grave. If there's a battle, maybe the strange fighters will be destroyed, when Ainnle and Ardan are against them.

Cries heard.

NAISI *wildly*: I hear Ardan crying out. Do not hold me from my brothers.

DEIRDRE: Do not leave me, Naisi. Do not leave me broken and alone.

NAISI: I cannot leave my brothers when it is I who have defied the king.

DEIRDRE: I will go with you.

NAISI: You cannot come. Do not hold me from the fight. *He throws her aside almost roughly.*

DEIRDRE *with restraint*: Go to your brothers. For seven years you have been kindly, but the hardness of death has come between us.

NAISI *looking at her aghast*: And you'll have me meet death with a hard word from your lips in my ear?

DEIRDRE: We've had a dream, but this night has waked us surely. In a little while we've lived too long, Naisi, and isn't it a poor thing we should miss the safety of the grave, and we trampling its edge?

AINNLE *behind*: Naisi, Naisi, we are attacked and ruined!

DEIRDRE: Let you go where they are calling. *She looks at him for an instant coldly.* Have you no shame loitering and talking, and a cruel death facing Ainnle and Ardan in the woods?

NAISI *frantic*: They'll not get a death that's cruel, and they with men alone. It's women that have loved are cruel only; and if I went on living from this day I'd be putting a curse on the lot of them I'd meet walking in the east or west, putting a curse on the sun that gave them beauty, and on the madder and the stonecrop put red upon their cloaks.

DEIRDRE *bitterly*: I'm well pleased there's no one in this place to make a story that Naisi was a laughing-stock the night he died.

NAISI: There'd not be many'd make a story, for that mockery is in your eyes this night will spot the face of Emain with a plague of pitted graves.

He goes out.

CONCHUBOR *outside*: That is Naisi. Strike him!

Tumult. Deirdre crouches down on Naisi's cloak. Conchubor comes in hurriedly.

They've met their death – the three that stole you, Deirdre, and from this out you'll be my queen in Emain.

A keen of men's voices is heard behind.

DEIRDRE *bewildered and terrified*: It is not I will be a queen.

CONCHUBOR: Make your lamentation a short while if you will, but it isn't long till a day'll come when you begin pitying a man is old and desolate, and High King also. . . . Let you not fear me, for it's I'm well pleased you have a store of pity for the three that were your friends in Alban.

DEIRDRE: I have pity, surely. . . . It's the way pity has me this night, when I think of Naisi, that I could set my teeth into the heart of a king.

CONCHUBOR: I know well pity's cruel, when it was my pity for my own self destroyed Naisi.

DEIRDRE *more wildly*: It was my words without pity gave Naisi a death will have no match until the ends of life and time. *Breaking out into a keen.* But who'll pity Deirdre has lost the lips of Naisi from her neck and from her cheek for ever? Who'll pity Deirdre has lost the twilight in the woods with Naisi, when beech-trees were silver and copper, and ash-trees were fine gold?

CONCHUBOR *bewildered*: It's I'll know the way to pity and care you, and I with a share of troubles has me thinking this night it would be a good bargain if it was I was in the grave, and Deirdre crying over me, and it was Naisi who was old and desolate.

Keen heard.

DEIRDRE *wild with sorrow*: It is I who am desolate; I, Deirdre, that will not live till I am old.

CONCHUBOR: It's not long you'll be desolate, and I seven years saying: 'It's a bright day for Deirdre in the woods of Alban'; or saying again: 'What way will Deirdre be sleeping this night, and wet leaves and branches driving from the north?' Let you not break the thing I've set my life on, and you giving yourself up to your sorrow when it's joy and sorrow do burn out like straw blazing in an east wind.

DEIRDRE *turning on him*: Was it that way with your sorrow, when I and Naisi went northward from Slieve Fuadh and let raise our sails for Alban?

CONCHUBOR: There's one sorrow has no end surely – that's being old and lonesome. *With extraordinary pleading.* But you and I will have a little peace in Emain, with harps playing, and old men telling stories at the fall of the night. I've let build rooms for our two selves, Deirdre, with red gold upon the walls and ceilings that are set with bronze. There was never a queen in the east had a house the like of your house, that's waiting for yourself in Emain.

SOLDIER *running in*: Emain is in flames. Fergus has come back, and is setting fire to the world. Come up, Conchubor, or your state will be destroyed!

CONCHUBOR *angry and regal again*: Are the Sons of Usna buried?

SOLDIER: They are in their grave, but no earth is thrown.

CONCHUBOR: Let me see them. Open the tent!

Soldier opens back of tent and shows grave.

Where are my fighters?

SOLDIER: They are gone to Emain.

CONCHUBOR *to Deirdre*: There are none to harm you. Stay here until I come again.

Goes out with soldier. Deirdre looks round for a moment, then goes up slowly and looks into grave. She crouches down and begins swaying herself backwards and forwards, keening softly. At first her words are not heard, then they become clear.

DEIRDRE: It's you three will not see age or death coming – you that were my company when the fires on the hilltops were put out and the stars were our friends only. I'll turn my thoughts back from this night, that's pitiful for want of pity, to the time it was your rods and cloaks made a little tent for me where they'd be a birch-tree making shelter and a dry stone; though from this day my own fingers will be making a tent for me, spreading out my hairs and they knotted with the rain.

Lavarcham and Old Woman come in stealthily on right.

Not seeing them. It is I, Deirdre, will be crouching in a dark place; I, Deirdre, that was young with Naisi, and brought sorrow to his grave in Emain.

OLD WOMAN: Is that Deirdre broken down that was so light and airy?

LAVARCHAM: It is, surely, crying out over their grave. *She goes to Deirdre.*

DEIRDRE: It will be my share from this out to be making lamentation on his stone always, and I crying for a love will be the like of a star shining on a little harbour by the sea.

LAVARCHAM *coming forward*: Let you rise up, Deirdre, and come off while there are none to heed us, the way I'll find you shelter and some friend to guard you.

DEIRDRE: To what place would I go away from Naisi? What are the woods without Naisi or the seashore?

LAVARCHAM *very coaxingly*: If it is that way you'd be, come till I find you a sunny place where you'll be a great wonder they'll call the queen of sorrows; and you'll begin taking a pride to be sitting up pausing and dreaming when the summer comes.

DEIRDRE: It was the voice of Naisi that was strong in summer – the voice of Naisi that was sweeter than pipes playing, but from this day will be dumb always.

LAVARCHAM *to Old Woman*: She doesn't heed us at all. We'll be hard set to rouse her.

OLD WOMAN: If we don't the High King will rouse her, coming down beside her with the rage of battle in his blood, for how could Fergus stand against him?

LAVARCHAM *touching Deirdre with her hand*: There's a score of woman's years in store for you, and you'd best choose will you start living them beside the man you hate, or being your own mistress in the west or south?

DEIRDRE: It is not I will go on living after Ainnle and after Ardan, After Naisi I will not have a lifetime in the world.

OLD WOMAN *with excitement*: Look, Lavarcham! There's a light leaving the Red Branch. Conchubor and his lot will be coming quickly with a torch of bog-deal for her marriage, throwing a light on her three comrades.

DEIRDRE *startled*: Let us throw down clay on my three comrades. Let us cover up Naisi along with Ainnle and Ardan, they that were the pride of Emain. *Throwing in clay*. There is Naisi was the best of three, the choicest of the choice of many. It was a clean death was your share, Naisi; and it is not I will quit your head, when it's many a dark night among the snipe and plover that you and I were whispering together. It is not I will quit your head, Naisi, when it's many a night we saw the stars among the clear trees of Glen da Ruadh, or the moon pausing to rest her on the edges of the hills.

OLD WOMAN: Conchubor is coming surely. I see the glare of flames throwing a light upon his cloak.

LAVARCHAM *eagerly*: Rise up, Deirdre, and come to Fergus, or be the High King's slave for ever!

DEIRDRE *imperiously*: I will not leave Naisi, who has left the whole world scorched and desolate. I will not go away when there is no light in the heavens, and no flower in the earth under them, but is saying to me that it is Naisi who is gone for ever.

CONCHUBOR *behind*: She is here. Stay a little back.

Lavarcham and Old Woman go into the shadow on left as Conchubor comes in. With excitement to Deirdre.

Come forward and leave Naisi the way I've left charred timber and a smell of burning in Emain Macha, and a heap of rubbish in the storehouse of many crowns.

DEIRDRE *more awake to what is round her*: What are crowns and Emain Macha, when the head that gave them glory is in this place, Conchubor, and it stretched upon the gravel will be my bed to-night?

CONCHUBOR: Make an end with talk of Naisi, for I've come to bring you to Dundealgan since Emain is destroyed.

Conchubor makes a movement towards her.

DEIRDRE *with a tone that stops him*: Draw a little back from Naisi, who is young for ever. Draw a little back from the white bodies

I am putting under a mound of clay and grasses that are withered – a mound will have a nook for my own self when the end is come.

CONCHUBOR *roughly*: Let you rise up and come along with me in place of growing crazy with your wailings here.

DEIRDRE: It's yourself has made a crazy story, and let you go back to your arms, Conchubor, and to councils where your name is great, for in this place you are an old man and a fool only.

CONCHUBOR: If I've folly I've sense left not to lose the thing I've bought with sorrow and the deaths of many. *He moves towards her*.

DEIRDRE: Do not raise a hand to touch me.

CONCHUBOR: There are other hands to touch you. My fighters are set round in among the trees.

DEIRDRE: Who'll fight the grave, Conchubor, and it opened on a dark night?

LAVARCHAM *eagerly*: There are steps in the wood. I hear the call of Fergus and his men.

CONCHUBOR *furiously*: Fergus cannot stop me. I am more powerful than he is, though I am defeated and old.

FERGUS *comes in to Deirdre; a red glow is seen behind the grave*: I have destroyed Emain, and now I'll guard you all times, Deirdre, though it was I, without knowledge, brought Naisi to his grave.

CONCHUBOR: It's not you will guard her, for my whole armies are gathering. Rise up, Deirdre, for you are mine surely.

FERGUS *coming between them*: I am come between you.

CONCHUBOR *wildly*: When I've killed Naisi and his brothers, is there any man that I will spare? And is it you will stand against me, Fergus, when it's seven years you've seen me getting my death with rage in Emain?

FERGUS: It's I, surely, will stand against a thief and traitor.

DEIRDRE *stands up and sees the light from Emain*: Draw a little back with the squabbling of fools when I am broken up with misery. *She turns round*. I see the flames of Emain starting upward in the dark night; and because of me there will be weasels and wild cats crying on a lonely wall where there were queens and armies and red gold, the way there will be a story told of a ruined city and a raving king and a woman will be young for ever. *She looks round*. I see the trees naked and bare, and the moon shining. Little moon, little moon of Alban, it's lonesome you'll be this night, and to-morrow night, and long nights after, and you pacing the woods beyond Glen Laoi, looking every place for Deirdre and Naisi, the two lovers who slept so sweetly with each other.

FERGUS *going to Conchubor's right and whispering*: Keep back, or you will have the shame of pushing a bolt on a queen who is out of her wits.

CONCHUBOR: It is I who am out of my wits, with Emain in flames, and Deirdre raving, and my own heart gone within me.

DEIRDRE *in a high and quiet tone*: I have put away sorrow like a shoe that is worn out and muddy, for it is I have had a life that will be envied by great companies. It was not by a low birth I made kings uneasy, and they sitting in the halls of Emain. It was not a low thing to be chosen by Conchubor, who was wise, and Naisi had no match for bravery. It is not a small thing to be rid of grey hairs, and the loosening of the teeth. *With a sort of triumph*. It was the choice of lives we had in the clear woods, and in the grave we're safe, surely. . . .

CONCHUBOR: She will do herself harm.

DEIRDRE *showing Naisi's knife*: I have a little key to unlock the prison of Naisi you'd shut upon his youth for ever. Keep back, Conchubor; for the High King who is your master has put his hands between us. *She half turns to the grave*. It was sorrows were foretold, but great joys were my share always; yet it is a cold place I must go to be with you, Naisi; and it's cold your arms will be this night that were warm about my neck so often. . . . It's a pitiful thing to be talking out when your ears are shut to me. It's a pitiful thing, Conchubor, you have done this night in Emain; yet a thing will be joy and triumph to the ends of life and time.

She presses knife into her heart and sinks into the grave. Conchubor and Fergus go forward. The red glow fades, leaving stage very dark.

FERGUS: Four white bodies are laid down together; four clear lights are quenched in Ireland. *He throws his sword into the grave.*

There is my sword that could not shield you – my four friends
that were the dearest always. The flames of Emain have gone
out: Deirdre is dead and there is none to keen her. That is the
fate of Deirdre and the Children of Usna, and for this night,
Conchubor, our war is ended.

He goes out.

LAVARCHAM: I have a little hut where you can rest, Conchubor;
there is a great dew falling.

CONCHOBOR *with the voice of an old man*: Take me with you. I'm
hard set to see the way before me.

OLD WOMAN: This way, Conchubor.

They go out.

LAVARCHAM *beside the grave*: Deirdre is dead, and Naisi is dead;
and if the oaks and stars could die for sorrow, it's a dark sky and
a hard and naked earth we'd have this night in Emain.

CURTAIN

IV

NOTES ON THE PLAYS

IN THE SHADOW OF THE GLEN

'In the Shadow of the Glen' was the original title in the 1904 Edition, and again in Volume I of the 1910 Dublin Edition. In the 1905 Edition the 'In' was dropped. Ellis-Fermor uses both forms; I have kept the original, since it seems to give a subtly-different shade of meaning.'

p.**82** *a stocking with money* (S.D.): both literally, for the peasantry kept (or keep) their money in stockings; and figuratively, as for savings or a girl's dowry. (*v. W.W.K.*, p.34.)

Brittas from the Aughrim Fair: This is probably Aughrim in Co. Galway, 4 miles S.W. of Ballinasloe, rather than the Wicklow Aughrim, which is only 20 miles away.

departed: Anglo-Irish peasant speech often has just this apparently stilted quality; here the euphemism is used out of respect for the dead.

God forgive him: this is a common pious ejaculation. Here (remembering certain ironies in *The Playboy*) it seems to me to have overtones, or ambiguities: forgiveness, not for sins only, but for dying and leaving her alone.

turf drawn for the winter: if the weather allows, the turf is brought from the bog, and stacked beside the cottages, by high-sided carts, or in panniers slung on donkeys.

queer: note the repetition of this keyword throughout the play.

not tidied, or laid out itself: Synge, always, is interested in such details, though I think it is wrong to call him 'necrologous', as P. M. Young does.

p. **83** *up on*: some editions read *upon*. Both rhythm and idiom seem to make the first reading preferable.

Lough Nahanagan: about 18 miles from Wicklow. It is a 'high' lake, some 1,400 feet up, and has the reputation of being inhabited by a piast or water-monster.

the like of a dead sheep: again a key-image, which links, in a curiously tenuous manner, Patch Darcy, Dan and Michael.

the Almighty God reward you: the usual beggar's thanks: see *W.W.K., passim.*

p. **84** *He lights his pipe* (S.D.): this is a dramatic moment; the struck match shows up the Tramp's haggard face, and Nora's response to his word throws some light on her character.

crossing the hills when the fog is on them: the magnified and eerie appearance of everything in white fog is a commonplace experience. But Nora has hinted at more than this.

Richmond Asylum: in Dublin. It was originally a prison: opened by the Duke of Richmond, *c.* 1810; now St Lawrence's Hospital. *v. W.W.K.*, p. 32.

Patch Darcy: this mysterious figure lurks in the background of the play; *v.* Introduction, p. 26. The source is a story told by an old man; of a man who had two glasses of whisky after reaping, and 'some excitement took him, and he threw off his clothes and ran away into the hills . . . Then there was nothing known of him till last night, when they found his body on the mountain, and it near eaten by the crows.' (*W.W.K.*, pp. 14-15.)

p.**85** *Rathvanna*: I have not been able to identify this. Many Wicklow names end in *–vanna*, but this does not appear. Probably he just liked the sound of it, for it comes again in *T.W.*

drift of mountain ewes: drift = small flock. But this was later to become part of the celebrated 'offensive' line, the trigger for the riots, in *The Playboy*: 'a drift of chosen females, standing in their shifts itself . . .'

with a half smile (S.D.): she recognizes her lover's ineptitude with the sheep, though wild ewes from the mountain would be difficult to handle on roads. (I have heard a proverbial expression for extreme competence and 'cuteness': 'Sure, he'd herd rats at a crossroads!')

a piece only: a short distance.

back to the west: it is customary to use points of the compass for direction, even inside the house, *v. Riders*: 'Did you hear that, Cathleen? Did you hear a noise in the north-east?'

p. **86** *sluigs*: mires or morasses, 'that which swallows'; contrasted with *bog*, which is usually walkable, and may be largely of the peat. The *red* bog (*v. infra*) has heather and bents on it, with black walls and trenches where the turf has been cut.

a piece of a grey thread and a sharp needle: any form of steel is a protection against evil; *v. A.I.*, p. 48: 'Yesterday he took me aside, and said he would tell me a secret he had never yet told to any person in the world. "Take a sharp needle," he said, "and stick it in under the collar of your coat, and not one of them [the fairies] will be able to have power on you."' Iron is a common talisman with barbarians; but in this case the idea of exquisite sharpness was probably present also, and, perhaps, some feeling for the sanctity of the instrument of toil, a folk-belief that is common in Brittany.

naked to the saints of God: v. (e.g.) Job i. 21.

dead man itself more company: note the irony in the light of what follows.

The tramp begins stitching one of the tags (S.D.): We might be tempted to read *rags*, but *tags* is good Elizabethan.

De Profundis: Psalm cxxx, one of the seven Penitential Psalms. It is a strong protection against evil or the supra-natural: *v. A.I.*, p. 161: 'then I remembered that I had heard them saying none of those creatures can stand before you and you saying the *De Profundis*, so I began saying it, and the thing ran off over the sand and I got home.' Curiously enough, its inclusion in the Missal is peculiar to Ireland, and dates from Penal days.

your honour: the Tramp is now thoroughly frightened, and uses the ceremonial address.

A long whistle is heard outside (S.D.): note this in the light of Nora's previous lie about her husband's signal to the young farmer.

drouth: thirst, dryness.

p. **90** *back hills*: the foothills of the glens, remote from the cottages: usually poor land, only fit for mountain sheep. The word *back* has overtones of backwardness and poverty as well as remoteness.

bits of broken trees were left from the great storm: events are often dated from some natural cataclysm, such as storm or flood, e.g. 'the year of the great wind'. We see how the poetry in Nora (which the Tramp has already noticed) is welling up: and Michael's complete incomprehension of it, and of her. His attention is all on the money.

baking a cake: soda-bread baked in shallow cast-iron lidded pans known as 'pot-ovens' in the hearth. *v. Riders.*

p. **91** *I'm no fool now . . . when my lambs are good*: note Michael's naïve self-complacency. *v. W.W.K.*, p. 44.

Seven Churches: Glendalough; which began as a religious centre in the sixth century under St Kevin. The ruins of the churches can still be seen.

a shake in your face: palsy.

your teeth falling: v. Deirdre: 'It is not a small thing to be rid of grey hairs, and the loosening of the teeth.'

and the white hair sticking out round you like an old bush where sheep do be leaping a gap: a countryman's image. Gaps in a fence or hedge are often stopped with thorn-trees, and sheep crashing through leave scraps of wool on the twigs.

his chin the way it would take the bark from the edge of an oak board: the countrymen shave but seldom, perhaps once a week for Mass.

(See, as relevant to the whole story, Chaucer's *The Merchant's Tale*, esp. II. 1820 et seq.)

we'll all be getting old, but it's a queer thing surely: consider Synge's translation from Villon, 'An Old Woman's Lamentations'.

p. 92 *a fine Union*: workhouse. 'In Wicklow, as in the rest of Ireland, the union, though it is a home of refuge for the tramps and tinkers, is looked on with supreme horror by the peasants. The madhouse, which they know better, is less dreaded.' (*W.W.K.*, p. 30.)

butt of a ditch: trough or hollow. This is where the sheep, and Patch Darcy, lay.

p. 94 *and I after driving mountain ewes*: note the subtle irony in Synge's reading of Michael's one-track mind. The sentence draws together the recurrent sheep-imagery and the wildness of the mountain, and Michael's desire for approval or pity.

RIDERS TO THE SEA

p. 96 *a clean burial, by the grace of God*: from time immemorial men have stressed the importance of the ritual burial, particularly of the drowned. *v.* Horace, Odes I, 18; and the reiterated stress on the deep grave, security and repose for the body.

The door . . . is blown open by a gust of wind (S.D.): this prepares the way for the discussion of the state of wind and sea by the girls. It is paralleled by the opening of the same door when Bartley's body is brought in.

Galway fair: Galway is the natural trade centre for the Islands; fairs for horses, cattle, sheep, etc. are held regularly in the larger towns.

when the tide's turned to the wind: to = against. There are usually heavy currents round islands; wind against tide raises a fierce steep sea. This is specially dangerous to curraghs (*v. infra*), which are safest in the long regular roll of the Atlantic. See also Introduction, p. 34 et seq.

p. 97 *green head*: headland or promontory that has grass on it.

the hooker: hookers were stoutly built sailing-cutters, extensively used in the coastal trade round the West, and into Galway. They carried hay and turf, cattle and horses.

new rope: to make a halter or nose-bridle for the horse. And see Introduction, p. 39.

the pig with the black feet: the phrase might almost be hyphenated, as the normal and personal description of the pig: in the Irish muck-na-gcrub-ndubha. It should not be played for a laugh. See *A.I.*, passim.

p. **98** *a star up against the moon, and it rising in the night*: perhaps a memory of *The Ancient Mariner*:

> The moving Moon went up the sky,
>   And nowhere did abide;
> Softly she was going up,
>   And a star or two beside –

another cock for the help: a cock is a conical-shaped mound, often used, of hay. Kelp is the seaweed and wrack torn off the reefs by storms, and washed ashore on the strands. It is used in Aran for manure; formerly it was burnt in long sloping pits, to give a rock-like tarry residue from which iodine was extracted. The process is described in *A.I.*, p. 45 et seq., and *W.W.K.*, p. 189.

p. **99** *and you'll see me coming again in two days, or in three days . . .*: v. *A.I.*, p. 87. 'A man who is not afraid of the sea will soon be drownded,' he said, 'for he will be going out on a day he shouldn't. But we do be afraid of the sea, and we do only be drownded now and then.'

The blessing of God on you: it is disastrous not to return the blessing to anyone who goes on a journey.

the turf from the cake: the round flattish loaves of soda-bread are cooked in heavy iron lidded pans, and the glowing embers of turf are piled on top. Notice the growing petulance of the two girls.

p. **100** *give her the stick . . . The stick Michael brought from Connemara*: the living and the dead seem to meet through their possessions; Bartley is wearing Michael's spare shirt.

poteen: illicit whisky of great strength. Synge noted that most of the drownings in Aran were caused by drunkenness; but 'their grey poteen, which brings a shock of joy to the blood, seems predestined to keep sanity in men who live forgotten in these worlds of mist'. (*A.I.*, p. 40.)

passing the black cliffs of the north . . . Donegal: perhaps the cliffs of Slieve League –

> That ocean-mountain steep;
>   Six hundred yards in air aloft,
> Six hundred in the deep.

– on the south shore of Donegal. But in any case it is a very long way for a body to drift: Synge seems at pains to explain the improbability, though it was in his 'source'. (Introduction, p. 35.)

the string's perished with the salt: a realistic touch, for salt contracts and hardens cord. Synge noted how much rheumatism was caused by the custom of washing clothes in sea water (fresh water was scarce in time of drought), for the salt lay in the clothes and kept them continually moist.

p. **101** *It's that number is in it*: this is the *anagnorisis*, the recognition of classical tragedy; followed by the lament. For the speculations as to the *stitches*, see Introduction, p. 40.

keen: the wail raised over the dead; *black hags*, shags or cormorants. Black birds are always of ill-omen; there is a passage in *A.I.* (p. 162) that tells of a flock of black birds, 'so many that they blackened the sky' which were clearly supra-natural.

a bit of an old shirt: the eternal cry of sorrow, of man's contraction in death: *v. Hamlet* V. i. 220:

> Imperious Caesar, dead and turned to clay,
> Might stop a hole to keep the wind away . . .

p. **102** *Bride Dara seen the dead man with the child in his arms*: I do not know the source, unless it be a variation of the story told to Synge by an old man:

'There was a young woman,' he said, 'and she had a child. In a little while the woman died and they buried her the day after. That night another woman – a woman of the family – was sitting by the fire with the child on her lap, giving milk to it out of a cup. Then the woman they were after burying opened the door, and came into the house. She went over to the fire, and she took a stool and sat down before the other woman. Then she put out her hand and took the child on her lap, and gave it her breast . . .' (*A.I.*, pp. 137-8.)

p. **103** *the grey pony behind him*: see Introduction, p. 39, for speculations as to the red and grey symbolism, beyond that of red for life or blood, grey for death.

but something choked the words in my throat: consider *Macbeth*, II. ii. 30.

with fine clothes on him, and new shoes on his feet: a kind of transfiguration. See Introduction, p. 40, and perhaps consider Revelations xxi. 5. and 'The Lyke-Wake Dirge'.

the young priest: notice the bitterness of Maurya when faced with the standard consolation; the theme is repeated from the beginning of the play.

Bay of Gregory of the Golden Mouth: Gregory Sound separates the Islands of Inishmore and Inishmaan. I cannot trace this bay on any chart.

p. **104** *curragh* (or curagh): the craft of the Islands and of the West Coast generally. They are long, with up-curved bow and very low freeboard; keel-less and made out of lath and tarred canvas. They will live in seas that are fatal for any other craft; but are fragile and unstable. Except in the most sheltered harbours, they are taken out of the water after use, and laid bottom-upwards on the shore. Synge

has several descriptions of his own passages in them in *A.I.* They
were originally of wickerwork covered with skins: compare the Welsh
coracle.

and he a baby lying on my two knees: consider the dramatic functions
of the Nurse in the *Choephoroe* and in *Romeo and Juliet*; and perhaps
Yeats'

> . . . You have lacked articulate speech
> To tell Your simplest want, and known,
> Wailing upon a woman's knee,
> All of that worst ignominy
> Of flesh and bone.
> 'A Prayer for My Son', *C.P.*, p. 238

There does be a power of young men floating round in the sea: v.
Introduction, pp. 34, 35.

nine days in the sea: the people always hope that if a body is not
washed up at once it will float on the ninth day. Fish, fowl and the
battering of the waves quickly make a body unrecognizable; *v. A.I.*,
pp. 137-8.

The old woman was keening by the fire.

'I have been to the house where the young man is,' she said, 'but
I couldn't go to the door with the air was coming out of it. They
say his head isn't on him at all, and indeed it isn't any wonder and
he three weeks in the sea.'

p. 105 *he was washed out*: perhaps a shade of contrast-irony is
perceptible, for Maurya has long been watching the surf for
Michael's body.

where there is a great surf on the white rocks: the ferocity of a big sea
breaking on a headland is incredible until one has seen it. I remember
that an old man used a Synge-like expression, in reproving me for
sailing alone: 'Remember this, Your Honour; there's mercy in the
sea, but there's no mercy in the rocks.'

dark nights after Samhain (pron. Sówin): All-Hallowtide (1
November), the feast of the Dead in pagan and Christian times.
(*Samhain* was also an annual publication, 1901-8, edited and largely
written by Yeats, which dealt with the Irish dramatic movement.
Riders was first published in it.)

Holy Water: it is usual to keep this in cottage homes, for ritual or
benediction.

fine white boards: the islands are treeless, and timber must come
from the mainland; *v.* Introduction, pp. 33, 36, and the opening of
the play. The episode of the borrowing of the boards is in *A.I.*, p. 137.
'They have no boards to make her a coffin, and they'll want to
borrow the boards that a man below has had this two years to bury
his mother, and she alive still.'

p. **106** *a new cake*: which Bartley should have had for his journey: we may remember, in many religious rituals, the provision of food for the dead.

nails: the traditional symbolism is emphasized by the speech of Another Man two lines later.

spring well: where Maurya was to have met Bartley. We may recall the Biblical symbol, e.g. Psalm lxxxiv. 6, Isaiah, xii, 3.

puts the empty cup mouth downwards on the table (S.D.): note the gesture, the renunciation of further need for consolation.

no man at all can be living for ever: this is taken from a phrase in a letter from an Islander, Martin McDonough, to Synge:

> It happened that my brother's wife, Shawneed, died. And she was visiting the last Sunday in December, and now isn't it a sad story to tell? But at the same time we have to be satisfied because a person cannot live always. (cit. Greene and Stephens, p. 105.)

THE TINKER'S WEDDING

ACT I

p. **108** *dram-shop*: a public-house.

p. **109** *ditch* (S.D.): in view of the frequent references (cf. also *The Shadow*) it is perhaps necessary to explain what Synge would have had in mind. First there is the 'dry' ditch, a hollow three or four feet across, by the roadside, often backed by a thicket of hazel or thorn. This is a favourite camping and living area: cf. *Macbeth*,

> Ditch-delivered by a drab

and Yeats'

> Because this age and the next age
> Engender in a ditch.

Then there is the 'wet' ditch of stagnant water, often foul: cf. Yeats again

> . . . if it be life to pitch
> Into the frog-spawn of a blind man's ditch . . .

But the 'butt of a ditch', as in *The Shadow*, would be merely the hollow at the foot of a turf, stone, or thorn hedge, often covered with branches of gorse or briar, and so capable of hiding a body.

mind: pay attention to it.

And it's you'll go talking of fools: 'you're a fine one to be talking about fools, when no one until today heard even a woman like you telling such a lying story'. 'Lying' has also the sense of 'false' and 'stupid'.

since the moon did change: the phrase becomes a dominant through the play; it is one clue to Sarah's unusual whim.

queer time . . . queer thoughts: the word (as in *The Shadow*) is very much stronger than in modern English; perhaps including ideas of *fey, fantastic as well as strange, peculiar*.

It's hard set you'd be to think queerer than welcome . . .: 'You would have difficulty in thinking any thought that I wouldn't be interested in.'

p. **110** *rich tinkers*: the hierarchy in the tinker's world is pronounced.

Tibradden to the Tara Hill: Tibradden is a mountain in Co. Dublin, 8 miles west of Bray. For Tara, See note to *Deirdre*, pp. 304-5.

a great smell coming from the thorn-trees: hawthorn in April-May is particularly pungent. Sarah's 'poetic' thoughts and speech may be compared with those of Nora in *The Shadow*. Cf. also The Song of Solomon, ii. 13.

the day I got you: v. Synge's description in *W.W.K.* of the tinkers' gatherings, at which their women were bartered or exchanged.

Rathvanna: v. note to *The Shadow*, p. 275.

lug: ear.

Ballinaclash: a hamlet in South Wicklow, 2 miles south-west of Rathdrum.

p. **111** *he with a grand eye for a fine horse, and a grand eye for a woman*: a traditional combination: cf. Yeats, 'The Gyres' (*C.P.*, p. 337):

> . . . Those that Rocky Face holds dear,
> Lovers of horses and of women . . .

the Beauty of Ballinacree: cf. Mary Doul in *The Well of the Saints*. Ballinacree is a small village in Co. Meath.

Arklow: a small town at the mouth of the Avoca River, some 50 miles south of Dublin.

easy pleased with a big word: cf. again Nora of *The Shadow*: 'but you've a fine bit of talk, stranger, and it's with yourself I'll go.'

Glen Malure (Glenmalure): the scene of *The Shadow*.

It's lonesome and cold you'll be feeling the ditch: v. *The Shadow*, p. 93.

playing cards, or drinking a sup, or singing songs . . .: v. Introduction, pp. 47-8.

a big boast of a man: large, arrogant, commanding, but with overtones of unwilling admiration.

p. **112** *it's great love the like of him have to talk of work*: there is double irony here, for tinkers are notoriously lazy, and the priest later does just what she predicts.

A holy pair surely!: 'holy' is often used merely to intensify; cf. Yeats'

> Being but holy shows

Hence (coming from the priest), the double irony again.

p. 113 *selling asses*: even today the herds of asses accompanying tinker caravans are a common sight in the West.

'*It's a cruel and a wicked thing to be bred poor*': v. Villon, and Shaw, *passim*. Note Sarah's histrionic ability (though it is the stock-in-trade of her kind) throughout this scene. Synge's translation of Colin Muset (p. 283) is also relevant.

making cans in the dark night: no tinker would do this, but the picture Sarah draws is a suitably pathetic one, from long practice in begging.

p. 114 *And when he asked him what way he'd die*: from 'The Night before Larry was Stretched', which is Mary's song for the curtain to Act I.

Let you not be falling to the flames . . .: I do not think that a double meaning is intended.

It's a bad, wicked song: the text has been lost. Perhaps it was a reminiscence of a ballad Synge had heard in West Kerry, about a priest whom a young woman attempted to seduce, who 'told how it was no fit life for a fine young man to be a priest, always saying Mass for poor people, and that he would have a right to give up his Latin and get married to herself'. (*W.W.K.*, p. 105.)

p. 115 *and you with a stack of pint bottles above reaching the sky*: v. again Synge's 'Epitaph' (*after reading Ronsard's lines from Rabelais*).

It's destroyed you must be hearing the sins of the rural people on a fine spring: a double-edged remark which the priest does not pick up. We may compare the story told to Yeats by a priest who had just confessed a convent of nuns: 'It was like being nibbled to death by ducks.'

I'll be singing you songs unto the dawn of day: cf. *The Shadow*: 'but it's fine songs you'll be hearing when the sun goes up.' We may criticize the poeticism of *unto*, which Synge uses also in *The Playboy*.

p. 116 *speaking Latin to the Saints above*: cf. the Latin malediction of the dénouement; and perhaps the confident assumption that the language spoken in Heaven was Irish.

hard abominations: I feel this phrase is Synge's rather than the priest's. Ezekiel xvi offers some possible parallels.

whisper-talk: flirtatious talk; *v. infra;* and note again below the influence of the moon. Cf. *Winter's Tale* I. ii. 284: 'Is whispering nothing?'

p. **117** *Dundalk*: a town on the coast, about midway between Dublin and Belfast.

with great queens in it: cf. again Synge's poem 'Queens', and, in general, *Deirdre*.

white shifts for the night: v. the production of *The Playboy*: 'Audience broke up in confusion at the word *shift*.' (Introduction, pp. 60-1.)

p. **118** *with white necks on them . . . and fine arms would hit you a slap*: Synge is fond of these violent contrasts: cf. 'Queens' again, and *Deirdre*, p. 251.

What good are the grand stories I have: v. Yeats' 'John Kinsella's Lament for Mrs Mary Moore' (*C.P.*, p. 383):

> And O! but she had stories,
> Though not for the priest's ear . . .

ACT II

p. **120** *it's a great stir you're making this day, washing your face*: v. Somerville and Ross, 'A Patrick's Day Hunt' (*Some Irish Yesterdays*). I wash meself every Sathurday morning, whether I want it or no and 'twas washing my face I was when William Sheehan came in the door, and it no more than ten o'clock in the morning . . . 'God bless the work!' says he. 'You too,' says I.

cuckoos singing and crying out on the top of the hills: note Mary's poetical speech, and cf. the Tramp in *The Shadow*.

the rich men do be driving early to the fair: Irish fairs start early, 5 a.m. or so; the 'rich men' would be the strong farmers, cattle jobbers, etc.

rousing cranky: waking up in a difficult mood.

parson's daughter below, a harmless poor creature: the Protestant clergy and their families were notoriously gullible; perhaps represented in malicious contrast to the priest's realistic treatment of the tinkers.

p. **121** *. . . and you the pride of women to destroy the world*: cf. *Deirdre*; and Marlowe's Helen of Troy.

the one did put down a head of the parson's cabbage to boil in the pot with your clothes: that is, she stole a cabbage from the parson (*v. supra*) and boiled it with her washing; an example of Sarah's sluttishness, which is superbly contrasted with the next sentence. The presence of an evil person could put out the altar candles.

my own complaint to the mitred bishop: Synge is fond of this phrase: v. *The Playboy*, p. 218.

p. **122** *with blood and blisters on my naked feet*: this is not a picturesque hyperbole; pilgrimages up Croagh Patrick and to the Stations of Lough Derg produce just this. Cf. *W.S.*, p. 169.

horses'd go licking the wind: beating, going faster than the wind, cf. the poetic diction of the Scottish ballads; though the sophisticated reader may find a poetic ambiguity.

selling songs to the men: ballads, such as Autolycus had in his wallet in *The Winter's Tale*.

p. **123** *speckled female*: *speckled* suggests the maculations of old age: *v.* Yeats' 'a speckled shin'.

black hovels above, would choke a mule: cabins or huts so smoky and confined that a mule (toughest of animals) would choke in them.

sitting up on the ends of barrels: outside public houses, where the empty barrels are stored.

p. **124** *Grianan*: Greenan or Greenane, some 2 miles west of Rathdrum.

she walking single in a lonesome place: the irony lies in Mary's age and appearance; and perhaps in the much vaunted chivalry accorded to women in Ireland.

p. **125** *butt of the hills*: foot, beginning.

hooshing: sweeping silently, spiriting away.

hardy: vigorous, in good health, as well as 'tough'. It is always complimentary.

p. **126** *pack of you*: a usual, and expressive, term for a gathering of tinkers. Cf. Malvolio: 'I'll be revenged on the whole pack of you'.

bet: beaten, especially in emulation.

and you near burst with the fat: he is a 'big boast of a man', and *v.* the 'Epitaph' again.

p. **127** *to put up block tin*: i.e. the tinkers will break all his windows, which will have to be replaced by heavy tin sheets.

Kilmainham: *v.* note to *The Playboy*, p. 297.

to the coast of Clare: i.e. across the width of Ireland, east to west.

bog-hole: soft places in the bog, usually at the foot of the turf banks where the peat has been cut. *v.* note to *The Well of the Saints*, p. 287.

p. **128** *airy*: perhaps 'complacent' + 'eager' is nearest to the sense. But *airy* can also mean eerie: *v.* Yeats, 'This is an airy spot'. There is a different usage in *Deirdre* (Notes, p. 303).

p. **129** *bias of the sacks*: folds or pockets.

Clash: 2½ miles from Rathdrum, in Co. Wicklow.

THE WELL OF THE SAINTS

ACT I

p. **132** (S.D.) *v.* Introduction, pp. 49, 50. The ruined church, or a part of it, is an effective adjunct to a stage setting; consider, e.g., eighteenth-century picturesque landscape, and the second act of O'Casey's *The Silver Tassie*.

late autumn: I do not think that any symbolism is intended.

the morning lost on us: wasted.

Clash: v. T.W., note, p. 285.

a queer cracked voice: the women's voices are a constant theme; *cracked* has overtones of insanity as well as of sound. Yeats' 'Crazy Jane' was originally 'Cracked Mary'.

sitting out all the year in the rain falling: *v.* Introduction, p. 54, and, *passim*, the whole background of *The Shadow*.

I do be thinking odd times we don't know rightly: 'there are times when I think we aren't certain . . .'

it was the ones with sweet voices were the best in face: we may remember echoes of this in Tudor literature. It is interesting to note that Yeats objected to this over-close recollection of Cordelia; compare his own 'Hound Voice; (*C.P.*, p. 385):

> The women that I picked spoke sweet and low
> And yet gave tongue . . .

p. **133** '*the beautiful dark woman*' . . . *in Ballinatone*: cf. the 'Beauty of Ballinacree' in *T.W.* There are many songs, in and from the Irish, on 'beautiful dark women'. I do not know the source of this one.

There is a *Ballinatone House* 2 miles west of Rathdrum; Synge would have enjoyed the euphony of the name.

the seven counties of the east: presumably Antrim, Down, Louth, Meath, Dublin, Wexford, Waterford.

they're a bad lot those that have their sight: blind people, and idiots, have been till comparatively recent times the subject of such jokes – horrible as they are – as have been played on Martin and Mary. This is echoed later: '*for the seeing is a queer lot, and you'd never know the thing they'd do*'.

p. **134** *Grianan: v.* notes to *T.W.*, p. 285.

it's scores would have had me and welcome: Mary is always introspective, concerned to justify herself in her own closed world.

pith: the very large green rushes that grow near water are easily peeled to give a white cellular pith, and were used as wicks for dips (rushlights).

p. **135** *as if you'd met a thing wasn't right*: something supernatural, perhaps a 'pishogue'. See *A.I.*, pp. 144-5, and Notes, p. 276.

cute a little fellow . . .: cute = 'clever' + 'sly-cunning'; e.g. 'he's as cute as a fox'.

and threw down his corpse into the bog: see the poem 'Danny' and note to *T.W.*, p. 285. To throw a corpse into a bog-hole is a normal way of disposing of a body; the semi-liquid peat closes rapidly and leaves no trace. It may be found centuries later, perfectly preserved. Many corpses were thus disposed of in 'The Troubles'.

putting up a still: the simple apparatus of a boiler, worm, etc. for making 'poteen', illicit whisky. See Introduction, and Notes to *Riders*, p. 278.

a great sight to see a man hanging by his neck: see Notes to *The Playboy*, pp. 298, 300.

p. **136** *with the help of God, you'll see a power hanged before you die*: for this ironic collocation, see Introduction, p. 9.

a place across a bit of the sea . . .: Aran.

naggin: noggin.

Patch Ruadh: Red Peter.

the bit of money we have hid in the thatch: cottage roofs were common hiding places; I have known arms to be concealed there. But Nora in *The Shadow* has a stocking, being of settled folk.

making blather till the fall of night: v. *The Shadow*, p. 93.

p. **137** *churches and high crosses*: great limestone crosses, of superb Celtic workmanship, are found alone or in churchyards. St Kevin's Cross at Glendalough is famous.

the big shawl: a heavy black shawl, draped like a hood over the head, is or was the normal Irish Sunday-best dress for this class of woman.

p. **138** *what way is he after trusting the holy water with the likes of you?*: Synge explains carefully why the Saint has entrusted the holy water to Molly – see Timmy's previous, and subsequent, remarks to Martin – but it is important dramatically that she should carry it.

young girls . . *are the cleanest holy people you'd see walking the world*: v. the traditional emphasis on the sanctity of virginity; and Mary Doul's snort of contempt at the Saint's simplicity. The phrase also gives some idea of the closeness of Synge's texture; consider Martin's previous remark, 'and yet I'm told it's a grand thing to see a young girl walking the road', and later 'and be showing us the big women and the young girls, and all the fine things is walking the world'.

p. **139** *unfolding Saint's cloak* (S.D.): the farce with the cloak serves to protract the tension until the Saint returns.

as the archangels below, fell out with the Almighty God: presumably the pun is intentional; *Paradise Lost* – 'Nine days they fell'. Molly's unintentional irony is lost on Mary Doul.

p. **140** *selvage* (selvedge) *of the wood*: woven edge, or border, as of cloth. But I have never heard it used thus in Ireland, though R. L. Stevenson has the same sense of the word in *Catriona*.

p. **141** *making game with them that likes it*: exchanging witty talk, badinage. Synge emphasizes delicately from time to time the happiness of the couple before they recover their sight.

    It's on a bare starving rock: v. Introductions, p. 33, and *A.I., passim. Starving* is partly transitive; as 'leading to starvation'.

    the grave of the four beauties of God: Introduction, pp. 49-50.

    curragh: v. Introduction to *Riders*, and Notes, p. 279.

    Cashla Bay: on Galway Bay, 15 miles south-west of Oughterard.

p. **142** *waving them back* (S.D.): the Saint's denunciation is impressive; he has already summed up Timmy and the chorus of girls; hence the *women and smiths* that follows.

    Did you watch him moving his hands?: a good piece of observation by Bride.

    I'm thinking it was bad work . . .: here, and in the next speech by Mat Simon, are the two essences of the situation.

p. **143** *it's more joy . . . than your own man will get from you*: Molly Byrne's character is emerging steadily through this scene.

    by the black of his head: a smith in a country forge is naturally black from the sparks and charcoal.

    gamy: v. Notes to *Deirdre*, p. 306.

    Oh, it was no lie they told me, Mary Doul: the protracted cruelty that follows before the *anagnorisis* is almost too painful.

p. **144** PEOPLE *jeeringly* (S.D.): the play has a sort of double chorus: the girls and the crowd. For the cruelty of that latter, see *The Playboy*, p. 225 et seq., and *A.I., passim.*

p. **145** *any grey mare on the ridge of the world*: the phrase is Tudor in its hyperbole; cf. 'I'd know his way of spitting, and he astride the moon' (*Playboy*, p. 215). But it is also visual, of the eerie effect of a solitary grey horse against a high sky-line.

p. **146** *you'll be having men and women with their knees bled*: v. pp. 122, 169.

    a hundred years or a thousand itself: cf. for the idiom *Riders*: '. . . if it was a hundred horses, or a thousand horses you had itself . . .'

    Let me hit her one good one, for the love of the Almighty God: cf. Introduction, p. 9.

    but on the splendour of the Spirit of God, you'll see an odd time shining out through the big hills, and steep streams falling to the sea: a good example of Synge's art. The colloquialism of *an odd time* breaks the rhythm away from his mannerism, as well as giving the intermittent nature of the mystics' apprehension of unity; while the last clause swings into the full alliterated cadence.

p. **147** *and let you not be raising your voice, a bad thing in a woman*: the Cordelia image again. But the scolding wife is a stock figure of comedy.

Annagolan: a townland N.W. of Wicklow.

Laragh: a village in Co. Wicklow, near Glendalough and 7 miles north-west of Rathdrum.

Glenassil: I cannot trace this; perhaps Glendas(s)an, near Glendalough.

the holy Kevin: the famous Saint, founder of the 'Holy City' of Glendalough. His 'bed' is still shown in his cell, some distance from his monastery, beside the Upper Lake at Glendalough. It is believed by some to be a prehistoric rock-tomb.

ACT II

p. **147** *your old thorns*: turf or peat is useless for ironwork; hard wood, though possible, would be inefficient. But the scene is set 'a hundred or more years ago' when coal slack might be unobtainable.

p. **148** *put a tuck in your sleeves*: roll up or fold back.

plucking your living ducks: to make the 'flock' beds and pillows of that age. Synge noted (*A.I.*, p. 143) the cruelty of this operation.

and it freezing since the moon was changed: a common belief (with some justification) in the West and elsewhere.

p. **149** *he cuts a stick and throws it away* (S.D.): note now the petulance of the action is fitted to the speech.

slipping each way in the muck: see Introduction to *The Shadow*.

pot-hooks (S.D.): S-shaped iron hooks to hold the cast-iron cauldrons over the fire; *v.* Introduction to *The Shadow*.

looking at him sharply (S.D.): the blindness may be returning.

p. **150** *the way you'd see a priest going . . .*: a vivid but not improbable image.

blowing in the forge: working the bellows, with a chain attached to a beam and counterweight.

p. **151** *for not a penny at all*: compare the bargaining for the priest's fee in *T.W.*

the like of you for dreepiness: generally, 'dishevelled and dirty', but the word includes Timmy's red nose, and 'eyes weeping and watering', that Martin had picked on before; a general impression of depressed rheum.

talking of nothing, and thinking of nothing, but the way they do be looking in the face: a strange twisted aspect of the miracle. Synge is, from this point onwards, working towards a morality play.

p. **152** *I've heard the priests say . . .*: perhaps Synge is remembering Oscar Wilde's fable, quoted by Yeats (Introduction, p. 50).

I'll tell your wife if you talk to me the like of that: Molly's vulgarity and cruelty are being steadily developed.

p. **153** *and the thatch dripping, maybe, and the starved ass braying in the yard*: v. Introduction, p. 17. The cadence is worth noting.

sop of straw: a wisp or handful.

a high room with dry timber lining the roof: the better-class cottages would have match-board ceilings: the attic room or space between being often used for storage (cf. *Riders*).

It's queer talk you have: we may remember the use of queer in *The Shadow*, and of all Synge's characters who turn poets: the Playboy, Nora, the Tramp, Maurya.

to be talking that talk with a girl: cf. Polonius' advice to Ophelia, and perhaps Yeats' 'The Wild Old Wicked Man' (*C.P.*, p. 356):

> . . . I have what no young man can have
> Because he loves too much.
> Words I have that can pierce the heart,
> But what can he do but touch?

Cahir Iveragh: 'Iveraghig' in the text seems to be a misprint for 'Iveragh', which is a mountain 6 miles south of Cahirciveen, in Kerry. *Cahir* is a common suffix, meaning height. In any event Iveraghig does not seem to fit Synge's cadence. So the *Reeks of Cork*, presumably the range of hills lying to the north of that city. The more familiar Macgillicuddy's Reeks are in Kerry.

till we'd have a fine life passing abroad: cf. the Tramp's speech to Nora in *The Shadow*.

p. **154** *Wouldn't any married man you'd have be doing the like of that?*: we may remember Molly's earlier cynicism as to the duration of married love. Then follows the impassioned ingenuity of Martin's plea, so that she becomes a little frightened.

like a high lamp would drag in the ships out of the sea: v. Introduction, pp. 13-15.

And you'd do right not to marry a man . . .: this is, rhythmically, a difficult speech; probably one of those that the actors found it hard to master in the initial production. I have left the punctuation, on the grounds that Synge meant this torrent of words to suggest Martin's emotion.

p. **155** *for I'm seeing you this day, seeing you, maybe, the way no man has seen you in the world*: the climax of Martin's intensity of imagination.

he's only to open his mouth to have a fine woman, the like of me, running along by his heels: again, perhaps, an Elizabethan reminiscence; e.g. *Two Gentlemen*, III. i. 104:

> That man that hath a tongue, I say, is no man.
> If with his tongue he cannot win a woman.

p. **156** . . . *tripping slightly over tin can* (S.D.): this, together with the growing darkness, is a subtle piece of irony.

till I'd grow an old wretched road-woman the like of yourself: v. Nora's soliloquy in *The Shadow*, and Villon.

It's them that's fat and flabby do be wrinkled young: Mary Doul, who is equally the target for Molly's cruelty, gives as good as she gets. Note the recurrent motif of the hair.

p. **157** *has no right to have her heart scalded with hearing talk – and queer, bad talk, I'm thinking – . . .: scalded*, cf. *The Playboy* 'scalded with the weight of drink': *queer*, cf. Patch Darcy in *The Shadow*.

p. **158** *I've a voice left for my prayers, and may God blight them this day*: note the typical Synge irony, and cf. *The Playboy, passim*.

and they twisting and roaring out . . . and each day always and ever: cf. St Augustine's description of the torments of Hell; and compare *A.I.*, p. 120: 'and talking with endless repetition of fishing, and kelp, and of the sorrows of purgatory'.

ACT III

p. **159** *till I'm an old woman with long white hair . . .*: the idea of this compensation in old age is working in her mind; as it shortly will in his.

and a little wind turning the sticks: *sticks* is used generically for anything from a twig to a tree.

a power of queer things to be stirring: v. The Shadow, and *A.I., passim*. Many stories of the Sidhe describe these signs of the nearness of the invisible.

p. **160** There's *a sweet tone in your voice . . . You're taking me for Molly Byrne, I'm thinking*: but he is not; and this moment, that another dramatist might have made sentimental, the beginning of a reconciliation, is cancelled by Synge's irony. Man and wife proceed to attack each other.

p. **161** *as bald as an old turnip you'd see rolling round in the muck*: a good example of Synge's doctrine of brutality, 'the clay and worms'.

p. **162** *There's the sound of one of them twittering yellow birds*: perhaps the yellowhammer or bullfinch? The thought of the white hair and beard has touched off the strain of poetry in both of them, much as the Tramp in *The Shadow* infects Nora.

p. **163** *The Lord protect us from the saints of God*!: it is strange that this line was not picked out by the early audiences as a 'cause of offence'.

if it was a hundred yeomen were passing itself . . .: *yeomen* denotes any armed men or 'military'; it occurs as such in popular 'rebel' songs. They are often associated with the police: *v. A.I.*, p. 135.

You're a grand man, the world knows, . . .: I have inserted commas here.

They grope over to church (S.D.): their pitiful attempt at hiding is emphasized by the contrast with the opening scene: which is linked to this by the peeled rushes that reveal their presence.

p. **166** *at the crossing roads*: I do not think this is meant to carry any symbolic value, though Maeterlinck might have made it do so.

the image of the Lord is thrown upon men: v. Genesis i. But this is the Protestant in Synge, as is the ironic rejoinder by Martin.

and the skies would be harsh . . .: contrast the alternating picture of his life in terms of the weather; and cf. the opening of Act II. The beasts with their 'hanging heads' in the north wind is good observation.

. . . and seeing no sight of the glittering seas: the Saint takes up the description, as it were counterpointed.

From this point onward the text follows the revisions made to the 1910 Edition.

p. **167** *when you'd the queer wicked grin in your eyes* . . . *making game with a man*: Molly Byrne's character is gradually filled in by Martin: cynicism, sexuality, and flirtatiousness. *Making game*; mocking repartee, often a prelude to courtship. Timmy the Smith and Molly, entering upon marriage, are used dramatically to counterpoint the marriage of the blind couple.

p. **168** *and keeping a watch on him day and night the way no other woman would come near him at all*: note that it is Mat Simon's suggestion, and not the poetical future that Martin has painted for them, that nearly wins her over to the healing by the Saint.

What call has the like of you . . .: reason, justification.

but you're a poor blind sinner, God forgive you, and I don't mind you at all: cf. the ending of *The Shadow*: 'but you're a quiet man, God help you, and I don't mind you at all'.

Let you take that man . . .: let is a common Jussive subjunctive in Anglo-Irish.

p. **170** *your worn feet, and your welted knees, and your fasting, holy ways*: note the rhythm, as well as the traditional rhetorical triad. *Welted,* calloused.

the grey days, and the holy men, and the dirty feet is trampling the world: again the cadence and the rhetorical triad. Note also the ironical values implied in the position in the phrase of the *holy men.*

the yelping lot of you: as of a pack of cur-dogs. Cf. also the way in which the crowd turns against Christy Mahon.

p.**171** *where you do have to be walking with a slough of wet . . .*: cf. *The Shadow*, though the term used there was *sluigs.*

where you do have to be lepping the stones: consider both the malice of Timmy's remark, *Deirdre*, p. 238. and the poem 'The 'Mergency Man':

> Then the peelers said, 'Now mind your lepping,
> How can you see the stones for stepping?'

There are many stepping-stones, easy in low water but dangerous after rain, in the rivers that flow in the Wicklow glens.

THE PLAYBOY OF THE WESTERN WORLD

ACT I

p. **176** *creel cart*: with high movable sides, used for carrying turf, sheep, pigs, etc.

Where's himself: the 'man of the house', husband or master.

wake: the 'watching of the dead'; a gathering in valediction, at which the corpse is laid out on a table. See Introduction to *The Shadow*.

scruff of the hill: slope below the summit; cf. *scruff of the neck.*

p. **177** *Father Reilly's dispensation from the bishops* is necessary because Pegeen and Shawn are being married in Lent.

peeler: a nickname originally given to the Royal Irish Constabulary, instituted under the Secretaryship (1812-18) of Sir Robert Peel. Hence any policeman.

six months for maiming ewes: a favourite device for paying off grudges on one's neighbours or landlord. Cf. cattle-hocking, hamstringing cattle by a knife or hatchet. *v*. Kipling's 'Cleared':

> They only paid the Moonlighter his cattle-hocking price . . .

a great warrant to tell: highly skilled and famous for telling.
stories of holy Ireland: *v*. Introduction, pp. 8-9.

Father Reilly has small conceit . . .: see e.g. *The Vanishing Irish*.

that murderer: the word is used familiarly and not ironically in all sorts of circumstances, e.g. 'I'm murdered with the heat'.

p. **178** *feeling* [there is] *a kind of fellow*: see *The Shadow*, p. 85, and the translation 'Laura is ever present to him'.

you're a daring fellow: the words are ironically used, but gain from the later repetitions in relation to Christy Mahon.

p. **179** *Stooks of the Dead Women*: rocks on the sea-shore, pointed like *stooks*, conical clusters of sheaves of oats set up to dry. 'Do you see that sandy head?' he said, pointing out to the east, 'that is called the Stooks of the Dead Women; for one time a boat came ashore there with twelve dead women on board her, big ladies with green dresses and gold rings, and fine jewelries, and a dead harper or fiddler along with them.' (*W.W.K.*, p. 119.)

knock the heads: emended from *knock the head*.

tinkers: with an ill reputation as beggars and thieves. *v. T.W.*

militia: the 'brutal and licentious soldier' of the time, roughly equivalent to Territorials.

stop alone in it: *v.* again *The Vanishing Irish*, and Introduction.

in the gripe: the hollow of.

p. **180** *Oh, Father Reilly, and the saints of God . . .*: note the conjunction.

penny pot-boy: a serving-man in a cheap public house. Cf. a Shakespearean 'drawer'.

p. **181** *a bona fide*: bona fide traveller, as such excepted from the licensing 'hours'; a concession much abused.

wanting: 'wanted' by the police for some crime.

strong farmer: of substance, having a farm which gives a good living.

p. **182** *the butt of his tail-pocket*: depths of the pocket of the old-fashioned swallow-tailed coat. With knee breeches and buckled shoes it was the ceremonial dress of the older men.

followed after a young woman: see again *The Vanishing Irish*.

the holy missioners making sermons: *v.* Honor Tracy, *Mind You, I've Said Nothing*, Ch. IX.

p. **183** *With the help of God I did, surely . . .*: *v.* Introduction.

I never used weapons. I've no [gun] *licence, and I'm a law-fearing man*: the irony is wholly unconscious.

p. **184** *hanged his dog from the licence*: because he could not afford to pay for it.

loy: a long thin spade; the pattern varies in different counties.

Aye, I buried him then: note the force of the stage direction *Considering*. Christy is now committed to a circumstantial story and its elaborations.

that man should be a great terror when his temper's roused: this is picked up later with varying emphasis. And consider the film *The Quiet Man*.

The peelers is fearing him: the men combine in the build-up of Christy's self-esteem.

poteen: illicit whisky, distilled from potatoes, oats or rye. Its manufacture was once a major industry in the West of Ireland, and the search for the stills or 'stored' whisky a major preoccupation of the police.

pitchpike: two-pronged fork used for pitching, e.g. hay or dung.

loosèd khaki cut-throats: note the reminiscences, here and elsewhere, of the Boer War.

walking dead: the irony of Old Mahon's reappearances, always at the most inopportune moments.

p. **185** *drouthy*: thirsty.

with a man killed his father holding danger from the door: note both the irony and the ellipsis; this for the sake of the rhythm.

p. **186** *a kind of a quality name*: one borne by the aristocracy. He promptly takes this opening that suggests he is 'landed gentry'; the Mahons were a famous military family.

p. **187** *You've said the like of that, maybe*: the eternal *riposte* of woman. Pegeen continues the attack in good feminine fashion.

scribes of bog: strips of peat country.

streeleen: chat.

the poets of the Dingle Bay: *v*. Tomás Ó Crohan's *The Islandman*.

p. **188** *a dung fork and stabbing a fish*: poaching salmon, usually on the spawning redds in winter.

a gaudy officer: in the striking Edwardian uniform of the Militia.

banbhs (pron. bannuvs, or bonhams): young pigs.

p. **189** *a seemly fellow with great strength in me . . .*: contrast Old Mahon's account of his son in Act III.

p. **190** *I've their word*: I have their orders.

priesteen: little priest; *-een* throughout is the diminutive, e.g. *bohir*, road – *bohireen* or *boreen*, track; *houseen*, little house. In the Widow Quin's mouth it is contemptuous, as in *squireen*.

penny poets: selling ballads at fairs. Cf. Autolycus in *A Winter's Tale*.

overed: got over it. The anti-heroic account is contrasted with Christy's 'murder'.

wiser comrade: pron. com-er-áde, often used merely in the sense of *pair, fellow*, e.g. the comrade of a shoe.

p. **191** *shebeen*: a low wayside public house.
her leaky thatch is growing more pasture: *v.* Chapman's continuation of *Hero and Leander*:

> – like ripe corn that grows
> On cottages, that none or reaps or sows . . .

Doesn't the world know: Pegeen's temper is released in these superb images of abuse. For the *kidney stew*, compare *Hamlet* IV. iii. 28-33.
grass tobacco: dried but uncured tobacco leaf. This slanging match between the older and younger women, pursuing the same man, is a standard feature of comedy: in particular of the Restoration. Some critics have felt that the imagery is too violent to suit the dialogue. To which we may reply that Pegeen is 'a wild young woman', that there are precedents in Elizabethan drama, and that this is Synge's kind of poetry.

ACT II

p. **194** *with nothing worth while to confess at all* . . .: see Introduction, and *T.W.*
cnuceen (or knockeen): little hill. So also *supeen*, little sup.

p. **196** *two hundred-weights and five pounds*: note the farmer's measure, as of sacks or pigs.

p. **197** *scythe . . . loy*: note how Christy's imagination is filling in the epic details of the fight.

p. **199** *lepping the stones*: crossing by stepping-stones. Synge has several such references.
frish-frash: froth-like substance, e.g. beaten eggs.
It's queer joys they have: Pegeen's anger at Christy's flirtation finds its outlet in a sadistic description of hanging.

p. **200** *kissing and talking deep love in every shadow of the ditch*: see again T. H. White, op. cit.
lonesome: this is a keyword for Christy, and perhaps for Synge himself. *v.* Introduction.

p. **201** *mitch off*: sneak away, play truant.
rinsing your ankles: girls such as Pegeen would go barefoot. The phrase may well have been another 'cause of offence', for several reasons. See, too, the poem 'On An Island'.

p. **202** *thraneen*: scrap of thread, shred.
cleeve (S.D.): cleave, a basket.

p. **203** *Kilmainham*: a notorious gaol in Dublin.
have courage to come behind him: again the irony.

p. **204** *rye path*: path by the side of a patch of rye.
turbary: right of cutting turf (peat) on a stretch of bog.
the long car: a kind of waggonette, once popular in the West for postal services, etc.
from Mayo to the western world: we may note the irony even in the title of the play. For the western world is Connaught *and* the United States.
one blow to the breeches belt: the hero's stroke becomes magnified steadily as the story is re-told.

p. **205** *not saluting at all*: not giving the conventional greeting, such as 'God bless the house!'
An ugly young streeler with a murderous gob: *Streeler*, rugged youth, used mainly by city urchins: *gob*, mouth, hence the whole face.
That was a great blow: here and elsewhere – as in Pegeen's description of the hanging – there is a strong element of morbidity.
mortified scalp: note the ironical reflection of the way in which the Widow Quin killed her man.

p. **206** *till there's nothing but distraction on me*: I have added *me* as an emendation.
a lier on walls: a curious phrase; perhaps of the groups of idle young men sitting on walls, or leaning against them, in evenings, gossiping and boasting. Maunsel edn. has *liar*, which is equally difficult.
felts: fieldfares.
making mugs . . . in the bit of a glass . . .: the recurrence of this episode (*v.* p. 193) is part of the irony: *v. Richard II*, IV. i. 265.
his two ears rising like a hare: Synge, a countryman, achieves some superbly vivid imagery of this kind; cf. the weasel, later.
the laughing joke of every female woman: the Widow Quin and Old Mahon between them develop a kind of satiric anti-masque: contrast the adulation of Pegeen and the girls.

p. **207** *an old weasel tracing a rat*: again the country image; a weasel works quickly and pertinaciously, weaving from side to side to pick up the scent.
a kind of carcass . . .: dead sheep and cattle are not buried but pushed over cliffs into the Atlantic. Cf. 'given the cliff' in Somerville and Ross.

p. **208** *May I meet with one tooth*: cf. the old lady of tradition: 'I've only two teeth in my head, but thank God they meet.'
spavindy ass: lame with spavin, disease of the hock-joint.

NOTES

There's poetry talk for a girl you'd see itching and scratching: the summit of Christy's achievement in infecting Pegeen with his new-found poetry. The lyric mood is sustained, a little improbably, in Act III.

handling merchandise in the heavens above: perhaps a reminiscence of Yeats' 'He wishes for the Cloths of Heaven'? (*C.P.*, p. 81).

hookers: a stout, heavily built sailing cutter; formerly much used in coastal traffic and carrying cargo to the islands. *v. Riders*, Maxwell's *Wild Sports of the West*.

p. **209** *at the corner of my wheel*: the old men come in to gossip while she is spinning.

through the Meadows of Ease: cf. *Antony and Cleopatra*, IV. xii. 51. Corkery (op. cit., p. 197) attacks this and similar phrases, perhaps offended by *Footstool of the Virgin's Son*.

We'll swear he's a maniac: she finally convinces Old Mahon that he is. And see the dénouement.

p. **210** *She's in the boreen making game of Shaneen Keogh*: *boreen* or *bohireen*, lane (*v. supra*); *making game of*, mocking at.

ACT III

p. **210** *cockshot-man*: who allowed sticks to be thrown at him, for a consideration, at fairs. There is a brilliant and sad painting of one by Jack B. Yeats.

p. **211** *A man can't hang by his own informing, and his father should be rotten by now*: this, and the macabre discussion of the skulls, may recall *Hamlet* and perhaps Webster; as well as Villon.

there was a graveyard: Irish graves, like Donne's, are often broken up 'Some second guest to entertain'. *v.* T. H. White, op. cit., on this also. See the poem 'In Kerry'.

winning clean beds and the fill of my belly: note the ironic counterpointing of Christy's rewards for the other half of the story of the 'murder'.

p. **212** *I knew a party was kicked in the head by a red mare*: *v. Riders*.

till he eat the insides of a clock and died after: note the magnificent 'metaphysical' image of the horses and the clock in conjunction.

p. **213** *slightly emotional from his drink* (S.D.): the effect of poteen, which may well be almost neat and unmatured alcohol, is rapid and violent. Self-pity prepares the way for his new rôle of 'heroic' madman, again counterpointing Christy's rise to greatness.

winkered mule: mule with blinkers on the bridle.

p. **214** *Mount there on the bench*: note the ingenuity of the stage-craft for reporting the races.

skelping: slapping, spanking.

p. **215** *sucking the life blood from the butt of my lug*: with teeth fixed in the lobe of the ear. Perhaps an image from weasels or ferrets, who usually fasten on rabbits at the base of an ear.

p. **216** *parlatic*: paralytic.

a terrible and fearful case: again the heroic delight in reported violence.

p. **217** *pacing Neifin in the dews of night*: Neifin is the mountain west of Loch Conn, on a line drawn between Newport and Ballina.

p. **218** *a kind of pity for the Lord God . . .*: here Synge's own poem 'Dread' is relevant. Bourgeois points out that the first image is taken from Douglas Hyde's 'Love Songs of Connacht':

> I had rather be beside her on a couch, ever kissing her,
> Than be sitting in Heaven in the chair of the Trinity.

astray in Erris, when Good Friday's by: Erris is a barony in north-west Mayo. A good Catholic does not make love in Lent.

stretched back unto your necklace, in the flowers of the earth: unto is curious. See the translation 'Laura is ever present to him', and perhaps *Antony and Cleo*patra, IV, xii, 51.

such poet's talking, and such bravery of heart: note the association of the two qualities.

spearing salmons: by torchlight, usually out of season.

Taking your death in the hailstones, or in the fogs of dawn: v. Nora's last speech in *The Shadow*.

paters: paternosters.

p. **219** *sailing the seas till I'd marry a Jew-man, with ten kegs of gold*: Yeats' ballad, 'Colonel Martin' (*C.P.*, p. 361) is perhaps relevant.

p. **220** *stretched out retching speechless on the holy stones*: the summit of 'brutality of phrase'. Stephen MacKenna quotes a Lenten Pastoral of 1908 warning the people that it was 'henceforth a mortal sin' to give out alcoholic drinks at a funeral or a wake.

throw him on the crupper . . .: the opportunity for a wake is not to be neglected. There is a story of a 'casual' corpse (of a tramp) being borrowed for this purpose by three successive parishes, until the priest had to intervene. v. Introduction, pp. 29, 30.

gilded dispensation: perhaps a pun on the lettering, sanctity, and cost.

'*dreading that young gaffer who'd capsize the stars*': v. Introduction, pp. 13-15.

p. **221** *picking a dirty tramp up from the highways of the world*: note the
rhythm and cadence.

drift of heifers: v. the famous 'drift of chosen females' below.

on the plains of Meath: the more fertile lands of the midlands and
south-east are proverbial in the west for their wealth.

Go on to the foreshore if it's fighting you want: v. the account of the
battle on the 'strand' in Somerville and Ross, *Experiences of an Irish
R.M.* ('The Boat's Share').

will wash all traces: the *Macbeth* image?

simmering in passions: a good adaptation of Elizabethan (and
earlier) flame-imagery.

p. **222** *Take the loy is on your western side*: points of a compass are often
used for direction; a man will, for example, talk of sitting on the north
or south side of his own fireside.

I'm mounted on the spring-tide of the stars of luck: v. 'There is a tide
in the affairs of men . . .' This is the moment of hubris.

for I swear to God I'll wed him, and I'll not renege: Bourgeois again
gives the source in Hyde's 'Religious Songs of Connacht':

Before the cock crows tonight you will reneague me three times.

But equally it is straight Elizabethan: as in, e.g., *King Lear*, II. ii. 78,

Renege, affirm, and turn their halcyon beaks . . .

an easy or a cruel end: v. again Yeats' 'Lament for Mrs. Mary
Moore':

A bloody and a sudden end,
Gunshot or a noose . . .

that all should rear up lengthy families: v. Genesis viii. 17, etc.

What's a single man . . .: v. Introduction, p. 17.

p. **223** *You're fooling, Pegeen!*: note how the Chorus turns against
Christy.

after lacing in my heart-strings: cf. *Othello*, III. iii. 261.

p. **224** *the sins of the whole world*: the phrase is perhaps a Protestant's.

Leave troubling the Lord God: v. Henry V, II. ii. 18:

'. . . now I, to comfort him, bid him a' should not think of God, I
hoped there was no need to trouble himself with any such thoughts
yet.'

old hen: influenza; *cholera morbus*: the peasantry love to pick up
scraps of medical language.

scorch my understanding at her flaming brow: an Elizabethanism that
seems over-rhetorical in this context.

skelped . . . pandied: beaten like a schoolboy. *v.* Joyce's *Portrait of the
Artist as a Young Man*.

p. **225** *for if you're after making a mighty man of men this day by the power of a lie*: perhaps the heart of the play.

show a blow: the phonetic clash is awkward; one is tempted to read *shove*, which is possible idiomatically.

would raise the top-knot on a poet in a merchant's town: compare Yeats' 'the stirring at the roots of the hair'; and Housman's *The Name and Nature of Poetry*. The merchant's town presumably suggests a Philistine environment.

What good'd be my lifetime if I left Pegeen?: but the irony is in his rapid abandonment of her: compare Michael's renunciation of Nora at the end of *The Shadow*.

p. **226** *a drift of chosen females*: see Introduction.

p. **227** *hanging is an easy and a speedy end*: contrast Pegeen's description on p. 199.

a great gap between a gallous story and a dirty deed: gallous (sc. gallows), a hanging matter, but with overtones of 'wildness', intensity; Christy's story of the murder is approved so long as it is a story only. The reversal comes when he attempts to translate his fiction into reality.

scorch his leg: 'I had defended the burning of Christy Mahon's leg on the ground that an artist need not make his characters self-consistent, and yet, that too was observation, for "although these people are kindly towards each other and their children, they have no sympathy for the suffering of animals, and little sympathy for pain when the person who feels it is not in danger".' (Yeats, *Essays and Introductions*, p. 326.)

p. **228** *hanging as a scarecrow for the fowls of hell*: perhaps a memory of 'L'Epitaphe Villon'. See Introduction. And we may remember Hardy's *Jude*, Housman's *Shropshire Lad*, and Wilde's *The Ballad of Reading Gaol*.

ladies in their silks and satins snivelling in their lacy kerchiefs: as in many popular 'hanging' ballads of the eighteenth century. That of 'The Night before Larry was Stretched' is used for the curtain of Act I of *T.W.*

hell's flags of welcome: perhaps a compound echo from Marlowe or Shakespeare.

p. **229** *picking cockles*: the coldest, wettest and most ill-paid of work.

By the will of God, we'll have peace now for our drinks: see, again, the ending of *The Shadow*.

DEIRDRE OF THE SORROWS

(*The spellings of various names, such as Cuchulain, are rendered from the Irish, and are therefore inconsistent. I have not attempted to standardize them.*)

ACT I

p. **232** *Slieve Fuadh* (S.D.): Sliabh Fuait, of the mountain-range now known as The Fews in Co. Armagh. The name is apparently used for Carrigatuke, the peak of the highest mountain, on the shoulders of which the road from Dundalk to Armagh passes.

a half-furnished piece of tapestry (S.D.): this is important; it depicts Naisi and his brothers in a hunting scene, for Deirdre has already watched them. *v. infra.*

later than the common: later than usual. The phrase is still in use.

above chasing hares: i.e. on the higher slopes of the mountain, with greyhounds.

Who'd check her like was made . . .: 'who would reprove anyone (as well-born) as she, who (one would have thought) was made only for a life of pleasure'. The ellipsis makes the speech obscure.

the way if there were no warnings told about her: *v.* Introduction, pp. 68-9.

without a thought but for her beauty and to be straying the hills: notice the early characterization of the 'child of nature'; and cf. the traditional evocative-pastoral, 'straying the hills'. ('Lycidas', *A Winter's Tale*, etc.)

Conchubor'll be in a blue stew: this seems to me unfortunate; more, perhaps, for the euphonic clash than because of a misplaced 'vulgar idiom'.

p. **233** *he should be in his tempers*: a common idiom.

but so long as she's gathering new life . . .: I do not think that any symbolism is intended by the flowers, nuts and sticks, though they are emphasized again later.

to singe the beauty of her like: the image of the moth or butterfly.

p. **234** *it raining since the night of Samhain*: Synge uses All Souls' Night as a kind of reference point, for the coming of autumn; as also in *Riders, The Shadow*. It is so used in the Saga. The month of Samhain is November.

throwing purple upon crimson, and she edging them all times with her greens and gold: the colours symbolize passion, nature, kingship; cf. also the pre-Raphaelite tradition.

the birds to school her, and the pools in the rivers: Deirdre has at first a Wordsworthian simplicity, that changes to royal womanhood when she declares her love.

white skin, and her red lips, and the blue water and the ferns about her:
this again suggests a pre-Raphaelite painting. Compare, perhaps,
Swinburne's 'Masque of Queen Bersabe'.

she'll be my comrade: v. Notes, p. 296.

a settled man . . .: mature, prosperous, as well as 'set in his ways'.

prying after her needles . . .: Synge brings out the possessive fussiness
of age.

p. **235** *light and airy*: the overtones are difficult to explain; there
is a suggestion both of Deirdre's grace, waywardness, and
irresponsibility.

Emain Macha: 'the twins of Macha', applied to the (originally)
two-topped prehistoric earthwork west of Armagh. The story of its
naming is in Hull, op. cit., p. 99, in 'The Debility of the Ultonic
Warriors'.

duns and grey: colours of the homespun cloth, as contrasted with
the royal dyes.

p. **236** *A man with his hair like the raven*, etc: a standard poetic image
of beauty (v. Song of Solomon, v. II) but of special significance here.
'Once on a snowy day it came to pass that her fosterer killed a calf for
her dinner: and when the blood of the calf was poured upon the
snow, a black raven swooped down to drink it. When Deirdre took
heed of that, she said to Lavarcham that she would desire a husband
having the three colours which she beheld, namely, the colour of the
raven on his hair, the colour of the calf's blood on his cheeks, and the
colour of the snow on his skin.' (Hull, p, 24.)

Three young men and they chasing in the green gap of a wood: hunting
in a glade or ride. This is Deirdre's first ominous act of defiance: she
has seen the Sons of Usna. Conchubor does not take her up at once,
but both realize that destiny has begun to takes its course.

you'll have little call to trouble for knowledge, or its want either: cf.
Yeats'

> . . . And is so lovely that it sets to right
> What knowledge or its lack has set awry . . .
> 'Coole Park and Ballylee, 1931' (*C.P.*, p. 275)

dry leaves are blowing back and forward: we may think, perhaps, of
the imagery of the dry leaves in Yeats' 'At the Hawk's Well'; and of
the 'Ode to the West Wind'.

p. **237** *the furze breaking and the daws sitting two and two on ash-trees by
the duns of Emain*: furze = gorse; jackdaws mate in late March or
April, *duns* (dúns) = forts or citadels.

What we all need is a place is safe and splendid: v. the ironic
anticipation of the time of the safety of the grave.

the five parts of Ireland: the kingdoms of Ulster, Munster, Leinster, Connaught and Meath (*v.* Hull, p. 33).

the people of the glens: perhaps the echo of Synge's much-loved Wicklow.

and you may take the word of a man has no lies: this speech seems to be confused in syntax and difficult in rhythm. Perhaps we may paraphrase: 'You can believe this of me, and I am not a liar, you would find no other man so mentally confused and disturbed when he comes to you, as I am now.' There is irascibility, fear and weakness in Conchubor's character: here he appeals to Deirdre's maternal feelings. Note the anticipatory irony.

Emer: daughter of Forgall the Wily, wooed by Cuchulain as the most beautiful of all maidens. See Hull, op. cit., pp. 57 ff.; and 253 ff.; Lady Gregory, *Cuchulain*, pp. 21 ff.; 276 ff.; also Yeats' 'The Only Jealousy of Emer'.

Maeve (Medb, 'she who intoxicates'): Queen of Connacht, wife of Ailell. She owned the White-horned Bull of Cuailgne, the subject of the great epic, *The Tain Bó Cuailgne*. See Hull, pp. III ff.: Lady Gregory, pp. 268 ff.

p. **238** *I'm a ripe man and in great love* . . .: notice Conchubor's pathetic attempts at self-justification.

it's no work the High King to be slipping on stepping-stones . . .: 'it is both unsuitable and dangerous for the High King . . .' The danger of the stepping-stones in flood seems to have impressed Synge; *v. The Well of the Saints* and the poem 'The 'Mergency Man'.

p. **239** *Lay them out quickly*: there is a new imperiousness in Deirdre now; we may think of Cleopatra's robing for her death:

> Give me my robe, put on my crown; I have
> Immortal longings in me . . .
>
> (v. ii. 278)

There are, perhaps, other resemblances in what follows. Yeats' Deirdre paints herself; it is of interest to compare his verse:

> These women have the raddle that they use
> To make them brave and confident, although
> Dread, toil or cold may chill the blood o' their cheeks.
> You'll help me, women.
>
> (*C. Plays*, p. 178)

p. **240** *Dundealgan*: Dundalk

Conall Cearneach: Conall 'the Victorious', one of the chief Ulster heroes.

p. **242** *Tara*: Teamhan na Riogh, the royal acropolis, which reached the height of its importance and fame in the third century A.D. It is in Co. Meath, south-west of Navan and east-north-east of Trim. The raths, earthworks, and some of the foundations can still be seen.

At your age you should know there are nights when a kind like Conchubor . . .: a famous example of Synge's *bravura*, wildness and brutality and exaltation.

cnuceen: hillock, *v. The Playboy*, note, p. 296.

p. **243** *Nessa*: mother of Conchubor, and daughter of Echaid Yellow-heel, king of Ulster. Her name was originally Assa, the 'gentle' or 'docile'.

Rogh: presumably Roigh, father of Sualtim, who was father of Cuchulain.

p. **244** *Fedlimid's daughter*: Fedlimid was Conchubor's story-teller; having, as such, prophetic gifts.

p. **245** *And we've a short space only to be triumphant and brave*: in this and the following speech lies much of the tragic theme. We may note Empson in *Seven Types of Ambiguity* on this: 'The language here seems rich in implications; it certainly carries much feeling and conveys a delicate sense of style. But if one thinks of the Roman or medieval associations of *triumphant*, even of its normal use in English, one feels a sort of unexplained warning that these are irrelevant; the word here is a thin counter standing for a notion not fully translated out of Irish; it is used to eke out that alien and sliding speech-rhythm, which puts no weight upon its single words.' (p. 6.)

the sun red with envy . . . the moon pale and lonesome: we may, if we will, find echoes of Shakespeare, Donne, Shelley.

Alban: Alba; sometimes applied to England, but here meaning Scotland and particularly that district that is now Argyllshire. Hence the 'little islands of the sea' and the references later to the Glens.

p. **246** *Brandon in the south*: Brandon Mountain is situated in the Dingle Peninsula, between Smerwick Harbour and Brandon Bay. On its summit is the beehive hut said to be the dwelling of St Brendan (*b*. A.D. 483) who left it to search for 'the land of promise of the saints', and is reported to have reached America. His miraculous voyage is reported in Lady Gregory's *A Book of Saints and Wonders*.

Will you wed us, Lavarcham? You have the words and customs: we may remind ourselves that Lavarcham was a poetess and a sage.

ACT II

p. **247** *curagh* (curragh): the light craft framed of wattles and covered with skins. See *Riders, passim*. But very large ones would be used for these voyages; such a one set out (1963) from N. Ireland to Iona.

Their like would go any place where they'd see death standing: part, but only a part, of the reason for the return of the brothers.

by the earth, and the sun over it . . .: this recalls the marriage ritual at the end of the first act.

p. **248** *I wouldn't care*: emended from *I didn't care*.
crows were stripping his thigh-bones: v. *The Shadow*, p. 84.
haggard: farmyard.
a happy and sleepy queen: see, perhaps, Yeats' 'Lullaby' (*C.P.*, p. 300): and Deirdre's 'Lament'.

p. **249** *to go walking lonesome by-ways with a gamy king*: again Synge's *bravura*; compare *The Playboy*: 'picking up a dirty tramp from the highways of the world'. *Gamy*: gaiety *plus* energy, athletic and/or virile.

talk the moon over to take a new path in the sky: perhaps compare Cory's 'Had tired the sun with talking, and sent him down the sky.'

p. **250** *The full moon, I'm thinking, and it squeezing the crack in my skull*: for the effects of the full moon, consider *T. W.*, and *Othello* v. ii. 108,

> It is the very error of the moon;
> She comes more near the earth than she was wont,
> And makes men mad.

the crack in my skull: the suture that closes during infancy? *v. In Memoriam*, 44.

Was there ever a man crossed nine waves after a fool's wife and he not away in his head?: Owen, the emissary of Conchubor, is full of violent speeches. The *nine waves* are presumably a reference to the seas and straits he has crossed to reach Deirdre. *Away in his head*: insane.

spancelled: linked together; commonly of goats, with iron rings round the necks, connected by a short chain. This is to hinder them from straying, since they will never co-operate in order to move in the same direction. For the image as applied to marriage, see, e.g., the coupled dogs in Hogarth's 'Marriage à la Mode', Pl. I.

are you well pleased that length with the same man snorting next you: the thought is common to *The Well of the Saints*, and *The Shadow*: cf. 'and there'll be no old fellow wheezing, the like of a sick sheep, close to your ear'. So too the brutality of the Donne-like *snorting*:

> Or snorted we in the Seven Sleepers' den.

We may contrast the description of Deirdre and Naisi, 'the two lovers who slept so sweetly with each other'.

Naisi should be stale and weary: it is difficult to convey the exact sense of *should*: 'it is certain, in the natural order of things, that Naisi will be . . .'

bleaching in a bog-hole: v. notes to *T.W.,* p. 287.

It's a poor thing to be so lonesome . . .: note the brutality of Owen's speeches, and his persistent harping on the Villon theme of the old age of men, women, queens. His rôle is that of the traditional Tempter.

p. **251** *and now she'd scare a raven from a carcass on a hill*: such death-imagery is always in Synge's mind. Perhaps the thought is of Villon's 'Ballade des Pendus', as well as from a sight common in all sheep-country.

It's because Naisi killed him: Owen gives *one* reason for his revenge.

p. **252** *You'll not be young always . . .*: Fergus reiterates, more gently, Owen's theme.

and getting in your children from the princes' wives: royal children would be put out to be brought up in princely households; hence the prevalence of the foster-brother in Celtic legend.

It is a poor thing to see a queen so lonesome and afraid: this, overheard by Deirdre, is the beginning of her determination to go back to Emain and her death.

p. **253** *throwing a line for salmon*: an anachronism that must have escaped Synge.

Glen Masain: for this, and the other place-names woven into the lyric structure, we may quote Deirdre's 'Farewell to Alba' (Hull, pp. 31-2):

> . . . Lovable are Dún-fidga and Dún-finn,
> Lovable the fortress over them;
> Dear to the heart Inis Draigende,
> And very dear is Dún Suibni.
>
> Caill Cuan!
> Unto which Ainle would wend, alas!
> Short the time seemed to me,
> With Naisi in the region of Alba.
>
> Glenn Láid!
> Often I slept there under the cliff;
> Fish and venison and the fat of the badger
> Was my portion in Glenn Láid.
>
> Glen Masáin!
> Its garlic was tall, its branches white;
> We slept a rocking sleep,
> Over the grassy estuary of Masán.

Glen Etive!
Where my first house I raised;
Beauteous its wood: – upon rising
A cattle-fold for the sun was Glenn Etive.

Glen Dá-Rúad!
My love to every man who hath it as an heritage!
Sweet the cuckoos' note on bending bough,
On the peak over Glen Dá-Rúad . . .

even when there's a bird in every bush making his own stir till the fall of night: this is good observation; small birds roosting in thickets move and twitter ceaselessly till it grows dark and they finally settle.

though we'd live the age of the eagle and the salmon and the crow of Britain: the eagle and salmon appear in Celtic sources as the 'oldest Animals'.

p. **254** *Glen de Ruadh*: (*v. infra*) It has been suggested that this is Gleann da Ruail in Lochaber and Cowal, Argyllshire. *Glean Laoigh* (= Glenn Laid): Glen Loy in the same district.

Would you have us go to Emain, though if any ask the reason we do not know it: this, the motive for Deirdre's return, is the weakness in plot that some critics have felt. She answers it, darkly, in her next speech.

p. **255** *throwing out the clay on leaves are bright and withered*: here the leaf-clay images seem to carry this load of symbolism; cf. Shelley and the Ode again.

a night where there is sleep for ever: perhaps remembering 'nox est perpetua una dormienda'.

when the tide turns on the sand: note how Synge uses, lightly, the charged evocatives of 'tide' and 'sand', the overtones of the archetypal images. (*v. infra.*)

It should be a poor thing to see great lovers and they sleepy and old: again the Villon theme.

p. **256** *I could stop them . . .*: the passage seems obscure.

He scatters gold pieces over Fergus (S.D.): this, and Owen's suicide, complete the Judas theme.

p. **257** *It's many times there's more sense in madmen than the wise*: cf. *Lear*.

p. **258** *Cuan*: I cannot identify this. Watson gives Cuan nan Orc, the Sea of Orc. Ainnle seems to have gone there, perhaps to the Orkneys; see the second quoted verse of Deirdre's 'Lament'.

we're going west: the metaphorical meaning is not stressed.

a poor, untidy thing: cf. his own poem 'Queens'; and Villon. Perhaps there is another Cleopatra-echo:

> Your crown's awry;
> I'll mend it, and then play.
> (v. ii. 316)

ACT III

p. **259** *It's a poor thing the way me and you is getting old . . . to be loitering this place getting your death, maybe . . .*: Lavarcham brings out Conchubor's age, cruelly and unconsciously underlined by her care for his health. Compare Nora and Dan at the end of *The Shadow*. And see the ending of both plays.

p. **260** *beauty goes quickly in the woods*: contrast Naisi's earlier 'Come away into the safety of the woods'. Lavarcham tries by every method to head off Conchubor.

sloppy face of trouble: I find this idiom false; though we may compare, e.g. death as the 'untidy' thing.

and now the worms is spying on his own inside: perhaps a less compelling version of the Shakespeare (Hamlet-Polonius), and Marvell images.

p. **261** *men from the clans that hated Usna*: the revenge-aspect of Conchubor's action is stressed in the sources of the play.

a horse-boy to call Fergus from the north: Fergus would have enforced the safe-conduct; but he had been detained (as part of the plot) by being placed under a 'prohibition' or *geasa* to attend a feast. (See Introduction, p. 71.)

I'll go into your high chambers: Lavarcham has changed from the rôle of nurse and confidante to that of prophetess: *v.* Introduction, p. 75.

p. **262** *The Red Branch House . . .*: one of the three royal courts of Conchubor at Emain. The other two were called the 'Royal Branch' and the 'Speckled Branch'. In the Red Branch were kept the spoils and trophies and the skulls taken from the enemies of Ulster.

He's likely making up a welcome for us: Deirdre's irony is at first unconscious – see her next speech.

p. **263** *we three who have conquered many*: the saga stresses the brothers' wide and continuous conquests in north-west Scotland.

You'd best keep him off, maybe . . .: at this point the prospect of the death of the three hero-comrades overwhelms Naisi. Now the gulf opens between the two lovers; on a common formula, each imagining the other's remarriage. Hence the 'distant' talk, that shows the 'great space between friends'. *v. infra.*

p. **264** *it's that grave when it's closed will make us one for ever*: in the Saga, Conchubor caused the bodies of Deirdre and Naisi to be buried in separate graves; yet each morning for some time one body was found to have passed to the grave of the other in the night. Finally a yew-tree grew out of each grave, and their branches met over Armagh Cathedral. (Hull, op. cit., p. 53.) The legend is widespread: the most famous version is that of Baile and Aillinn, of which Yeats made a poem (*C.P.*, p. 459): cf. also his 'Three Bushes' (*C.P.*, p. 341).

knacky fancier: this again I find out of key. So far as it can be paraphrased it suggests 'deceitful and clever chooser of women to satisfy your superficial desires'.

mottled goose neck: the image is justified by its aptness and cruelty; Conchubor's neck is maculated (cf. the 'speckled shin'), wrinkled and pimpled. Cf. Yeats' 'Crazy Jane and the Bishop' (*C.P.*, p. 290):

> The Bishop has a neck, God knows,
> Wrinkled like the foot of a goose . . .

p. **265** *Do not leave me, Naisi*: this is the crucial point; Naisi's bonds with his brothers in the fighting are stronger than his love. Hence the 'hardness of death has come between us'.

p. **266** *Let you go where they are calling*: these are 'the words without pity'.

the madder and the stonecrop . . .: vegetable dyes from lichens; until recently in use. Madder gives a deep red, stonecrop or 'crottle' a vivid orange.

p. **268** *like straw blazing in an east wind*: for the image generally *v.* 'Lycidas', and Yeats' 'Elegy on the Death of Major Robert Gregory'.

It's you three will not see age or death coming: the elegiac lament, with the two crouching women as audience, recalls Maurya in *Riders*.

p. **269** *Is that Deirdre broken down that was so light and airy?*: gay, carefree; *v.* Notes, p. 303.

the voice of Naisi that was sweeter than pipes playing:

Though they gave forth a sound of melody,
The pipes and the flutes that month by month are played before you,
It is mine in truth to tell you today
I have heard sounds sweeter far than these.
In the house of Conachar they are delightful,
The flutes and horns played by the musicians.
Yet I found greater pleasure hearkening to the songs
Famous and enchanting, sung by the sons of Usnach.
Like the sound of the wave the voice of Naisi,
Was a music that wearied not the listener . . .

(Hull, p. 50)

p. **270** *a torch of bog-deal for her marriage* . . .: the pine-wood dug out of the bog is full of resin, and flares like a torch. The bog-oak is hard, black, and will not burn.

many a dark night among the snipe and plover: birds often make their way into Synge's lyric passages: cf. *The Shadow*. Snipe and plover move ground at dusk; snipe feed, in calm weather, at night.

when the head that gave them glory is in this place: I have inserted *in* as an emendation.

Draw a little back from the white bodies:

> His absence is the secret of my grief.
> In place of the forms of the sons of Usnach
> I see only a dark tomb: it covers a white body:
> Well known to me and more to be desired than every other!
>
> (Hull, p. 51)

p. **271** *I see the flames of Emain starting upward in the dark night*: this, the most famous speech of the play, is highly wrought in language and rhythm. Synge's imagination owes little to its sources here. Weasels and wild cats are the haunters of ruins, as well as archetypes of ferocity; cf. Yeats' 'The Gyres' (*C.P.*, p. 337):

> . . . shall,
> From marble of a broke sepulchre,
> Or dark between the polecat and the owl,
> Or any rich, dark nothing disinter . . .

p. **272** *I have put away sorrow like a shoe that is worn out and muddy*: Deirdre's lyric continues its biblical imagery.

It is not a small thing to be rid of grey hairs, and the loosening of the teeth: a distillation of the theme of the horrors of old age.

I have a little key to unlock the prison of Naisi: cf. Cleopatra

> What poor an instrument
> May do a noble deed! he brings me liberty . . .
>
> (v. ii. 235)

and, for the converse of Deirdre's image, v. ii. 4,

> and it is great
> To do that thing that ends all other deeds,
> Which shackles accidents, and bolts up change . . .

p. **273** *I have a little hut where you can rest, Conchubor; there is a great dew falling*: consider the deliberate 'falling close' of high tragedy, the contrast with Fergus' heroic speech, the echo of Lavarcham's speech at the beginning of this act.

Methuen Contemporary Dramatists
include

Peter Barnes (three volumes)
Sebastian Barry
Edward Bond (six volumes)
Howard Brenton
  (two volumes)
Richard Cameron
Jim Cartwright
Caryl Churchill (two volumes)
Sarah Daniels (two volumes)
Nick Darke
David Edgar (three volumes)
Ben Elton
Dario Fo (two volumes)
Michael Frayn (three volumes)
Paul Godfrey
John Guare
Peter Handke
Jonathan Harvey
Declan Hughes
Terry Johnson (two volumes)
Bernard-Marie Koltès
David Lan
Bryony Lavery
Doug Lucie
David Mamet (three volumes)

Martin McDonagh
Duncan McLean
Anthony Minghella
  (two volumes)
Tom Murphy (four volumes)
Phyllis Nagy
Anthony Nielsen
Philip Osment
Louise Page
Joe Penhall
Stephen Poliakoff
  (three volumes)
Christina Reid
Philip Ridley
Willy Russell
Ntozake Shange
Sam Shepard (two volumes)
Wole Soyinka (two volumes)
David Storey (three volumes)
Sue Townsend
Michael Vinaver (two volumes)
Michael Wilcox
David Wood (two volumes)
Victoria Wood

For a complete catalogue of Methuen Drama titles
write to:

Methuen Drama
215 Vauxhall Bridge Road
London SW1V 1EJ

or you can visit our website at:

www.methuen.co.uk